VOID

Library of
Davidson College

Boston's Lower Criminal Courts, 1814–1850

Boston's Lower Criminal Courts, 1814–1850

Theodore Ferdinand

Newark: University of Delaware Press
London and Toronto: Associated University Presses

© 1992 by Associated University Presses, Inc.

All rights reserved. Authorization to photocopy items for internal or personal use, or the internal or personal use of specific clients, is granted by the copyright owner, provided that a base fee of $10.00, plus eight cents per page, per copy is paid directly to the Copyright Clearance Center, 27 Congress Street, Salem, Massachusetts 01970. [0-87413-422-6/92 $10.00 + 8¢ pp, pc.]

Associated University Presses
440 Forsgate Drive
Cranbury, NJ 08512

Associated University Presses
25 Sicilian Avenue
London WC1A 2QH, England

Associated University Presses
P.O. Box 39, Clarkson Pstl. Stn.
Mississauga, Ontario,
L5J 3X9 Canada

The paper used in this publication meets the requirements of the American National Standard for Permanence of Paper for Printed Library Materials Z39.48-1984.

Library of Congress Cataloging-in-Publication Data

Ferdinand, Theodore N.
   Boston's lower criminal courts. 1814–1850 / Theodore Ferdinand.
     p.   cm.
   Includes bibliographical references and index.
   ISBN 0-87413-422-6 (alk. paper)
   1. Criminal courts—Massachusetts—Boston—History. I. Title.
KFX1147.F47   1992
345.744′6101—dc20
[347.4461051]   90-50595
                                                                                      CIP

PRINTED IN THE UNITED STATES OF AMERICA

Contents

Acknowledgments	7
Introduction	9
1. The Early Criminal Courts	21
2. Responsive Law and Police Power	38
3. The Prosecutor Assumes Control	67
4. The Judges	99
5. Crime in Antebellum Boston	135
6. The Offenders	149
7. Modernizing Boston's Lower Courts	181
8. The Future of America's Responsive Courts	194
Appendix A: The Method	211
Appendix B: Judges of the Municipal Court	216
Notes	220
Bibliography	225
Index	231

Acknowledgments

Many people have made important contributions to this work and richly deserve recognition. First, the National Institute of Justice was wise enough to fund such a project as this one (79-NI-AX-0001) and deserves my undying gratitude for its vision. In particular Dick Rau of NIJ was especially kind and helpful at every step of the way. The staffs at the Municipal Court and Social Law Library in Boston offered useful guidance during the beginning stages, and Beth Hart, Pat Dooley, Terri Rooney, Rick Laurence, and Mary Bularzik were all invaluable in coding the data flawlessly under less than ideal conditions. Dottie Frank was selfless in her good natured willingness to type and retype portions of the manuscript at a moment's notice. Professor Simon Dinitz deserves major thanks for his steadfast encouragement during latter stages of the work, and Professor Don Newman at the end of his long, outstanding career provided an important boost toward completion. Finally, my warm colleague Ruth Cavan along with several anonymous reviewers made many valuable suggestions. Without these fine, generous people as well as unnamed but appreciated others this work would not have been possible.

Introduction

This monograph is primarily a study of Boston and its lower criminal courts from 1814 when the War of 1812 was drawing to a close, until the eve of the Civil War in 1850. Even though we know very little about Boston, its courts and criminality during these years, it was a pivotal period in all respects. In a few short years Boston was transformed from a small, preindustrial, provincial seaport to a thriving cosmopolitan center of commerce, finance, and small industry. During this period the city showed all the strains of rapid economic growth including those associated with a tidal wave of immigration: its crime rate soared, and soon it had an organized police department, congested criminal courts, a professional corps of lawyers and jurists, and a law school to instill not only the technical foundations of law but professional values and ideals as well. The legal institutions of Boston, along with the community changed dramatically during this period.

The Early Courts

Following the Revolution, the law was regarded as a sacred statement of tradition and convention, supreme over all—judges, lawyers, and public alike. It sorted out the innocent from the guilty, and its outcomes were virtually above question. The Municipal Court, which had been established in 1800 as a lawyers' court with a professional style and formal decorum, tried between two hundred and three hundred felony or misdemeanor cases a year before juries and sat only three or four days a week. It punished offenders with prison or jail terms and fines but not with the death penalty, which only the Supreme Judicial Court could impose.

On Friday 26 July 1822, for example, two Boston merchants, Samuel Upton and William Barnes, were brought to trial in the Municipal Court on a charge of fraud. Their attorney, Daniel Webster, was on the threshold of an important career in national politics. The presiding judge in the Municipal Court was Josiah Quincy, who would begin a highly successful six terms as Boston's second mayor within a year and then move on to Harvard's presidency. The prosecutor, James T. Austin, was the Suffolk County Attorney, and in a few years would become the Commonwealth's first Attorney General. The indictment charged that the two defendants fraudulently offered a cargo of coffee and tobacco as security for a loan of $12,000. When their business failed, the loan and the cargo were lost, and the indictment ensued.

The case is noteworthy more for the caliber of the actors, the high-minded tone of the arguments, and the manner in which the case was tried than for its legal substance. Webster stuck close to the law in presenting his defense, but in his conclusion he was reminded of the novel, *The Pirate*, in which a great whale was driven onto a shoal in the Orkney Islands. When the islanders discovered the animal, they bound him with rope and set upon him with harpoons, spears, and pitchforks. Despite his wounds and exhaustion, the whale gave a great lunge, snapped his bindings, upset their boats, and with a single stroke of his tail leapt over the sandbar and was once again free in the open sea. Webster felt that he and his clients were being harassed unnecessarily by little men.

When his turn came, Austin lectured the jury that:

> The principles of the law are the doctrines of morality and religion; and no man better understands than that worthy gentleman [Webster], how infinitely superior are its general provisions, to the purpose of temporary profit—the loose and demoralizing expedients of cupidity and avarice—the money making schemes of artifice and deception. In vain is it that you expect an honorable and high minded community unless the administration of the law conforms to the sternest principles of integrity. If there is any variation between them, the Commonwealth is disgraced and the public is ruined. In vain will it be that you support churches and preach religion on the Sabbath. It is the court, and not the Church, that supports your reputation. Moral precepts, it is said, come with a cold and unfeeling application from the pulpit, but men smart under them practically when we lawyers are preachers.

Near the end Austin commented on Webster's allegory,

> "It is for the jury to decide how . . . far the great whale may disport himself in waters where inferior inhabitants of the same element may be captured and destroyed."

And he went on to note that:

> an intelligent and high minded jury [will] see no distinctions but those of law, and [will] give no indulgences that justice could not sanction. They [will] preserve the impartiality of the judicial character that the words of the poet may continue to be fiction.

Finally he ended with a quote from Shakespeare's *King Lear:*

> Plate sin with gold, and the strong lance of justice
> Hurtless breaks—clothe it in rags,
> A pigmy straw may pierce it.

In his final comments Judge Quincy warned the jury that "Both the public and the accused have a right to expect a calm and dispassionate inquiry and a verdict founded on a firm and discriminating perception of the facts in the case without any fear or favor." Despite Austin's eloquence the jury found the defendants not guilty after only sixteen minutes of deliberation (from the *Boston Daily Advertiser and Reporter*, Saturday 27 July 1822: 2).

The Police Court, (the other court of this study,) was established in 1822 when Boston town was reorganized as a city. In the early years it handled about 2,500 cases each year. It was more informal with personalities and routines playing a larger role in outcomes. The judges, although lawyers, were less professional, and cases were usually argued by the complainant who was often the victim or, if not, the constable. The offenses themselves were mainly misdemeanors, and the punishments were jail terms or fines. Consider the following account published by a court reporter in 1856:

> Twenty-five years ago, the Police Court of Boston presented a very different appearance from the Court at the present time. Then, three of four cases a day were the average number brought for trial, and occasionally, when six or seven prisoners were arraigned, the Justices, Clerks and officers, seemed to talk and act as though it was almost an impossibility to get through so many cases in one day. Now, how changed the scene. Instead of five or six cases, we sometimes have between fifty and sixty. I am inclined to think that thirty-five is about the average number. Two-thirds of these cases, at least, are arraigned for rioting and drunkenness, and are very rapidly disposed of. The unfortunates are called up to the prisoners' bar, and sometimes the Clerk will read the complaint to them, and sometimes he will omit it, simply holding the document in his hand and saying to the prisoner: "You was brought here for being drunk, last night! Was you drunk?"
> If the prisoner says, "Yes," the Clerk immediately adds, "The court find you guility, and sentence you to pay a fine of three dollars and costs, for want of which you stand committed."
> But if the victim says "No!" two or more policeman rush to the stand, with surprising agility, and, raising their right hands, stand ready to swear, as fast as their tongues can wag, that the prisoner was not only drunk, the night previous, but that he was noisy and quarrelsome. If the prisoner has no counsel, the Judge will ask him if he wants to ask those witnesses any questions. The poor, bewildered devil will commence talking, perhaps very

incoherently, while the Judge is recording his sentence, and passing the same over to the Clerk; the victim finds himself "booked" for a free ride in a safe commodious vehicle, which runs regularly every day (Sundays excepted) between the Court House and South Boston, called the "Black Maria." (Fenner: 26-28)

As time wore on, the Police Court became less and less important in Boston's criminal justice system.

We also know that during the 1840s a rejuvenated bar struggled to improve its professional status by tightening admission requirements, and the training of young lawyers shifted from the traditional apprenticeship method to enrollment in established law schools. The lower courts were redefining their mission, especially the Municipal Court, by adding large numbers of regulatory cases and by diverting a growing volume of minor disputes, which were not really criminal cases, into nonlegal channels.

Just before the Civil War the lower courts were reorganized to approximately their modern form. In 1855, in place of the Municipal Court, a new Superior Court was created, and in 1866, instead of the Police Court, today's Municipal Court was established. As Boston grew seven collateral district courts were established to assist the Municipal Court, but the court structure that Boston works with today essentially took shape during the Civil War period. This reorganization was an administrative move to clarify and redistribute the lower courts' jurisdictions and to strengthen their legitimacy, but it also marked the debut of Boston's modern court system.

The period of this study, 1814-50, therefore, focuses basically on the formative years of Boston's modern criminal court system. It was during this period that its lower courts established their distinctive jurisdictions, defined their special procedures, and organized their separate staffs. During this period they assumed their modern form.

We know in rough terms how the city of Boston developed during this period. The Revolution severed English control of American commerce, and after the War of 1812 the economic take-off gathered speed. The city became more stratified with a highly visible aristocracy; it also became politically polarized and religiously divided. The religious and social institutions of colonial Boston could no longer digest the strains of rapid economic change, and other institutions—political and legal—were badly needed.

The mounting wealth of the community during this period gave some basis for its growing sense of pride, but the challenge of crime and the best ways to organize a criminal justice response were gnawing problems that were difficult to solve. The city fathers could hardly feel proud about these problems.

Some Significant Changes

This monograph attempts to answer some of the broader questions regarding Boston's legal system by looking closely at its lower criminal courts. Along the way we will learn that the galloping crime rate had very little direct influence on the legal system of Boston. Indeed, the reverse was the case, the developing legal system seems to have been an important factor in the rising crime rate.

As the state courts assumed an expanding role in economic development—resolving riparian disputes, overlapping franchises, and the like—the local courts began to supervise the activities of vice purveyors on a broad front. Among the first areas they began to monitor were prostitution, gambling, and the sale and consumption of alcoholic spirits.

The campaign against vice got underway during Josiah Quincy's term as mayor. In September 1823 he organized a raid on a cluster of establishments devoted to vice—brothels, dance halls, and grog shops, centered on the Hill—a notorious area on the north side of Beacon Hill in Boston. After he closed down the area, Quincy took steps to insure that it remained closed by organizing regular patrols of the area by Boston's small constabulary force.

This was the beginning of Boston's efforts to regulate its more "enterprising" businessmen. When the campaign was extended in later years to include taverns and related establishments, it added substantially to the regulatory responsibilities of the courts and to their criminal caseloads. These regulatory responsibilities in turn forced the courts and their agents, the police, into a new proactive stance vis-à-vis misbehavior generally.

The police quickly assumed primary responsibility for crime prevention from the constables and the night watchmen, but despite their heroic efforts to sweep the city clean of drunks, prostitutes, and gamblers, their overall impact on the courts was minimal. It was probably the constables who invented plea bargaining in the 1830s, but apart from this notable contribution, they had little direct influence on the dramatic changes that were underway in the city's legal system.

This new proactive stance in criminal justice, however, set the stage for a dramatic growth in the prosecutor's office. Thanks to his new role in ferreting out malefactors, the prosecutor assumed control of the crime control machinery in Boston. His duties had grown from a simple presentation of the Commonwealth's case in court against a handful of defendants in the 1810s to the investigation of vice and regulatory offenses and disposal of the vast majority of defendants through such extrajudicial mechanisms as dismissal, probation, or plea bargaining.

The crime problem itself also took some interesting turns. Youth crime emerged as a problem in the city for the first time in the 1830s, and by 1850 it accounted for the bulk of Boston's property losses. Public drunkenness, gambling, and prostitution also grew rapidly during the 1830s and 1840s. Although the mushrooming Irish population certainly aggravated some of these problems, they were by no means solely responsible.

The big story of this period, however, was the explosion of regulatory offenses, that is, violations of regulatory laws. The Commonwealth made a concerted effort to limit the sale of spirits in the late 1830s and 1840s through licensing, and liquor violations grew by leaps and bounds. The prosecutor was a key factor in the campaign against tavern owners, and this campaign, in turn, was a major reason behind the sudden emergence of his office.

As the prosecutor's responsibilities multiplied, however, the jurisdictions of both the Municipal Court and the Police Court began to realign themselves so that the Municipal Court became the main criminal court of Boston and the Police Court assumed a relatively minor role in the campaign against crime. Since the Police Court had no professional prosecutor, it used complainants or the arresting officer to prosecute its cases. The prosecutor, therefore, did the bulk of his business in the Municipal Court where he presented the Commonwealth's case against offenders. When he became deeply involved in the fight against vice and drunkenness, virtually all these cases shifted to the Municipal Court, where the caseload zoomed. The Police Court's caseload also grew in response to a growing crime problem albeit more slowly, and the crucial cases, i.e., those that most alarmed the community, almost disappeared from the Police Court after 1840. The Municipal Court was where the action was, and though the Police Court did three times the business of the Municipal Court, it was still a court of amateurs dealing with minor cases in a routine fashion.

Finally, criminal trials were growing longer, appeals were becoming more common and being upheld more frequently, fewer jury trials and guilty verdicts were being recorded, and punishments were getting slightly milder.

Some Larger Currents

How were these wondrous changes accomplished? Did they grow out of the individual efforts of practicing jurists and lawyers who saw the problems of the courts and devised practical, everyday solutions? Or did they stem basically from the leaders of the profession who evaluated correctly the outmoded practices of the day and worked out more effective methods for dealing with the shifting problems of the profession? A little bit of both seems to have been the case.

The shift to a more aggressive, proactive posture in the courts was probably a direct result of a deeply held belief among Boston's statesmen and moral leaders—including, for example, John Adams, John Quincy Adams, Josiah Quincy, Judge Lemuel Shaw, and William Ellery Channing—that the state and its policies should be guided foremost by its responsibility for the moral, intellectual, social, and economic betterment of the people. Borrowing from John Locke they believed deeply in the notion of a commonwealth—government's purpose was to serve the highest aspirations of the people. The courts and criminal justice were simply one aspect of a very broad governmental responsibility to uplift the people. As industrialization gathered momentum and entrepreneurs demanded greater flexibility in the law, the courts assumed an important role in furthering economic growth.

At the other end of the court system, plea bargaining was invented by constables in the Police Court who adapted the timeworn practice of negotiating with suspects issues of mutual interest regarding the dual problems of adjudication and sentencing. It worked so well, however, that it was soon adopted more generally, particularly by the progressive jurists of the Municipal Court.

The early decades of the nineteenth century witnessed the beginning of Boston's modern legal system—that is, of high volume, multi-purposed criminal courts using pretrial procedures to dispose of a large number of cases. Paradoxically, as the courts moved toward informal, extralegal methods, the officers of the court—the judges, the defense attorneys, and the prosecutors—were becoming more professional and more technically competent, while legal procedures were becoming more intricate. They were obviously not closely related. Or were they?

Although the courts used plea bargaining extensively to dispose of their minor cases, the Municipal Court was also where the more novel, complicated cases were held. They were tried there by professionals in terms of the evolving rules and doctrines of the profession. The Police Court was largely unaffected by these developments and continued to handle its routine cases in routine ways. Thus, the growing professionalism and evolving due process of the courts were concentrated largely in the Municipal Court, and it (along with the Supreme Judicial Court) became the vessel of Boston's legal development. The Police Court simply atrophied.

We can learn much from history. How and why particular changes were ushered in, and what they meant for the people enveloped by them. This study focuses on the criminal courts of nineteenth-century Boston, but it is not a historical study in the usual sense. Historians identify the flow of events by piecing together the actions and comments of all the significant actors. Diaries, letters, speeches, books, and articles of notables are scrutinized for their viewpoints on the issues of the day, and from these materials a picture of what happened emerges.

At the same time, many historians avoid speculation regarding the whys and wherefores of history. Thus, even though much of their work is guided by personal whim or curiousity, they rarely give voice to their intuitions regarding the broad meaning of their work. They rarely attempt to define the larger social, political, or economic forces that were also moulding the actions of the personalities they report. They gather mountains of information on individuals but relatively little on the larger issues that made these individuals.

This study paints a portrait of the city's courts, its officers, its constables, and its criminals, and it presents a record of their activities form 1814 to 1850. But it does not stop there. The oceanic changes that engulfed Boston during this period were clearly reflected in the action of its criminals and its courts. I have attempted here to interpret the findings of my research in terms of authoritative perspectives drawn from the social sciences.

My explanations as to why the courts and criminals acted as they did should spark focused research into the detailed circumstances that underlay the broad changes in the courts depicted here. History and historians can benefit from a broader sense of social currents, and I have attempted to place the day-to-day activities of the courts within the eddies and whirlpools of these broader currents.

Some readers may object to my method, but to wait until all the facts have been gathered and their patterns clearly delineated before suggesting their probable structure is to perpetuate the weaknesses of an aimless gathering of historical facts with little awareness or concern for the key events that guided historical development. Thus, I have attempted to explain why the courts grew increasingly aggressive in searching out violators, though my explanations are inferences drawn not only from the historical record but also from the broader social and political movements that shaped these courts and criminals and made them what they were. That is the method of science: the linking of idiographic research with nomothetic explanation. To be sure, this link must be carefully documented, but explanation that guides fact-gathering is the key. Orderly cumulation of knowledge and efficient gathering of evidence become the norm as a discipline evolves into a science.

The links between broad social currents and day-to-day activities are sometimes difficult to document, particularly where the personal documents of most of the people involved no longer exist, but I have provided a limited documentation of these links, and further research will provide more. Once the right questions have been framed, the method to be used in answering them is often clear, and that is what I have attempted here: to ask the right questions of the historical record, and as some answers became clear to pose even more pointed questions.

Boston's Lower Criminal Courts, 1814–1850

1
The Early Criminal Courts

The criminal courts provide a fine measure of a community's civilization. Dangerous villians, social deviants, petty offenders, fearful victims, and innocent defendants all stream through the courts where they are dealt with by duly authorized agents of conventionality and order. Taken together, the offenders and their accusers offer a composite picture of the forces for change and dissipation in the community as well as the forces for stability.

The courts, however, offer more than a window on society. They have evolved a method for resolving the most fundamental conflicts so that all parties are bound by the outcome, even if it means serious sacrifice for the accused. The system of due process coolly assesses both prosecution and defense arguments and provides an objective, authoritative decision regarding their legal merit. Today the courts stand as a symbol of fair play, of a commitment to justice over social or political privilege. The quality of the courts, therefore, is a clear barometer of the extent to which a community has installed justice at the center of its social and political life.

Not all courts balance the demands of justice and politics in the same way. Some cleave tightly to the rules of due process while others respond to the demands of factional politics, but all of them reflect in some fashion both the state of the law and the condition of the community.

The Objectives

This study reveals how the lower criminal courts in antebellum Boston adapted to a rapidly changing community, while also undergoing far-reaching changes in their own right. Much can be learned through studies that use court records to identify the level and patterning of their criminal work. Care must be taken to tease apart those changes that arise through the influence of the larger politico-legal system from those that develop within the courts themselves, and from those that reflect social change in the community.

In this chapter we shall concentrate on the changing context of the courts—the dramatic changes that Boston as a whole was undergoing as well as the fundamental changes in the broader legal system that affected Boston's lower courts very directly. Specifically, we shall review how the Commonwealth's courts were drawn into an activist, responsive role in shaping the development of Massachusetts, and how the local courts, in turn, assumed a central role in the effort to control the sale of spirits in Boston.

We shall also review the shift in legal training in New England from apprenticeships in law offices to formal curricula in established law schools, and we shall estimate its effects upon the quality of the legal profession. We shall survey the recent history of procedural law in the United States, and finally we shall recount the structural growth of the courts in Boston during the antebellum period. In subsequent chapters we shall focus more narrowly on Boston's lower courts themselves, and how they changed.

The Evolution of Early Boston

The early nineteenth century, roughly between the War of 1812 and the Civil War, was a pivotal period in the development of Boston and the country. During this era the nation as a whole was moving rapidly toward full industrialization, and Boston transformed itself from a small seaport of 33,000 in 1810 into a metropolitan center of 137,000 in 1850. During this forty-year period, satellite cities that produced everything from firearms to cotton and woolen textiles to shoes sprang up around Boston. They provided a strong economic base for Boston's emergence as a commercial, financial, and light manufacturing center before the Civil War. In the midst of all this, a tidal wave of Irish-Catholic immigrants broke upon the city, which forced Bostonians to face a conflict between their universalistic ideals and their particularistic religious and ethnic loyalties. In 1830 only 19.4 percent of Boston's population had been born in the British Isles, but by 1850 fully 43.4 percent had (Knights 1978, 36), and the vast bulk of these immigrants had come from Ireland. Between 1841 and 1850, nearly 76,000 people landed in Boston from Ireland (Handlin 1968, Table V, 242).

The economic transformation of the community, together with its growing heterogeneity, meant a gradual change in its crime patterns. In the early 1700s prosecutions for both property and assaultive offenses were much lower than in the early part of the nineteenth century, and property cases outnumbered assaultive cases by more than three to one (Ferdinand 1980, 198). The most common cases by far involved crimes against chastity, morality, or decency (Faber 1977–78, 99–103).

By the early 1820s criminal cases per 1,000 had multiplied by a factor of eight, and assaultive cases now outnumbered property cases by nearly two to one! Cases involving crimes against morality were still common, but now they were followed closely by assaultive cases (Ferdinand 1980, 198; but see Nelson 1975, 471–72). Prosecutions for violent crimes had increased substantially since the eighteenth century; prosecutions for property crimes also increased but at a slower pace; and prosecutions for crimes against chastity, morality, or decency increased slightly even if liquor violations are left out.

What are we to make of these changes? First, there can be little doubt that broad changes in the Boston community during the eighteenth century affected its crime patterns. The fact that all measures of criminality point to sizable increases suggests that the underlying crime rate did, in fact, move up sharply.

At the same time, it is clear that shifts in prosecution policy were also a factor. Interest was shifting from crimes involving sin or personal frailty, e.g., fornication or adultery, toward those connected with organized vice, e.g., prostitution, keeping a gambling house, or illegal taverns. As the cohesiveness and homogeneity of the community declined, sin became less important, but as the city sought to control itself more closely through governmental structures, regulating vice became a major focus (Foucault 1979, Part Three, chap. 1). Public drunkenness was an obvious exception, but it was also a symptom of the pressing problem of controlling the sale of alcohol.

No doubt the growing attention given to vice stemmed from the rapid growth of a vice industry in Boston, but it also reflected a growing commitment to controlling the problem; and in the early decades of the nineteenth century, brothels, gambling dens, and illegal taverns all came under pressure. In absolute terms there was no decline in crimes against morality in Boston, even when we exclude drunkenness arrests that were growing rapidly, but relative to other crimes, their prominence had clearly lessened in comparison to the eighteenth century.

The fact that prosecutions for violent crimes far outnumbered property prosecutions in the Police Court during this early period (see fig. 5.8) is also of some interest, since other studies of European and American cities have discovered a similar pattern during periods of rapid industrialization (Zehr 1975; Ferdinand 1978). Zehr, for example, found that relative to property offenses, prosecutions for violent offenses rose sharply during early stages of industrialization in several German and French cities, but that as industrialization advanced, violent offenses reverted just as rapidly to their former ratio with property offenses.

Looking at the Boston data, instead of reflecting an underlying shift in criminality, it now appears that these changes stemmed largely from a growing reluctance of the court to accept minor assault and battery cases. Basically, as the Police Court gathered experience, it became wary of minor assault and battery cases, which were mainly private disputes, and their numbers, relative to minor property offenses, declined. Thus, large swings here were largely the result of a changing policy in which the officers of the Police Court became convinced that minor assault and battery cases were not criminal and could not be controlled effectively by court action.

The Emergence of Responsive Law

The antebellum period witnessed a fundamental change in the broader legal system as well. Not only were the common law concepts of justice and due process being refined, but a whole new legal focus—positive, responsive law—was forming in which the aim was not simply to adjudicate criminal complaints but to identify and resolve serious problems in the community (Nonet and Selznick 1978, chap. 4). Traditionally, the courts had served as the ultimate arbiter to whom citizens might bring their complaints against malefactors and receive a degree of satisfaction. Traditionally as well, the courts had passively awaited these complaints and adjudicated them largely unmindful of the result in society. The courts had played a reactive role, leaving the citizens to decide when a civil tort or a criminal offense had been sufficiently grievous to justify mobilizing legal institutions.

Horwitz, a legal historian, writes regarding eighteenth-century America[1]:

> common law rules were not regarded as instruments of social change; whatever legal change took place generally was brought about through legislation. During this period, the common law was conceived of as a body of essentially fixed doctrine to be applied in order to achieve a fair result between private litigants in individual cases. Consequently, American judges ... almost never employed the common law as a creative instrument for directing men's energies toward social change. (1977, 1)

Several forces converged during the early industrial period to alter permanently the development of America's legal institutions. The Revolution had demonstrated conclusively that a determined people, united behind a common purpose, could chart their own destiny. This fact, together with a long cherished belief in New England that government and its leaders were to foster the common virtues of the people, prompted the American people in the early decades of the nineteenth century to use government and its agencies to help build an industrial nation.

It all began in Massachusetts when a commonwealth form of government committed to the people's welfare was created in 1780 (Handlin 1968, chap. 1; see also Smith 1966, 3–11). Drawing mainly on the ideas of John Locke, New Englanders believed in the perfectibility of mankind, and they bestowed upon the new Commonwealth in Massachusetts the duty of accomplishing this purpose. John Quincy Adams, sixth president of the United States, expressed this philosophy of government in his annual address to Congress in 1825.

> Moral, political, intellectual improvement are duties assigned by the Author of Our Existence to social no less than individual man. For the fulfillment of these duties governments are invested with power, and to the attainment of the end—the progressive improvement of the governed—the exercise of delegated powers is a duty as sacred as the usurpation of powers not granted is criminal and odious. (quoted in Pickett 1969, 47–48)

In Boston this philosophy meant strengthening such beneficial institutions as the family and schools and suppressing such human frailties as vice and crime. The idea of a commonwealth meant, therefore, that government must play a large role in human affairs if the people were to fulfill their social and moral potential.

In particular it meant that public officials, while creating a healthy, beautiful city, must at the same time earnestly suppress drunkenness, prostitution, and gambling. The first to take up this mandate was Mayor Josiah Quincy (1823–29) who not only built Quincy Market and the Juvenile House of Reformation, organized Boston's first Fire Department, widened the streets of Boston, and kept them free of animal waste, but also systematically harassed West End brothels and tavern owners who sold spirits illegally (Lane 1967, 23–25).

Shortly after taking office, Mayor Quincy organized a series of raids on the brothels, and in August 1823 he arrested more than one-hundred inmates of such places and filed twenty-three liquor law violations in the Police Court. Later, in July 1825, a similar raid took place against the Beehive, a notorious, three-story, cone-shaped brothel in the North End, but this time it was organized by local residents who pulled down the tenement and attacked other brothels for three nights running, despite the efforts of the mayor and the city marshal to control the riot. Much property damage was reported but no one was injured (Hobson 1987, 11, 23).

Mayor Quincy's son, Josiah Quincy, Jr., resumed the battle when he became mayor of Boston in 1846 with frequent raids of brothels and gambling dens (Lane 1967, 64–65), but it was public drunkenness that alarmed Bostonians most in the 1830s and 1840s. Drunkenness was widespread and growing, and by the mid-1830s control of public drunkenness had become a major public goal.

On the national scene, distilled spirits had become a convenient form for bringing surplus grains to market, and by 1830 consumption per capita had grown to more than five gallons a year (Barney 1987, 103). As the temperance movement gathered strength in the 1840s, however, ascetic evangelism, the middle class, and feminine groups joined forces on behalf of prohibition. In Boston during the 1840s meetings were held almost nightly by temperance supporters or their opponents, and erratic swings of public policy during the 1830s and 1840s must be understood in this light. The politicization of the issue made the solution more elusive but at the same time more extreme.

Before 1835 common drunkards were arrested only when their public behavior had become a notorious disgrace, and the maximum penalty was set at a twenty dollar fine and sixty days in the House of Correction. When the problem began to spread in the 1830s, the statute was broadened in 1835 to include simple drunkenness and the punishment was changed for a second offense to a fine of ten dollar and three months in the House of Correction (Lane 1967, 49).

A parallel effort focused on vendors of spirits—the tavern owners. In 1786 the legislature passed a law prohibiting the sale of liquor in quantities of less than twenty-eight gallons without a liquor license. This law served the Commonwealth well, and it was not substantially changed until 1832 when it was relaxed.

The license fee was cut back; the smallest quantity that could be sold without a license was reduced to ten gallons; and the restrictions of sales to servants, minors, and common drunkards were no longer closely controlled. The policing of the liquor laws was not aggressive, and in 1830 upwards of three-hundred dealers were dispensing spirits without a license (Lane 1967, 41).

The more permissive 1832 law, however, only seemed to spur temperance forces into action. In 1833 the Board of Aldermen began restricting the number of vendor licenses in the city, and by 1835 the number of licensed taverns had dropped by half to about three-hundred (Lane, 1967, 42). In 1838 a "Fifteen-Gallon Law" was passed by the legislature in which the minimum sale of liquor by licensed vendors was set at fifteen gallons. Sales by the glass were prohibited, and the number of licenses was restricted to one for every two-thousand inhabitants or only about forty-three for all of Boston.

This new law, however, was repealed in 1840, and during the rest of the decade, in the absence of controlling state legislation, the Board of Aldermen in Boston regulated the sale of liquor through its licensing power. The number of licenses waxed or waned as political pressures dictated (Lane 1967, 78). In 1850, however, the state again insisted upon tighter control, and in addition to distilled spirits, for the first time wine, beer, and cider were included under its restrictions. Finally, in 1852, prohibition was established by law in which the private sale of alcohol in any amount in Massachusetts was forbidden, and violators were liable to a jail sentence upon a third conviction.

Vice was a vexing problem to Boston's antebellum leaders. It was widespread and growing, but it diverted the people from their broader purpose of building a commonwealth. For the most part, these leaders assumed a harsh, puritanical attitude toward it, and they spent the decades of the 1830s and 1840s trying to eradicate it.

The police are an indication of the serious effort that was devoted to stamping out vice in Boston (Hobson, 1987, 17–20). As the campaign to control drunkenness and prostitution gathered momentum, the idea of an organized police force equipped to deal not only with riots and crime but also with vice gathered support (Lane 1967, chap. 4). The city fathers viewed the police as a source of moral reform in the community: by cleansing the social environment, they made it easier for the citizens to follow a moral path (Lane 1967, 48). Constables and the night watch had handled all problems in this area since the beginning, but now it was decided that a force responsive to city officials and not to the courts, as the constables were, was badly needed. In 1838 nine police officers were appointed under the City Marshal, Benjamin Pollard, and in 1846 their number was increased to thirty with three detectives. It was clear that one of their primary responsibilities was to uphold the recently enacted liquor control statutes (Lane 1967, 44).

As the city expanded and prohibition gathered support, the police force also grew. Since no one was willing to abolish the constabulary or the night watch, during the 1840s the city had three distinct police arms. The mission of the watch was to maintain peace and order in the community after dark, but its police functions were definitely secondary to its duty to protect the community against fire (Lane 1967, 96). The constabulary, though primarily a police force, were officers of the court and not even city employees. Only the new police could be relied upon to enforce the vice laws as the city fathers wanted them enforced.

The police are not our primary concern here, but it is worth noting that the emergence of the police during the 1840s signaled a substantial shift in the lines of authority in enforcing the law. The constables had enforced the law at the bidding of the courts and were responsible ultimately to the chief judge. The police reported through the city marshal to the mayor and the city council. The courts were attuned to the limits of police power then as now, but the city's governing cadres were *more* interested in seeing city policy carried out. Only the city had the resources to establish an organized police force, but in so doing the city also changed fundamentally the basic purpose of the police.

Several developments, however, served to divert state government away from a repressive stance toward vice and crime and toward the constructive commonwealth ideal announced in the state's first constitution. As the industrial revolution gathered force in the 1830s, private firms became much more aggressive in pursuing economic opportunity. They utilized the waterways for irrigation, power, and transportation and in the process sparked innumerable disputes regarding water rights (Horwitz, 1977, 34–42). The courts were increasingly drawn into these conflicts and forced to revise the law regarding the uses of waterways so as to permit a more efficient utilization of this natural resource.

In addition small businesses in Boston began to use a variety of illegal practices (dishonesty in accounting, inaccurate weights and measures, misrepresentations in advertising and merchandising) that required constant supervision both by the courts and the new police (Lane 1967, 53). The business community was coming under a close scrutiny from the legislature and the courts as it exploited the environment for economic purposes.

As the Commonwealth assumed responsibility for guiding economic growth, the Supreme Judicial Court began to broaden the role of Massachusetts's legal institutions in the nineteenth century. Instead of viewing the courts's mission as one of defining the rule of law authoritatively and holding defendants precisely to it, the Supreme Judicial Court began to see it more as one of identifying the purposes of the community and helping the citizens to realize these purposes. Where the law obstructed this goal, the court was increasingly willing to review and reinterpret it. Where the law failed to curb unscrupulous entrepreneurs, it was strengthened. Thus, the state's legal institutions took their place alongside administrative government in helping the people achieve the idea of a commonwealth.

> by 1820 the process of common law decision making had taken on many qualities of legislation. As judges began to conceive of common law adjudication as a process of making and not merely discovering legal rules,

they were led to frame general doctrines based on a self-conscious consideration of social and economic policies. . . . This increasing preoccupation with using law as an instrument of policy is everywhere apparent in the early years of the nineteenth century. (Horwitz 1977, 2–3)

Industrialization helped to liberate the courts and law from dealing narrowly with vice and crime to a much broader conception of the law as a means of reshaping the institutions of the community for the general welfare. The problem of vice offered a very convenient issue to those who saw the main responsibility of government as that of protecting the people from obnoxious temptations, but the industrial revolution showed that government and the courts must also act positively on behalf of emerging forces within the community. The responsibility of the courts was broader than that originally envisioned by their early spokesmen: it was to encourage and channel positive forces within the community so that their fullest potential might be realized. In this way the courts laid the foundations for responsive law in the United States.

Llewellyn has called this period the Golden Age of American law, and Gilmore described it as the Age of Discovery in which,

an extraordinary degree of judicial power . . . had rooted itself in our practice well before the Civil War . . . with great judges deciding great cases greatly, aware of the lessons of the past but conscious of the needs of the future, striking a sensitive balance between the conflicting claims of local autonomy and national uniformity in an immense, diverse, and rapidly growing country, creating a new law for a new land. (Gilmore 1977, 35, 41)

As the courts began to focus on the business community, they assumed a regulatory stance—a stance that called for supervisory and repressive powers over business. This new responsibility, in turn, contained a number of important implications for legal institutions in the United States (cf. Teubner). It highlighted the need for purposive laws oriented to the peculiar needs of the community. We have already seen how Massachusetts shaped its legislation to combat public drunkenness during the 1830s. It also fostered more flexible criminal procedures that allowed greater individualization in adjudication and sentencing.

Businessmen were not simply members of the dangerous classes who bowed easily to criminal prosecution. They were sometimes powerful members of the community who had considerable financial and political resources to throw into their defense. Moreover, many of their crimes were not *mala in se* so much as *mala prohibita*. Thus, not only would prison sentences be difficult to impose, they would also often be inappropriate. Fines were needed to sanction their misbehavior. In addition much of their enterprise was devoted to novel activities where the law was vague. The degree of their guilt was unclear, and the proper dispositions for their cases were not well defined. In this context plea bargaining emerged (see chap. 5) during the 1830s to help the courts sanction the overly aggressive activities of businessmen without subjecting them at the same time to rigid procedures or punishments that ignored the individuality of their cases.

The new regulatory powers of the courts contributed to the growth of a more active prosecutor. Under the common law, private citizens or arresting constables prosecuted most criminal cases, but as the complexity of regulatory laws grew, the difficulties of enforcement and prosecution in Boston forced a more effective prosecutorial arm, and the prosecutor's office assumed at mid-century a dominant position in the fight against crime in general and regulatory crime in particular.

Developments in probation and parole also heralded the emergence in the criminal courts of more proactive policies vis-à-vis the community. As minor criminals began to inundate the courts in the 1830s, their poverty made it clear that simple, dispassionate punishments geared to their offense would only compound their misery and aggravate their criminality. Social support was needed more than condemnation. Josiah Quincy had led the way in establishing the Juvenile House of Reformation in 1826 and in response to his plea, the state legislature in 1835 opened the door to early prison release for morals offenders who promised to mend their ways and who posted a small surety as a guarantee with the court. Shortly after, in 1841, John Augustus—the father of probation—began his efforts to redeem the downtrodden of Boston by assuming custody over derelicts and others who promised to reform themselves in return for kindly words, subsistence, and shelter.

These small measures in Boston were the forerunners of a vast progressive movement that led ultimately to the Juvenile Court in 1899 in Chicago. They reflected essentially the new, positive stance of the courts as they confronted conditions in the community that seemed to demand legal intervention. In short a responsive, constructive orientation took shape during this period that led the courts to assume an activist stance toward the community and its problems.

The Evolution of the Common Law

While these changes were taking shape, the definitions of criminality were being sharpened, and gaps in due process were being plugged.

Recruitment to the bar was being more strictly regulated by a rejuvenated bar organization, and the training of lawyers was becoming more systematic and rigorous. Since these developments also shaped the course of justice in Boston, they should be explored in some detail to assess how they may have affected the criminal courts.

THE PREPARATION OF LAWYERS

Prior to the American Revolution, colonial lawyers were admitted for the most part to the English bar. Accordingly, they served an apprenticeship in English law offices while also participating in the Inns of Court at Westminster. After the Revolution, American lawyers were still trained via apprenticeships, but the English bar and Inns of Court were no longer available, and of necessity, their training was carried out almost exclusively in American law offices.

After the war, however, the American bar became progressively weaker (Hurst 1950, chap. 12; Chroust 1965, chap. 3). Its important centers were scattered along the Atlantic seaboard from Boston to Richmond, and its ability to shape the professional experience of American lawyers was much weaker than its English counterpart centered in London.

The prerevolutionary bar organization in Boston, the Suffolk Bar Association, seems to have had some influence on legal students, and its immediate successor, the Bar Association, played an even more important role. On 6 February 1771, the Bar Association agreed that no one should be recommended to the Superior Court as an attorney "who has not studied with some barrister three years at least" and that "the consent of the bar shall not be ... given to any young gentlemen who has not had an education at college, or a liberal education in the judgement of the bar" (Davis 1895, 110). After the Revolution, the Bar Association lapsed into inactivity and was finally dissolved in 1836 (Davis 1895, 114), when it lost the right to recommend candidates to the court for admission to practice (Gawalt 1979, 186).

Even though the Bar Association insisted on at least three years of apprenticeship, the training of American lawyers was still very uneven (Chroust 1965, chap. 4). Different law offices had different types of legal business and presented their apprentices with different qualities of expertise. Although much depended on the quality of the fledgling lawyer, much also depended on the legal skills of those who served as mentors as well as on the richness of their practice.

The apprenticeship method of training young lawyers could not help but produce an inferior bar, especially where the legal profession itself was dispersed and had only a weak tradition of authoritative service. The need for a different method of training young lawyers was painfully apparent.

At first, the need was answered by individual lawyers and judges giving ad hoc lectures for a fee to anyone who was interested. Soon, however, faculties of law were established to provide an integrated curriculum. The Litchfield Law School was established in 1784 and served the needs of more than one thousand law students during its forty-nine years of existence (Warren 1966, chap. 14). Finally, the older universities began to respond to the cry for systematic legal training. Harvard established its Law School in 1817, and Yale followed with a law school of its own in 1824,

The training that reputable law faculties could provide far exceeded that generally available to apprentices in law offices at the time, and although many of these early experiments failed, university-based law schools ultimately replaced the apprenticeship method of training young lawyers. In 1833, the Litchfield Law School closed its doors, and the preparation of law students was left primarily to reputable law faculties in established universities. An apprenticeship was still required in many states, and some states (Warren 1970, 345–46) even reduced the residence required in law school if the student had already served an apprenticeship. The apprenticeship method, however, was gradually abandoned and after the Civil War, the training of American lawyers assumed its modern form.[2]

Although there is little firm evidence that these changes brought any substantial improvement in the quality of new lawyers, it is a plausible thesis. The displeasure and even contempt with which the traditional method was regarded (Warren 1966, 133–50), the steady growth of the new method, and the comments of those close to these legal innovations suggest that there was a distinct improvement. Harvard's first law professor, Asahel Stearns, wrote that,

> This measure was adopted with the hope of providing a more systematic and thorough course of legal instruction and a better preparation for the practice than is generally attainable in the usual way of acquiring a law education. (Warren 1970, 304)

Nevertheless, for a period after it opened its doors, the Harvard Law School itself was in danger of failing. Declining enrollments, faculty instability, and a legal requirement that candidates to the bar in Suffolk County must undergo an apprenticeship in a law office for one year preceding their admission severely hampered its effectiveness (Gawalt 1979, 154). By the 1830s, however, it had recovered and was well on its way to the preeminence it enjoys today.

But if, indeed, the quality of training and the quality of lawyers improved in New England as a systematic curriculum in law replaced the apprenticeship method, it must have been reflected in improvements in the processing of criminal cases through the legal system. Whatever other changes were occurring in the courts during this period, it is important that a secular improvement in the professional skills of lawyers practicing in the criminal court be taken into account.

AN EVOLVING CRIMINAL PROCEDURE

During the colonial period the courts of Boston, as branches of the courts of England (Baker 1977, 21–22), administered a rough sort of justice in terms of the English common law and local standards of propriety and morality (Ferdinand 1978, 263–64; Oberholzer 1954). Following the Revolution, however, changes in the rules of evidence imposed greater structure upon criminal trials.

In seventeenth-century England, it was still possible for the king and his royal justices to punish jurors who found an unwelcome verdict, and complaints about the manipulation of juries and their verdicts by judges were common (Baker 1977, 23–25; Langbein 1978, 284–287; 291–95). Not until 1848 were the lower courts of England brought clearly and systematically under appellate review. Previously, review of criminal court decisions had been rare, and unjust verdicts were very difficult to reverse.

Defendants in England were not permitted defense witnesses until the end of the seventeenth century, and they were denied defense counsel until the eighteenth (Langbein 1978, 307–14; Beattie 1986, 341–43). The jury was seen as capable of separating valid evidence from invalid evidence, and little care was taken to limit what the jury could hear until 1675–90, when the first hearsay rules were formulated.

U.S. courts also followed very loosely defined procedures before the Revolution. The hearsay rule restricting second hand testimony was not given wide authority in U.S. courts until the early part of the nineteenth century (Friedman 1973, 134–37), and criminal defendants were not permitted formally to testify in their own behalf until the middle of the nineteenth century (Warren 1966, 472–74). As these procedures evolved, however, they contributed to more tightly defined due process and strengthened the court as it sought to establish procedural fairness.

NEW RESPONSIBILITIES

During the antebellum period, Boston's criminal courts began to assume a variety of new responsibilities that brought them very close to the multipurposed pattern of today's courts (Sarat 1979, 59–70). Since the beginning U.S. courts have been charged with the responsibility of setting standards of conduct through their sanctioning power. At first, they shared this responsibility with other institutions, that is, the church and town meeting (Ferdinand 1978, 262–63), with the result that minor deviancy was controlled largely through extra legal means (Oberholzer 1956, chap. 7 and 8). As the church lost its influence and the town meeting fell into desuetude, the courts became the only public agency capable of defining and maintaining minimum standards of conduct in the community.

They assumed this responsibility only hesitantly. Throughout the eighteenth century, noncapital criminal cases in Boston had been heard by a single court, the Court of General Sessions of the Peace. This court was established on 27 June 1699, and continued until 1800 as the primary criminal court in Boston. Between 1800 and 1822, however, four distinct courts were formed at different times to deal with different segments of the criminal spectrum.

On 4 March 1800 the Municipal Court of Boston was created and assumed the criminal jurisdiction of the Court of General Sessions. The new Municipal Court was funded by Suffolk County, but its officers (judges and prosecutor) were appointed by the governor. The Court of General Sessions had been funded mainly by fees and fines collected by the court.

At first the Municipal Court handled the entire criminal jurisdiction of the Court of General Sessions, but in 1809 it shared this jurisdiction with a quick succession of lower courts that held bench trials and could sentence defendants for only limited terms to the House of Corrections. The first of these, the Court of Common Pleas, assumed the lower end of the Municipal Court's criminal jurisdiction on 19 June 1809, and only two years later on 25 June 1811 the General Court of Sessions was formed to take its place. These several courts were all funded and staffed by the Commonwealth.

Nevertheless, the town of Boston had a pressing need to police its own ordinances, and steady pressure was brought by town officials to establish a local court staffed and funded by the town (Sprague 1890, 14–21). The General Court of Sessions was inadequate not only because it was a state court, but also because its justices were paid basically from the fees and fines that left them open to charges of manipulating verdicts to strengthen the court's financial base (Sprague 1890, 25–31). The Police Court, which was established in 1822 when the town was incorporated as a city, solved these problems by assuming the Court of Sessions's criminal jurisdiction as well as all cases involving violations of city ordinances and by-laws, and by paying its justices fixed salaries.

The courts obviously had some difficulty in deciding how to divide up the spectrum of criminal cases, and the different levels of government had difficulty in creating just the right mix of courts to serve their distinctive interests.[3] Confusion and uncertainty were apparant as the courts moved into a jurisdiction where they had never had clear authority before, i.e., the lower end of the criminal spectrum that had been controlled for the most part during the eighteenth century by the church and town meeting.

As the courts assumed jurisdiction over minor criminality, the standards of behavior they upheld, at least in the beginning, were those that had prevailed when Boston was still a small village dominated by an organized clergy. Although the structure of the community had changed substantially, by the 1820s its concepts of deviancy and minor crime had not, and Boston, through its lower courts, was attempting to maintain the same high standard of public behavior that had prevailed during the earlier period.

But the lower courts were not a church, and for a variety of reasons they could not fill the gap left by the receding influence of the church and town meeting. In the first place, the courts were a secular institution in a democratically organized community and were, therefore, much more accessible to outside influence (Klonoski and Mendelsohn 1979, 17–18) than the church and clergy in a theocratic community. Thus, if the courts in the nineteenth century were requiring a level of public behavior that was unacceptable to community leaders, the courts could be adapted to community sensibilities much more easily than could the church or its clergy in the eighteenth (Neubauer 1974, chap. 12). Second, the courts had no congregation and, therefore, no fine fabric of personal relationships to reinforce the standards of behavior they were seeking to maintain. They had only a force of constables to police the community and the formal sanctions of a fine or confinement with which to punish offenders. Thus, the formal punishments meted out by the lower courts for minor deviance (i.e., small fines) were so much less effective than the informal punishments of the church for similar offenses (i.e., public reprimands from the clergy) that considerable pressure undoubtedly accumulated within the city, as in England, to lift minor deviancy out of the jurisdiction of the court altogether.[4] Thus, as the Municipal and Police Courts assumed basic responsibility for minimal standards of public behavior, they encountered growing pressure to abandon minor deviance and to concentrate on more serious forms of criminality.

In addition, as the courts assumed sole responsibility for deviant conduct, Bostonians began to make full use of them to achieve their private goals. Most communities, and Boston was certainly no exception, nurture a continuing round of disagreements, quarrels, and even feuds among their citizens. These quarrels are generally settled either by informal consent or by communal intervention. Before the criminal courts assumed primary responsibility for justice and tranquility in the community, there were a variety of less formal methods for settling these disputes. The village pastor was usually available to mediate them, but agreements were sometimes achieved through out-and-out bullying. The strong ruled the weak in these instances, and the weak had no alternative but to accept the forceful terms of the strong.

As the courts became readily available to citizens, however, many disagreements that would have been resolved earlier by threat or actual violence were now taken to the courts for prosecution as criminal offenses. In short, when the courts became the primary instrument of justice in the community, they received a wave of cases that essentially represented minor criminal offenses stemming from serious private quarrels.[5] The distinction between offender and victim in many of these disputes was blurred, but since the court was responsible for preserving justice, initially at least, it had the responsibility for hearing these cases. Thus, in the early years of the courts, they were deluged with private disputes that were more a matter for mediation than criminal prosecution.

The legislature worried about the problem from time to time, and in 1843 formed a committee to consider whether "it be expedient to provide that the complainant shall in these trifling cases, be compelled to give security for payment of costs, if the prosecution be unfounded" (House Document No. 63, 1843, 3). No such authority was given Massachusetts courts, but it is clear that trivial cases were a problem.

As the lower courts carried out a campaign to rid themselves of trivial cases, their caseloads and particularly their minor criminal cases slowly shrank in volume. These adjustments undoubtedly hit the Police Court hardest, since its primary jurisdiction was minor crime, and probably explain why minor crime fell so much more rapidly in the Police Court during the 1820s than in the Municipal Court.

The Antebellum Legal Threshold

Sometime during the early 1830s Boston's lower criminal courts passed an important legal threshold. As they widened their jurisdictions during the 1830s and 1840s, growing numbers of lawyers, court clerks, and probation officers were needed, and new constituencies began to appear that favored one or the other of the courts' emerging roles as guardian of justice, mediator of private disputes, regulator, and provider of social services. Simultaneously, the officers of the courts — the judges, prosecutors, and defense attorneys — were becoming more professional and skilled as the procedures they followed grew more encompassing and the sanctions they administered became more humane.

In short the lower criminal courts were being transformed into multi-purposed agents of the community and the Commonwealth, and new personnel, both in terms of specialization and professional commitment, were needed to carry these changes out. The basic aims of this study are to identify how the community and the Commonwealth helped to shape the lower courts; to show how professionalization of the bench facilitated these changes; and to document the courts' response.

2
Responsive Law and Police Power

Legal scholars are largely in agreement that sometime during the antebellum period the law in Massachusetts was transformed from a rather rigid institution upholding minimal standards of social intercourse to a vehicle for advancing the moral and social welfare of society. Before the Revolution the common law was regarded as sovereign, and the community and its citizens were obliged to bow to its authority (Horwitz chap. 1). The law was administered for the most part in terms of subtle common law doctrines but with little regard for its impact on the parties involved, and the court felt no obligation to adjust its rulings to any particular end other than that of justice. To be sure, colonial administrative law was designed to serve the mercantile interests of the mother country, but the common law was regarded as useful only for the pursuit of justice.

Following the Revolution, a new spirit gripped the United States. In writing to a friend, John Adams observed that

> We are trying, by a thousand experiments, the ingenuity as well as virtue of our people. Imagine four hundred thousand people without government or law, forming themselves in companies for various purposes.... You must allow for a great deal of the ridiculous, much of the melancholy, and some of the marvellous. (Handlin 1968, 6)

After their victory in the Revolutionary War, New Englanders felt they had embarked upon a great enterprise, and they eagerly set about building a civil society guided by Christian, especially Enlightment, ideals — a society directed by its united citizens toward their common purposes; a society that was self-governing with a wide range of civil liberties for the individual. Most of the leading clergy in New England at the time — Lyman Beecher, Thomas Hooker, Albert Barnes, Timothy Dwight, William Ellery Channing, and Theodore Parker — thought and preached along these lines, and all of them envisioned the law as the basic instruments of a benevolent state shepherding its people towards an upright life (Armeo 1985, 61–73). William Ellery Channing, the great Unitarian preacher, wrote that "the chief end of the social state is the elevation of its members as intelligent and moral beings" and he welcomed the "great approaching modification of society under which every man will be expected to contribute to this object according to his ability" (Handlin 1968, 190).

Few recognized the paradox of a free people being *directed* toward any broad set of ideals because Locke's concept of the body politic provided just the right formula for sidestepping the issue. The body politic was based upon a unified citizenry who were self-consciously creating a just and civil society through responsive governmental ministers. The people were the creative force, and legal institutions and their lawful agents were the instruments whereby the people's will was realized.

If law was primary in their purpose, education was certainly a close second. Dr. Benjamin Rush, the architect of medical reform in the early United States, regarded the Revolution as only "the first act of the Great Drama.... We have changed our forms of government but it remains to effect a revolution in Principles, opinions, and manners so as to accommodate them to the forms of government we have adopted" (quoted in Messerli 1967, 417–18). Education was to provide the foundation for civic virtue, and a tightly organized political party was to finish the process by fostering republican ideals in its candidates, organization, and policies (Baker 1985, 544–49).

In Massachusetts postwar debates led by John Adams advanced the idea of a new commonwealth in which the social and moral aspirations of the people served as the foundation for a government dedicated to their general welfare. The Massachusetts Constitution of 1780, which Adams wrote almost single-handedly (Homans 1981, 287), proclaimed that:

> The body politic is formed by a voluntary association of individuals: It is a social compact, by which the whole people covenants with each citizen, and each citizen with the whole people, that all shall be governed by certain laws for the common good....
>
> Article VII. Government is instituted for the common good; for the protection, safety, prosperity, and happiness of the people; and not for the profit, honour, or private interest of any one man, family or class of men: Therefore the people alone have an incontestable, unalienable, and indefeasible right to institute Government.

Boston's world renowned public school system is a good example of the way in which the social state was to elevate its citizens, and Bostonians made sure that their children would have easy access to a primary education (see chap. 3). Public education was the responsibility of enlightened leaders acting in the name of the commonwealth to further the moral well being of all the people. It is no accident that Boston became a pioneering center of public education in the early years of the nineteenth century.

In Europe, where society was more complex, there was greater awareness of the differences between the aristocracy and the people as well as between the government and its subjects, but in the United States government was viewed simply as the arm of a unified people, expressing their common will, and seeking their common ends.

Today, it seems romantic, even naive, this notion of a single-minded people working as one for the welfare of all. In all honesty it could not survive the early nineteenth-century drumbeat of factional politics, religious strife, industrial conflict, and Civil War, but for a brief period after the Revolution many, particularly in Massachusetts, embraced it with great fervor.

The commonwealth idea, rooted as it was in John Locke's concepts of the social covenant and the body politic, and in the Puritan ideal of a moral community, carried with it the notion that the legislature had a responsibility to shape society to the social values of the people (Haskins 1968, 16–18). The law, as formulated in the legislature, no longer simply defined abstract justice; it provided the bridge to a new society. The legislature then became the instrument of the common will, and in this capacity it needed an agency to carry forward its initiatives.[1]

The district courts, which were staffed and largely funded by the state, became the chief arm for perfecting legal and social institutions. Together the legislature and the courts defined and implemented the common will with the legislature reactively pinpointing ways to improve the community, and the courts actively helping to realize these improvements in the everyday lives of citizens.

The Bostonian Commonwealth

The first hint of this new activism in government came during Josiah Quincy's term as second mayor of Boston, 1823–29. Mayor Quincy led a vigorous, forceful administration and sought to elevate the community by curbing vice—particularly prostitution and public drunkenness (McCaughey 1974, Chap. 7). As we have seen, Mayor Quincy led raids on taverns and houses of ill fame, and the suspects were tried mostly in the Police Court—the city's court. When Quincy retired from the mayor's post, he felt that he had contributed substantially to the safety and well being of the city and its people (see chap. 5).

There can be little doubt that Quincy's primary inspiration for his moral campaign against vice was founded in the commonwealth idea. Gusfield (1963, 42–43) has traced the origins of the temperance movement to the 1810s and New England's aristocratic, Federalist leaders of which Quincy was a prominent member. Gusfield saw it essentially as a movement to perpetuate traditional values among the common people, but in addition it was clearly an expression of the Federalist's sense of political responsibility. They felt obligated not simply to govern but to provide a government that would nurture the social and moral well being of the people. Quincy made the best of his opportunity to do that in city government.

But the state also had an interest in vice and drunkenness. Throughout the antebellum period the state passed legislation controlling gambling, prostitution, and the sale of spirits, and it policed them through the district courts. The mandate to forge a better society forced a confrontation with vice, and the powers to enforce these legislative initiatives in Boston were vested in both the Police Court and the Municipal Court.

The newfound responsibilities of the legislature and the courts to help fashion a commonwealth were largely sustained by the euphoria and moral convictions of the Revolutionary period (Handlin 1968, chap. 1). As the nineteenth century wore on and the Civil War loomed, the broader vision narrowed to a much more pragmatic view: the government could best serve the interests of the community by furthering economic development.

In Massachusetts, for example, riparian rights had traditionally meant that land and any attendant water rights were basically private property to be used as the owner wished. There was no requirement that water rights serve any productive purpose; only that their use did not limit or interfere with the rights of others (Horwitz 1977, 34–37).

During the 1830s, however, rivers became a convenient source of power for textile mills throughout Massachusetts, and as more and more mill owners came to a given river, the dams they erected weakened the flow for those below them. Those who were impaired in this fashion regularly sued their malefactors, and in 1844 the Supreme Judicial Court of Massachusetts ruled that those whose riparian rights were injured by the damming of the river for industrial purposes had no recourse as long as the original dam made a reasonable use of the river, that is, as long as a dam turned the river to useful pursuits without fundamentally altering it. Those who first exploited a given resource enjoyed priority in utilizing it against claims by late-comers.

The ancient common law view of property that its owner enjoyed its unrestrained use so long as he did not injure others was qualified to permit an owner to use property in ways that were somewhat injurious to others, if the owner was first to make productive use of it (Horwitz 1977, 40–41). There are other examples of adjustments of the common law to serve economic purposes throughout the nineteenth century, and they all testify to the basic shift in philosophy that had occurred.

This fundamental shift—founded as it was on an understanding that the law had a basic obligation to further the interests of the community by promoting economic development—carried implicitly the assumption that the *law* must correct those faults and obstacles that *prevented* sound economic growth. If the law was to facilitate development, it must be a positive factor in the community. It must identify the purposes of the community; it must redirect institutions accordingly; and it must shepherd citizens toward these purposes.

The common law was an ideal instrument for community development: it was bound basically by flexible precedent; it could cut easily through the ambiguities of conflicting claims to a decision that served not simply the needs of the parties but also the long-term interests of the community; and it was not bound to confounding compromises or political settlements. As an instrument of economic development, the common law served very nicely, and through its liberating touch the American people experienced an extraordinary release of energy (Hurst 1956).

As with all things it was not an unmixed blessing. A responsive, purposive law was led by its broad social mission into the thickets of political conflict, and it was forced to expand its sanctioning powers to herd the community and its citizens toward communal purposes. As the courts assumed a purposive stance in the community, they encountered entrenched groups that fought change and sought to restrict the courts and their decisions. The courts themselves became an arena within which political forces confronted each other to force the community in one direction or another (Horowitz 1977, chap. 1). For our purposes the most interesting transformation was the need for the courts to develop their capacity to nudge the community along lines that were consistent with its (the community's) own ultimate values and goals.

The police power of the courts swiftly became a force to reckon with in the early part of the nineteenth century (Handlin and Handlin 1969, chap. 9). This can be seen most clearly in the evolution of the eminent-domain law (Scheiber 1973) in the antebellum period, but it also is evident in a series of rulings by Lemuel Shaw, chief justice of the Massachusetts Supreme Judicial Court, indicating clearly the authority of the legislature and courts over banks, tavern owners, railroads, and mill owners. In each case Shaw and the Supreme Judicial Court upheld the right of the legislature to set the basic terms of business for private companies even to the extent of eliminating their right to do business altogether if the common good required it (Levy 1957, 153-54). The welfare of the community was the ultimate consideration, and that determined who deserved protection under the law and who needed to be curbed.

This was the legal climate within which criminal justice developed in Boston during the antebellum period, and it helps to explain why the Municipal Court became so responsive to the temperance movement in the late 1830s. Many believed that intemperance was not only a serious vice in itself but also that it spawned many other forms of crime and vice as well. The proper way to attack crime and vice in general was to suppress drunkenness (Quincy 1822). A convenient way to accomplish this goal was by controlling the sale of alcoholic beverages. Following this line of reasoning, the courts were enlisted in the regulation of tavern owners by the legislature as it attempted to control the sale of liquor, beer, and wine.

The Police and the Commonwealth

This shift to a responsive stance in the higher courts may help to explain the emergence of a centralized police force in Boston in the late 1830s. The first City Marshal, Benjamin Pollard, had been appointed in 1823 with the authority to prosecute minor crimes and city ordinance violations in the Police Court and to supervise the quality of the city streets, the common sewers, and "whatever else affects the health, security, and comfort of the city" (Lane 1967, 17). Specifically, the City Marshal was responsible for the crime control functions of the constables and deputy marshals as well as an army of teamsters and cartmen who kept the city streets free of rubbish and animal droppings, but the bulk of his time was occupied with policing the numerous licensing ordinances of the city. He issued dog licenses (and disposed of dogs without licenses); he regulated truckmen, hackneys, and cartmen; he licensed parades, exhibitions, public shows, and shopkeepers as they erected buildings, signs, and conducted business; and he supervised the construction and maintenance of public sewers (Lane 1967, 18-20). As the office of the city marshal was defined in 1822, much of his responsibility was in the regulatory category. To be sure it was not concentrated on businesses, but it was only natural that, when intemperance became the focus of regulatory legislation, the police should assume responsibility for enforcing these regulatory laws.

In 1838, the same year in which the restrictive Fifteen Gallon Law had been passed, the Legislature passed a bill allowing Boston to form

TABLE 2.1 THE ARREST PATTERNS OF FOUR ACTIVE CONSTABLES

Ebenezer Shute	Public Drunkenness		Liquor Law Violations		Total Arrests	Jacob Tallert	Public Drunkenness		Liquor Law Violations		Total Arrests
	N	%	N	%			N	%	N	%	
1826	61	28.6	3	1.4	324						
1828	87	18.3	1	0.2	475						
1832	115	27.6	11	2.6	417						
1834	96	21.7	21	4.8	442						
1836	103	24.6	38	9.1	419						
1838	187	34.6	22	4.1	541		3	37.5	—	—	8
1840	173	32.7	20	3.8	529		98	47.6	16	7.8	206
1842	79	26.7	1	0.3	296		168	36.9	2	0.4	455
1844	153	34.7	23	5.2	441		204	30.8	43	6.5	663
1846	308	53.3	9	1.6	578		349	50.1	12	1.7	696
1848	266	37.4	0	0	712		313	37.4	1	0.1	836
1850	—	—	—	—	—		334	33.4	1	0.1	1001

Jonas Shutter	Public Drunkenness		Liquor Law Violations		Total Arrests	Sam Vialle	Public Drunkenness		Liquor Law Violations		Total Arrests
	N	%	N	%			N	%	N	%	
1838	3	33.3	—	—	9		3	60.0	1	20.0	5
1840	173	40.3	11	2.6	429		60	32.4	0	0.0	185
1842	183	31.7	0	0.0	578		171	32.1	4	0.8	532
1844	192	44.8	15	3.5	429		226	37.2	36	5.9	607
1846	362	55.4	4	0.6	653		351	52.9	7	1.1	663
1848	329	39.5	1	0.1	832		330	36.7	1	0.1	898
1850	362	34.2	1	0.1	1058		349	34.9	0	0.0	999

a municipal police department of nine officers to supplement the constables and night watch. The new force turned quickly to policing public drunkenness among other things, and arrests rose from the 1836 low to a new high in 1846 (fig. 4.2). During the 1840s public drunkenness was the preeminent offense handled by the police, and it constituted 36.8 percent of all arrests brought before the Police Court during this period. There can be little doubt that Boston's constables and police were concentrating on the problem.

By way of illustrating the intensity of the effort, the relevant arrests of the four most active constables are displayed in Table 2.1, and we can see that all four reached their personal highs in 1846, when collectively they made 1,370 arrests for public drunkenness—95.1 percent of all public drunkenness arrests that year. At no time did such arrests fall below one-fourth, and in most years they were more than one-third of each constable's total.

It is interesting that liquor law violations were also relatively common in the early years. In 1840, these four officers made forty-seven of the forty-nine arrests in this category that were brought before the Police Court. After 1844, however, the number of liquor law arrests dwindled to nearly none. At first the constables and the Police Court handled these violations, but after 1844, they fell within the jurisdiction of the Municipal Court and no longer appeared in the Police Court.

Of even greater import, however, is the heroic effort of these four constables to suppress generally crime in Boston. In 1848—the last year in which all four were on the force—they made 2,162 arrests, that is, 60 percent of the 3,626 complaints brought before the Police Court. They accounted for 96 percent of the public drunkenness arrests in that year and for all fifty-nine of the prostitution arrests. In 1850, Shutter, Tallert, and Vialle (Shute had retired) made 3,058 arrests, averaging better than 3.2 arrests per day (based on a six-day week and no holidays)! Although there were more than sixty constables and policemen on the force at this time, these three clearly carried the burden of law enforcement in the central city of Boston.[2]

To carry out their expanded mandate the police needed a bigger force and a larger budget. By 1851 the original force of nine officers appointed in 1838 had grown to nearly seventy (Lane 1967, 60–61). In 1848 some constables were made police officers; and the remainder were no longer permitted to carry out full policing functions. Finally, in 1853 the nightwatch was merged with the day police so that policing was brought under one command (Lane 1967, 97–98). By 1854 the force had increased to one hundred and ninety-seven men.

Police budgets kept pace (see fig. 2.1). In 1825 $8,898 was spent on all phases of policing in Boston—only 2.4 percent of the total city budget. From that point police budgets rose steadily to a figure in 1845

Figure 2.1: Total Expenditures for Police in Boston: 1826-1850.
Source: Huse, 1916, Appendix I, 354.

more than eight times the earlier level—$73,362—and to more than triple its earlier share of the city's budget—7.5 percent (Lane 1967, 238). Boston's responsive courts required a proactive police force.

The Municipal Court and the Commonwealth

The new regulatory powers of the criminal justice system, however, were channeled primarily through the Municipal Court. The Police Court experienced a gradual increase in public drunkenness cases during the 1830s (see fig. 5.11), but in all regulatory categories (liquor law violations, offenses against religion, or city ordinance violations) and in vice arrests (see fig. 5.10 and 5.12) it exhibited a decline during the 1830s and 1840s. The Police Court could not provide jury trials, and the legal talent available in that court was limited. The arresting constable was the prosecutor, the defendant was often unrepresented by legal counsel, and the judge usually pronounced the verdict after only a brief hearing. Very few trials extended beyond a single day. The Police Court was not organized to undertake a regulatory role in the community.

It lacked an effective means whereby the constables and the police could be coordinated with the regulatory focus of the courts.[3]

The Municipal Court, on the other hand, was a trial court and was staffed by a county attorney who prosecuted most, if not all of the cases that came before the Municipal Court. The county attorney could and did coordinate the activities of the police and constables in pursuit of regulatory offenders, and since the Municipal Court was his arena, that is where these offenders were handled. Offenses that required a proactive investigation, arrest, and prosecution, that is, victimless crimes, were brought to the Municipal Court.

It is interesting that in addition to its traditional jurisdiction, the Municipal Court began in the 1840s to handle several victimless crimes as well. Prostitution and city ordinance violations had been part of the Police Court's jurisdiction. After 1840, however, city ordinance violators and brothel keepers were shifted to the Municipal Court, where they contributed to sharp rises in its caseload (see fig. 5.9, 5.10, 5.12, and 5.13). Public offenses that did not involve a serious investigative effort such as public drunkenness or street walking, on the other hand, remained part of the Police Court's jurisdiction.

In response to these jurisdictional shifts the expenditures of the

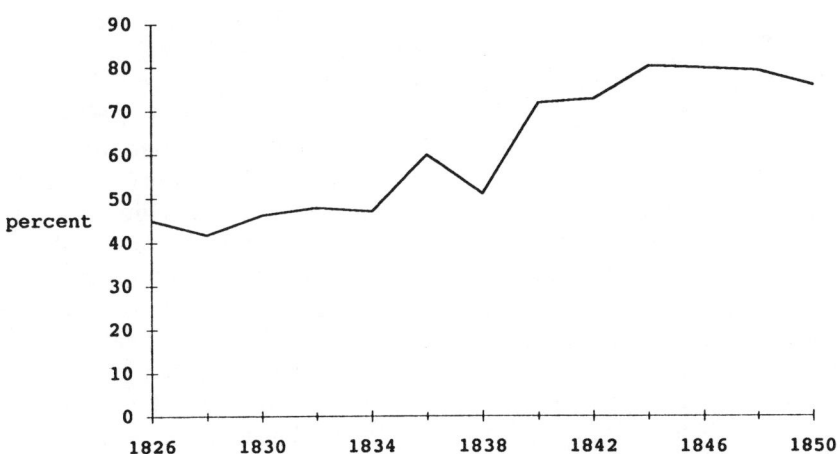

Figure 2.2: Expenditures for Jurors, Witnesses, and Constables as a Percentage of Total Expenditures for Suffolk County: 1826-1850.

Source: Huse, 1916, Appendix I, 349-53.

Municipal Court mounted rapidly. In comparison with total county expenditures, payments to jurors, witnesses, and constables grew especially rapidly during the 1840–50 period. Those court personnel who, next to the prosecutor himself, were most important to effective prosecutions were becoming increasingly active, and by the late 1840s they accounted for a substantial portion of the county's annual budget (see fig. 2.2).[4]

As the prosecutorial function became crucial in fulfilling the function of the court, its scope broadened. One area in which the prosecutor assumed more authority was in charging suspects. Traditionally, the prosecutor had been expected to charge primarily in terms of the circumstances of the offense and the condition of the victim (Langbein 1978). As the prosecutor involved himself more fully in the investigatory phase, other considerations began to play a more important part. The willingness of the accused to assist in prosecuting the instant offense or other offenses became a consideration in his charging. If the accused was resistive, he might be charged with a cluster of related offenses and prosecuted for them all; if he was cooperative, he might be charged and prosecuted for only the essential charge. In return for testimony against others or for guilty pleas to other charges, the instant charge might even be dismissed.

It was only a short step from this expansion in prosecutorial discretion to the invention of plea bargaining—that is, to the manipulation of charging to facilitate the conclusion of a case (Mather 1979). The investigatory responsibilities of the county attorney began to dominate his prosecutorial responsibilities once this step had been taken.

My argument to this point holds that the police powers of the state courts were expanded considerably when a responsive philosophy became dominant among key political and legal spokesmen during the antebellum period, and as a matter of course, the county attorney's office and the municipal police found their services in growing demand.

In Boston the Municipal Court became the instrument of this responsive philosophy because it was attended by a county attorney, and it held jurisdiction over state laws.[3] Vice and regulatory offenses increased dramatically during the 1840s in this court. The Police Court, which was not served by the county attorney and had a more limited jurisdiction, registered declines in vice and regulatory offenses except for public drunkenness. Accompanying these broad shifts in the two courts, there was a sharp expansion in prosecutorial discretion in the Municipal Court during the late 1830s and 1840s and a substantial increase in dismissals, informal probation, and plea bargaining. The Police Court, because it was largely peripheral to this new philosophy, exhibited much less change in charging and prosecuting cases.

The County Attorney's Changing Responsibilities

Changes in the County Attorney's role can most readily be seen by comparing the four broad streams of complaints that made up the Municipal Court's caseload: common law crimes, private disputes, vice, and regulatory violations. Each of these streams called upon a different form of prosecutorial discretion, and by examining how the county attorney handled each of them, we can begin to recognize how his role developed during the antebellum period.

Common law crimes, which included mainly serious crimes that were punished severely, demanded a vigorous prosecution. Several—murder, arson, robbery, forcible rape, and burglary—were subject to the death penalty until 1839, when robbery and burglary were removed from the list of capital offenses, and the others were punishable by long prison terms. The prosecutor's purpose in common law crimes was to provide an effective marshaling of the evidence and witnesses; a careful, professional application of the law; and a convincing courtroom presentation of the case. The prosecutor's role in investigating the case was usually minimal since victims readily came forward with complaints and willingly provided crucial evidence. His primary responsibility was to provide an effective prosecution of these cases to see that justice was done.

These crimes made up about half of the cases (see Table 2.2) coming before the Municipal Court during the 1814–50 period. They were tried before a jury more often than any other category (52.6 percent), and they were found guilty more often as well (38.2 percent). Few were dismissed (2.7 percent) or left on file (8.2 percent), and only 7.4 percent were not resolved by the Municipal Court. Had all capital cases, which were transferred to the Supreme Judicial Court, been excluded, the percentage of cases left on file or left unresolved would have been even smaller. Guilty pleas were accepted at a high rate, but there is no evidence that these pleas were induced by anything other than the defendant's own remorse. Common law crimes were shepherded along toward trial with a minimum of case attrition, and they were prosecuted effectively to a verdict.

Private disputes, however, were handled differently. The prosecutor had to decide whether the complaint reflected a criminal offense or simply a private disagreement in which one party sought to enlist the court on his or her side. If it was a criminal offense, it was prosecuted; if it was a private dispute, it was left to other, nonlegal means of resolution. Most of the assault and battery cases were taken to trial (56.7 percent), and most were found guilty (39.2 percent). But a sizable portion of these cases were also dismissed (5.9 percent), left on file (5.5

TABLE 2.2:
OUTCOME OF FOUR STREAMS OF CASES IN THE MUNICIPAL COURT AGGREGATED FROM 1814 THROUGH 1850

	Guilty N	Guilty %	Not Guilty N	Not Guilty %	Dismissed N	Dismissed %	Left on File N	Left on File %	Complaint Withdrawn N	Complaint Withdrawn %	Default N	Default %	Guilty Plea N	Guilty Plea %	No Outcome Indicated N	No Outcome Indicated %	Total
COMMON LAW CRIMES																	
Felony Against the Person	259	38.0	123	18.0	18	2.6	25	3.7	8	1.2	16	2.3	139	20.4	94	13.8	682
Minor Property Crime	1,054	39.7	321	12.1	46	1.7	205	7.7	4	0.2	78	2.9	780	29.4	165	6.2	2,653
Burglary	220	34.0	120	18.5	31	4.8	58	9.0	1	0.2	6	0.9	171	26.4	40	6.2	647
Counterfeiting	98	32.7	39	13.0	16	5.3	55	22.5	3	1.0	14	4.7	53	17.7	22	7.3	300
Felony Property Crimes	64	41.0	34	21.8	7	4.5	23	14.7	1	0.6	5	3.2	14	9.0	8	5.1	156
Total	1,695	38.2	637	14.4	118	2.7	366	8.2	17	0.4	119	2.7	1,157	26.1	329	7.4	4,438
PRIVATE DISPUTES																	
Fraud	47	15.9	40	13.5	16	5.4	65	25.9	30	10.1	9	3.0	25	8.4	64	21.6	296
Assault & Battery	213	39.2	95	17.5	32	5.9	30	5.5	22	4.0	21	3.9	10	1.8	121	22.2	544
Total	260	31.0	135	16.1	48	5.7	95	11.3	52	6.2	30	3.6	35	4.2	185	22.0	840
VICE OFFENSES																	
Prostitution	134	18.2	73	9.9	34	4.6	79	10.6	11	1.5	38	5.2	188	25.5	180	24.4	737
Gambling	26	30.2	2	2.4	1	1.2	5	5.9	0	0.0	8	9.4	22	25.6	22	25.6	86
Total	160	19.4	75	9.1	35	4.3	84	10.2	11	1.3	46	5.6	210	25.5	202	24.5	823
REGULATORY OFFENSES																	
Offenses Against Religion	52	10.9	41	8.6	21	4.4	18	3.8	9	1.9	9	1.9	189	39.6	138	28.9	477
Liquor Law Violations	124	12.3	55	5.5	45	4.5	71	7.1	11	1.1	32	3.2	507	50.3	162	16.1	1,007
City Ordinance Violations	116	14.6	80	10.1	35	4.4	69	8.7	12	1.5	29	3.7	205	25.9	247	31.1	793
Total	292	12.8	176	7.7	101	4.4	158	6.9	32	1.4	70	3.1	821	36.1	647	28.4	2,277

percent), or withdrawn by the complainant (4.0 percent); and an even larger share (22.2 percent) were left unresolved. Altogether nearly three-fifths of assault and battery cases were treated as criminal offenses, and nearly two-fifths were treated as private disputes.

Fraud was even more clearly a private dispute masking as a criminal complaint. Fifty-three percent of these cases were dismissed, left on file, or left unresolved, and another 10.1 percent were withdrawn by the complainant before trial. Only about 30 percent of these cases were taken to trial, and nearly as many were acquitted (13.5 percent) as were found guilty (15.9 percent). Nearly two-thirds of the fraud cases were at bottom private disputes; only one-third were treated as criminal offenses and even these were not prosecuted aggressively.

The prosecutor's responsibility with these kinds of cases clearly centered on whether to prosecute or to dismiss, and whether to prosecute vigorously. If he decided that the defendant's criminality was minimal, his course was clear: dismissal. But even those cases that offered some evidence of criminality were regularly acquitted by the jurors. Private disputes, like common crimes, were not proactively investigated by the prosecutor. For the most part, they were brought to court by private citizens, and the prosecutor's main responsibility was prosecution—not investigation.

Vice and regulatory offenses differed substantially from these more traditional kinds of criminal offenses, and as they grew more numerous, they forced the prosecutor into a new, more proactive role in the criminal justice system. Neither vice nor regulatory offenses resulted in a direct loss or injury to anyone, and therefore did not ordinarily provoke an instant sense of outrage or pain. To be sure, both offenses affronted the moral and social values of the community, and in the 1830s a widespread demand for their suppression arose. Neither vice nor regulatory offenses ordinarily produced the same kind of pressure for prosecution that burglaries or frauds did, and neither sparked the same kind of public cooperation that these more traditional crimes did. If vice and regulatory offenses were to be controlled effectively, a much more proactive prosecutor was required—particularly one that gave more attention to the investigatory phase. Thus, in addition to carrying out an effective prosecution of cases brought to the court, the prosecutor was obliged to *investigate* vice and regulatory offenses prior to bringing them into court.

The investigation of vice was spearheaded during the early years by the mayor and his city marshal (Lane 1967, chap. 2 and 5), but their attention was easily diverted to other pressing issues and their effort at best was sporadic. The county attorney, on the other hand, focused his whole attention on crime. He could readily pinpoint investigations so that only serious offenders were prosecuted, and he could maintain a steady campaign geared more to the realities of the law and offender patterns than the vagaries of politics or public opinion. Slowly, responsibility for vice and regulatory offenses shifted to the county attorney's office and the Municipal Court, which he served.[4]

As the prosecutor became involved in the active investigation of vice and regulatory offenses, however, a subtle shift in his approach to crime began to develop. When the prosecutor encountered difficulties in finding evidence or witnesses against known vice operators, it was convenient to promise them (the operators) a favor during the prosecution phase in return for cooperation in the investigatory phase, that is, if they would provide evidence against other offenders or above all would plead guilty. Since the prosecutor controlled both phases—the investigation as well as the prosecution—it was a simple matter to use the one to facilitate the other. As the investigation narrowed to a given suspect, the county attorney could easily negotiate a guilty plea to ease his prosecution of the case. Plea bargaining was a natural outgrowth of the prosecutor's investigatory responsibilities and was probably used to simplify both his investigatory and prosecutory duties. By the 1850s, therefore, the prosecutor's discretion broadened to permit drastic reductions in the prosecutorial effort in return for the suspect's cooperation in the investigatory effort.

This expansion of his discretion was a natural extension of the prosecutor's ability in private disputes to decide whether they involved criminal behavior or were simply private disputes that did not merit prosecution. His authority to dismiss private disputes was also used to adjust the prosecution where the defendant's demeanor seemed to warrant it. His experience in private dispute cases pointed the way for the prosecutor's handling of vice and regulatory offenses.

As can be seen from Table 2.2, both vice and regulatory offenses gave rise to an extraordinary level of guilty pleas. Nearly one-third of all regulatory offenses and more than one-quarter of all vice offenses resulted in guilty pleas, and both types of offenses also exhibited an unusually large number of unresolved cases (28.4 percent and 24.5 percent respectively). In addition, regulatory offenses displayed a weak conviction ratio in jury trials: 1.7 guilty verdicts for every not guilty verdict, the lowest for any offense category.

There is considerable evidence that the county attorney was not prosecuting vice or regulatory offenses with his usual vigilance. Guilty pleas were readily accepted; many cases were never resolved; and those that were tried before juries frequently resulted in acquittals. It might appear that the county attorney was not making a serious effort to convict such defendants, but the truth is he was finding it difficult to gather sufficient evidence to convict in many of these cases. As a result he was forced to lower his goals. At the same time, the legislature's mandate to the courts to deal effectively with these social problems forced him to control them as effectively as the evidence allowed. His dilemma was resolved by expanding the range of alternatives open to defendants—specifically to permit guilty pleas where the evidence was weak in return for reduced punishments (see chap. 3).

If this view of the prosecutor's changing role is valid, these several broad streams of cases—that is, common law crimes, private disputes, vice offenses, or regulatory offenses—should reveal distinctive changes in the ways in which they were resolved over the years. Specifically, there should be a growing level of dismissals among private disputes as the prosecutor redefined the functions of his office, and the number of plea-bargained cases should increase as the prosecutor encountered an expanding volume of vice and regulatory cases that could not be easily prosecuted or conveniently dismissed. At the same time common law crimes should show little evidence of prosecutorial discretion since the prosecutor's handling of these cases did not change substantially over the years.

The Prosecutor Emerges

Common law crimes embraced a wide range of offenses but the more numerous ones in the Municipal Court were minor property crimes, burglary, and violent crimes. The major changes here included a steady decline in the percentage of guilty verdicts; an increase in not guilty verdicts after 1840; and an increase in guilty pleas during the late 1830s and 1840s (see fig. 2.3–2.7).

Since the percentage of guilty verdicts was bound to fall as the number of not guilty verdicts and guilty pleas rose, the more basic question becomes why did guilty pleas and not guilty verdicts increase?

Guilty pleas among common criminals, although not negotiated with any regularity, may well have been prompted by a desire to generate good will with the prosecutor. Guilty pleas were not as common among these defendants as among, for example, city ordinance violators or liquor law violators, nor were defendants who pleaded guilty treated more leniently than those found guilty after a trial. But many defendants, no doubt, were well aware of plea bargaining in other cases and hoped to receive some measure of mercy by pleading guilty.

The increase in not guilty verdicts can also be readily explained. During the antebellum period the definition of due process received increasing attention, and several measures expanding the defendant's protections were inaugurated: the hearsay rule and the right to testify,

Figure 2.3: The Percentage of Guilty and Not Guilty Verdicts for Felony Against the Person in the Municipal Court: 1814-1850.

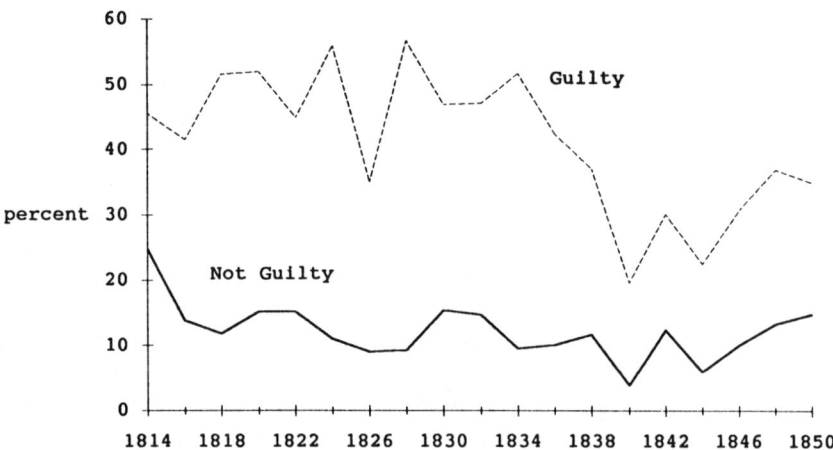

Figure 2.4: The Percentage of Guilty and Not Guilty Verdicts Among All Minor Property Crimes in the Municipal Court: 1814-1850.

Figure 2.5: The Percentage of Guilty and Not Guilty Verdicts Among All Burglary Cases in the Municipal Court: 1814-1850.

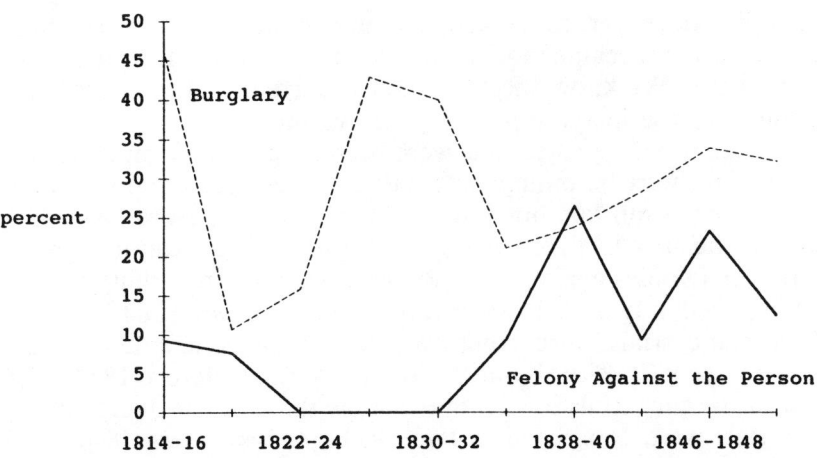

Figure 2.6: Guilty Pleas as a Percent of All Cases for Burglary and Felony Against the Person in the Municipal Court: 1814-1850.

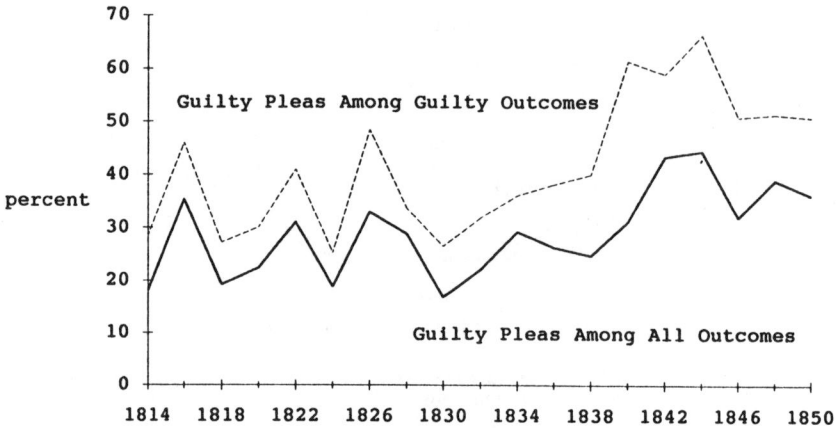

Figure 2.7: The Percentage of Guilty Pleas Among All Outcomes and Among All Guilty Outcomes for Minor Property Crimes in the Municipal Court: 1814-1850.

for example. Moreover, as the bar generally became more professional, defense attorneys became more skillful in using the law for the benefit of their clients. We know these changes occurred, and they probably contributed to the increase in not guilty verdicts.

But, if due process protections were becoming more comprehensive and defendants were becoming more difficult to convict, not only should there be more acquittals but longer trials as well. Before 1834 93.0 percent of the jury trials involving burglaries, misdemeanors against property, or felonies against a person and resulting in a guilty verdict were completed in two weeks or less. After 1846, however, 84.8 percent of these same trials were completed in the same length of time. Conversely, acquittals took only a little more time. Before 1834, 91.5 percent of the jury trials involving the same three offenses and ending in acquittals were completed in two weeks or less; after 1846, 87.8 percent.

The prosecution of common crimes was clearly changing, but in general these changes were beyond the power of the prosecutor to control. Defendants were becoming more difficult to convict, and they were more willing to plead guilty to certain offenses. These changes affected the ways in which common crimes were processed by the prosecutor, but they do not reflect basic changes in policy. The basic changes were occurring among the other broad streams of cases the prosecutor handled.

The prosecutor first began to test his powers with private disputes (for a full account of these powers see chap. 3). As with common law crimes, guilty verdicts decline and guilty pleas increase among private disputes, particularly after 1840, but dismissals (the trademark of private disputes) did not increase as expected for assault and battery cases.

Figure 2.8: The Percentage of Dismissed Cases for Assault and Battery in the Municipal Court: 1814-1850.

Assault and battery cases were common in the 1820s and early 1830s, and as the prosecutor learned to recognize private disputes among these cases, dismissals rose. When complainants began to discover that trivial disputes were no longer welcome in the Municipal Court, complaints dwindled in the 1840s and with them, dismissals.

Fraud cases, were rare before 1832 and probably did not contain many frivolous complaints. When commerce began to expand in Boston during the 1830s, however, entrepreneurs became increasingly the target of fraud complaints. During the 1830s, as the prosecutor had to dispose of a growing volume of trivial fraud cases, dismissals in fraud cases

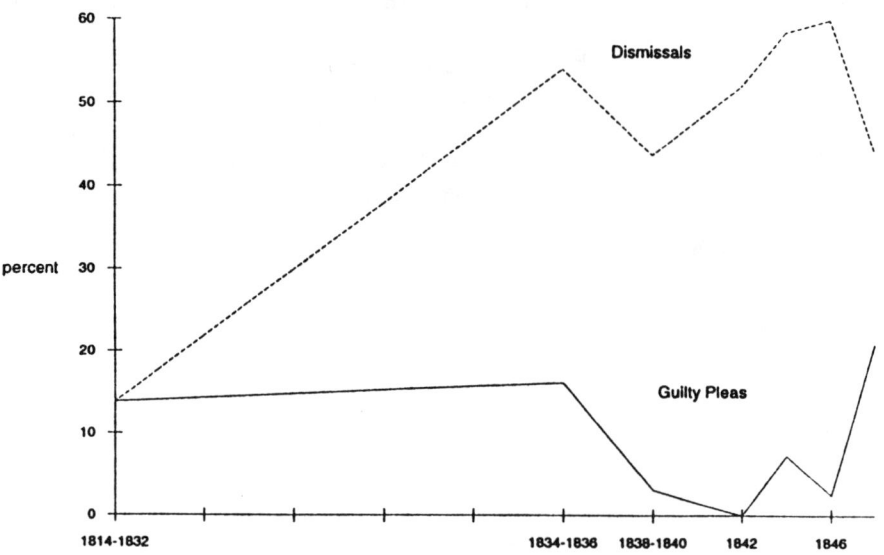

Figure 2.9: The Percentage of Cases Dismissed and Guilty Pleas for Fraud in the Municipal Court: 1814-1850.

became relatively common. By the 1840s the bulk of the cases were settled in this manner (see fig. 2.9), and if complaint withdrawn by complainant is added to dismissals, the majority of fraud cases were disposed of in this fashion before reaching a decision.

The county attorney was getting more skilled in separating criminal cases from private disputes and more confident in disposing of the latter through noncriminal channels. His acceptance of this responsibility represents a significant expansion of his authority within the criminal justice system.

When we look at regulatory cases (see Table 2.3), we note that guilty pleas took a decided turn upward after 1840, no doubt (see chap. 3) because of the growing use of plea bargaining in the Municipal Court. Accompanying this shift in pleading, jury trials became less common (dropping from 32.0 percent of all regulatory cases before 1841 to only 14.0 percent after); and cases left-on-file (a type of informal probation) and defendant defaults both showed sizable increases.

These several increases all suggest that the prosecutor was beginning to develop extraordinary new powers. Plea bargaining indicates his

TABLE 2.3: OUTCOME OF VICE AND REGULATORY OFFENSES BY YEAR IN THE MUNICIPAL COURT.

	Guilty		Not Guilty		Dismissed		Left on File		Complaint Withdrawn		Defendant Defaults		Guilty Plea		No Action Indicated		Total
	N	%	N	%	N	%	N	%	N	%	N	%	N	%	N	%	
Regulatory Offenses[a]																	
1814–1840	93	21.7	46	10.3	34	7.6	11	2.5	0	0.0	10	2.2	108	24.2	110	24.6	447
1842–1850	146	9.2	77	4.8	67	4.2	138	8.7	27	1.7	66	4.1	879	55.2	195	12.2	1,592
Vice Offenses[b]																	
1814–1820	12	22.2	9	16.7	5	9.3	2	3.7	0	0.0	1	1.9	14	25.9	11	20.4	54
1822–1828	32	49.2	5	7.7	3	4.6	3	4.6	0	0.0	2	3.1	8	12.3	12	18.5	65
1830–1836	18	22.5	8	10.0	7	8.9	7	8.9	0	0.0	3	3.8	18	22.5	19	23.8	80
1838–1840	21	26.9	6	7.7	2	1.3	4	5.1	4	5.1	2	2.6	16	20.5	23	29.5	78
1842–1844	21	21.0	11	11.0	4	4.0	9	9.0	3	3.0	7	7.0	33	33.0	12	12.0	100
1846–1848	38	18.6	23	11.3	9	4.4	35	17.2	4	2.0	17	8.3	71	34.8	7	3.4	204
1850	14	11.1	10	7.9	8	6.3	32	25.4	0	0.0	14	11.1	44	34.9	4	3.2	126

[a] Regulatory offenses include liquor law violations, offenses against religion (blue law violations), and city ordinance violations.
[b] Vice offenses include gambling and prostitution.

expanding role in moving cases, and his greater use of left-on-file probably points to a growing acceptance of informal probation in special cases. The increase in defaults probably means that he was more willing for defendants to post bond in support of their promise to refrain from misbehavior—a more formal type of probation.

In essence, then, the county attorney was more inclined in regulatory cases to adjust his prosecution effort to the characteristics of the defendant. Negotiation with defendants both explicit and implicit was becoming routine in regulatory cases, and the county attorney was beginning to exercise an extraordinary degree of discretion.

The fact that all these trends were apparent in the prosecution of vice cases (see Table 2.3 and fig. 2.10) only strengthens the argument. Regulatory offenses and vice violations were both victimless crimes in antebellum Boston, and their discovery and prosecution depended upon a proactive investigation. Since few victims followed the prosecution of these cases or took note of their resolution, regulatory and vice cases offered a wide latitude for experimentation. As the county attorney gained experience, he discovered broad areas to exert influence.[7] The county prosecutor was learning, in other words, how to manipulate

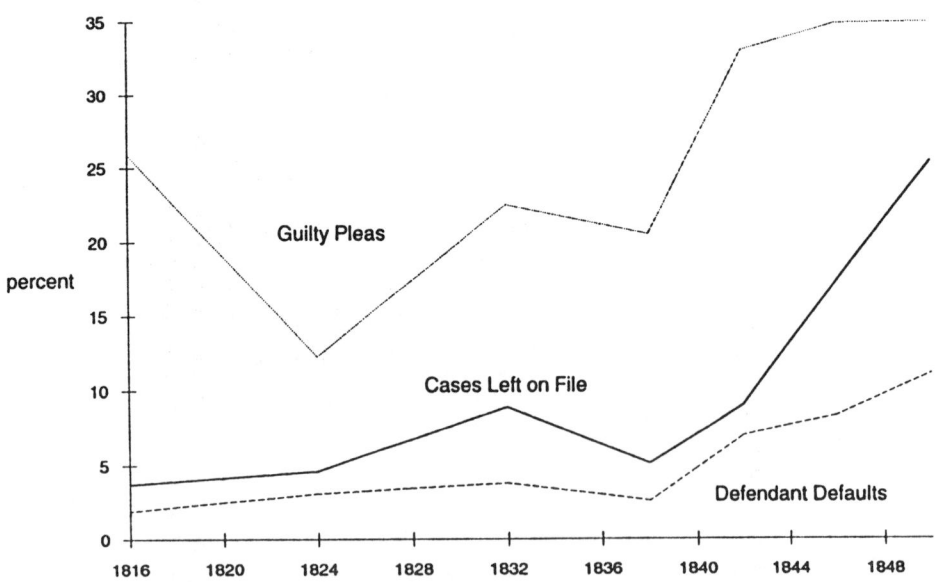

Figure 2.10: The Percentage of Guilty Pleas, Cases Left on File, and Defendant Defaults Among Vice Offenses in the Municipal Court: 1814-1850.

the basic sanctions at his disposal, how vigorously to prosecute and how severely to punish Boston's citizens. In this way the modern prosecutor's office took shape.

The Police Court

I have suggested that most of the changes encountered in the Municipal Court would not be found in the Police Court since it had no professional prosecutor and since its jurisdiction in vice and regulatory offenses was shrinking, but the Police Court had its own policies and procedures.

The same four streams found in the Municipal Court—common law crimes, private disputes, vice, and regulatory cases—were also found in the Police Court, but in different proportions. Whereas common law crimes were the primary case stream in the Municipal Court, vice (34.3 percent) and private disputes (39.6 percent) were most common in the Police Court. Vice included public drunkenness as well as prostitution and gambling, and private disputes embraced assault and battery and larceny. Common law crimes made up only 6.5 percent of the total, and regulatory offenses only 9.7 percent.

Despite the differences in their case streams, these several types were handled in the Police Court much as they were in the Municipal Court. Large numbers of the private disputes were either dismissed or left unresolved by the court, especially during the 1830s (see Table 2.4); and relatively few were tried or allowed to plea bargain. More than half of these complaints were not prosecuted, but those that were were resolved for the most part through bench trials and not through guilty pleas. Defendants pleaded guilty in fewer than 20 percent of these cases.

Vice cases, on the other hand, were rarely dismissed (see Table 2.5), and after 1832 the bulk of them were resolved in one way or another. They were prosecuted vigorously, and when taken to trial, fewer than 10 percent were found not guilty. Guilty pleas and plea bargaining became increasingly common after 1840.

Regulatory offenses—particularly those relating to the sale of spirits—were infrequent in the Police Court, constituting only 9.7 percent of the total. Most of them were city ordinance violations, and before 1836 the largest percentage was dismissed or never taken to a conclusion (see Table 2.6). Few were tried, but those that were were very likely to result in guilty verdicts. Guilty pleas and plea bargaining were common after 1834, and most cases were resolved in this fashion.

TABLE 2.4:
OUTCOME OF LARCENY AND ASSAULT AND BATTERY VIOLATIONS IN THE POLICE COURT: 1826–1850

	LARCENY										ASSAULT AND BATTERY									
	Guilty		Not Guilty		Guilty by Plea		Dismissal		No Outcome		Total	Guilty		Not Guilty		Guilty by Plea		Dismissal		No Outcome		Total
Year	N	%	N	%	N	%	N	%	N	%		N	%	N	%	N	%	N	%	N	%	
1826	2	0.8	1	0.4	0	0.0	0	0.0	229	98.7	232	6	7.4	3	0.7	0	0.0	0	0.0	454	98.7	460
1828	34	16.4	24	11.6	19	9.2	3	1.4	127	61.4	208	196	44.2	66	14.9	26	5.9	22	5.0	133	30.0	443
1832	4	2.8	4	2.8	7	5.0	8	5.7	119	84.9	140	8	2.1	3	0.8	10	2.7	15	4.1	329	90.3	364
1834	76	25.8	4	1.4	17	5.8	46	15.6	156	52.9	295	163	34.3	9	1.9	13	2.7	85	17.9	213	44.8	475
1836	99	35.0	2	0.7	35	12.4	34	12.0	112	39.6	283	160	40.3	5	1.4	39	9.8	56	14.1	142	35.7	398
1838	114	32.1	1	0.3	51	14.4	17	4.8	170	47.9	355	121	37.0	2	0.6	33	10.1	15	4.6	155	47.4	327
1840	92	28.3	1	0.3	42	12.9	33	10.2	156	48.0	325	135	38.1	3	0.9	20	5.6	44	12.4	155	43.7	355
1842	91	28.3	2	0.6	76	23.6	27	8.4	125	38.8	322	169	39.2	1	0.2	44	10.2	48	11.1	165	38.3	431
1844	96	26.3	0	0.0	69	18.9	24	6.6	156	42.7	365	143	33.6	36	8.5	58	13.6	36	8.5	129	30.4	425
1846	159	38.8	23	5.6	80	19.6	0	0.0	130	31.8	409	206	40.7	50	9.9	71	14.0	0	0.0	178	35.2	506
1848	193	30.5	18	2.8	133	21.0	40	6.3	249	39.3	634	229	36.7	49	7.9	90	14.4	29	4.6	211	33.8	625
1850	216	28.7	31	4.1	168	22.3	21	2.8	313	41.6	753	273	31.8	55	6.4	135	15.7	26	3.0	296	34.5	858

TABLE 2.5:
OUTCOME OF PUBLIC DRUNKENNESS AND PROSTITUTION VIOLATIONS IN THE POLICE COURT: 1826–1850

PUBLIC DRUNKENNESS

Year	Guilty N	%	Not Guilty N	%	Guilty by Plea N	%	Dismissal N	%	No Outcome N	%	Total
1826	15	4.2	7	2.0	0	0.0	0	0.0	336	95.7	358
1828	204	60.9	13	3.9	27	8.1	0	0.0	88	26.3	335
1832	4	.9	0	0.0	21	4.8	9	2.1	401	92.0	435
1834	303	72.5	8	1.9	37	8.7	24	5.7	7	1.6	423
1836	286	70.0	4	1.0	36	8.7	29	7.0	62	14.9	415
1838	518	69.4	11	1.5	154	20.6	7	0.9	64	8.6	747
1840	445	65.8	0	0.0	151	22.4	22	3.3	56	8.3	675
1842	376	53.6	3	0.4	259	36.9	26	3.7	37	5.2	701
1844	360	44.1	1	0.1	435	52.5	6	0.7	15	1.8	828
1846	662	46.5	19	1.4	732	51.4	0	0.0	9	0.6	1,424
1848	572	44.3	26	2.0	671	51.9	5	0.4	18	1.4	1,293
1850	642	45.3	15	1.1	731	51.6	4	0.3	12	0.8	1,416

PROSTITUTION

Year	Guilty N	%	Not Guilty N	%	Guilty by Plea N	%	Dismissal N	%	No Outcome N	%	Total
1826	5	2.4	0	0.0	0	0.0	0	0.0	214	90.7	219
1828	95	60.5	6	3.8	21	13.4	1	0.6	34	21.7	157
1832	6	10.3	0	0.0	1	1.7	1	1.7	50	86.2	58
1834	52	55.4	1	1.1	18	19.1	6	6.4	18	19.1	94
1836	38	66.7	1	1.8	11	19.3	1	1.8	6	10.5	57
1838	95	76.6	3	2.4	13	10.5	2	1.6	14	11.3	124
1840	75	44.4	0	0.0	46	27.2	9	5.3	39	23.1	169
1842	92	45.5	0	0.0	51	25.2	23	11.4	36	17.8	202
1844	23	37.1	5	8.0	13	21.0	5	8.1	16	25.8	62
1846	17	56.7	0	0.0	10	33.3	0	0.0	3	10.0	30
1848	22	37.3	3	5.1	33	55.9	0	0.0	1	1.7	59
1850	33	36.3	1	1.1	43	47.3	1	1.1	13	14.3	91

TABLE 2.6: OUTCOME OF CITY ORDINANCE VIOLATIONS IN THE POLICE COURT: 1826–1850

CITY ORDINANCE

Year	Guilty N	Guilty %	Not Guilty N	Not Guilty %	Guilty by Plea N	Guilty by Plea %	Dismissal N	Dismissal %	No Outcome N	No Outcome %	Total
1826	1	1.0	0	0.0	0	0.0	0	0.0	99	99.0	100
1828	22	34.4	4	6.3	12	18.8	1	1.6	25	39.1	64
1832	0	0.0	0	0.0	14	24.6	1	1.3	41	71.9	56
1834	18	14.4	0	0.0	24	19.2	14	11.2	68	54.4	125
1836	28	19.0	0	0.0	75	51.0	6	4.1	38	25.9	147
1838	50	20.1	0	0.0	103	41.4	2	0.8	94	37.8	249
1840	40	18.1	0	0.0	100	45.2	20	19.1	61	27.6	221
1842	47	24.2	0	0.0	88	45.4	16	8.2	44	22.2	194
1844	48	16.6	6	2.0	166	57.6	39	13.5	28	9.7	288
1846	28	26.4	2	1.9	68	64.2	0	0.0	8	7.5	106
1848	67	13.2	27	5.3	265	52.3	3	0.6	140	27.6	507
1850	81	16.1	20	4.0	340	67.5	4	0.8	60	11.9	504

Many common law crimes came before the Police Court, but most of them were simply bound over to the Municipal Court, leaving too few to analyze meaningfully. The other streams, however, were handled in much the same way as in the Municipal Court. Private disputes were rarely prosecuted to a conclusion in either court, and although vice and regulatory cases were prosecuted vigorously, they were increasingly resolved via plea bargaining.

There were, at the same time, some marked differences. Few private disputes were tried in either court, but those that were tried in the Police Court were found guilty at a much higher rate than in the Municipal Court, particularly before 1844 (see Table 2.2 and 2.4).

Similarly, in the Police Court relatively few vice cases were left unresolved (see Tables 2.2 and 2.5). This difference may reflect the ease with which cases could be tried in the Police Court. Bench trials were much easier and quicker than jury trials, and many more were tried and fewer were left unresolved in the Police Court.

The interesting question, however, is why did the practices of the Police Court parallel those of the Municipal Court as closely as they did? The Police Court administered a different jurisdiction (local ordinances); and it was not served by a professional prosecutor who actively organized criminal investigations, particularly before 1838 when a centralized police force was instituted in Boston. The Police Court initiated plea bargaining as early as 1836 with regulatory cases, and in 1844 it began to plea bargain vice cases as well. The Municipal Court, however, only began to use plea bargaining in 1842 with regulatory cases, and the practice spread to vice cases in 1846. The Police Court seems to have preceded the Municipal Court in plea bargaining by several years. Why?

The Police Court initiated plea bargaining for the same reason that it was developed in the Municipal Court: to ease the burdens of prosecution. McDonald (1979, 25–36) argues that police courts, in which the responsibility for prosecution rested with private citizens or the police, developed a pattern of negotiating with offenders at a very early period by offering thieves a portion of the reward for returning a particularly valuable stolen article. When the article was returned, the detective and the thief usually shared the reward money. Such arrangements were common in antebellum Philadelphia and New York as well as in Boston (Johnson 1979, 22–24), as was the practice of granting informants a certain license in their criminality in return for useful tips (Lane 1967, 10, 56–58). Although it was not plea bargaining in the usual sense, constables and police officials were involved regularly in intensive negotiations with the underworld.

The police must have realized very early, therefore, that regulatory and vice cases could be readily resolved by guaranteeing light fines for guilty pleas.[8] Such bargains, of course, required the assent of the Police Court bench, which willingly granted it. Once the techniques had been perfected in the Police Court, knowledge of them must have spread quickly throughout the Boston bar, which numbered only a few hundred lawyers. Shortly thereafter, these techniques were adapted to the Municipal Court and its caseload.

In essence, plea bargaining was devised in the Police Court during the 1830s by constables and police who had already developed considerable experience in negotiating with the underworld on a variety of issues. With these earlier negotiations as a model, plea bargaining was attempted, first with city ordinance violators, and then with public drunks and prostitutes. It was then adopted by the county attorney because it offered a convenient way of merging his investigatory and his prosecutory duties and because it was very compatible with the expanding scope of his office. Although lower courts rarely shape the formal law or procedures of the higher courts in a positive sense, they can at times directly affect the practices of the higher courts. Plea bargaining offers a good example.

3
The Prosecutor Assumes Control

As an instrument of the emerging responsive legal system in Boston, the prosecutor's office expanded sharply in the 1830s and 1840s. We have already seen that the prosecutor's caseload grew from 228 cases in 1830 to 1,532 in 1850 and that the costs of prosecution shot up in the 1840s to become the chief item in the annual budget of Suffolk County. Things got so hectic by 1849 that the county attorney, Samuel D. Parker, beseeched the legislature for relief.

> The excessive and unremitting pressure of official duty has already undermined my health; unremitting professional labors night and day with no vacation and no assistance and perpetual confinement daily and all day in badly ventilated court rooms, will breakdown the best constitution, and I hesitate not to...ask for relief.... If it cannot be obtained, I must retire from office. (*Boston Evening Transcript*: 1849, 2)

He got no relief and ultimately retired in 1852 after twenty-two years of service, at the age of 72.

These changes however, only outline the scope of the prosecutor's expansion. We must still chart its impact on the actions and policies of the prosecutor as his office assumed control of the criminal court and its business.

During much of the eighteenth century, juries had been the principal agency of justice in Boston's criminal courts. Through the grand jury, criminal complaints were examined for their merit, and if voted "true bills," the grand jury also specified the precise charge. If the case was brought to trial, the petit jury interpreted the criminal laws, evaluated the evidence, and issued a verdict of guilt or innocence. The judge or the prosecutor assisted the jury in its deliberations at each stage, but their contributions were only advisory. In addition, the judge supervised the courtroom conduct of the prosecutor, defense attorney, defendant, and others, and the prosecutor assembled and argued the case against the defendant. But when all was said and done, the jury had control (Greenberg 1976, 172; Nelson 1975, 3–4).

Shortly after the turn of the eighteenth century, however, the jury's powers began to wane. By the 1820s the judge had assumed responsibility for interpreting the law during trial (Nelson 1975, 168–69), and during the 1830s the prosecutor began to assume several of the jury's other responsibilities. He began to evaluate the substance of complaints, to specify charges, to determine guilt, and to set the level of punishment. By mid-century the prosecutor had replaced the jury as the right arm of justice in Boston.[1]

How was this revolution accomplished? Why did the prosecutor assume many of the functions of both the jury and the judge? The answers to these questions reflect more shifting mandates within the court than a willful attempt by the prosecutor to expand his powers. The prosecutor's responsibilities were broadened because he was in a unique position to formulate and implement crime control policy. Neither the judge nor the jury could do both in a large, cosmopolitan center, and as the jurisdiction of the criminal courts broadened, the prosecutor undertook to fulfill the mandate as a responsible public servant.

The Prosecutor's Expanding Powers

The scope of the office expanded in three distinct directions. The prosecutor began to dismiss minor cases before they reached the grand jury; he began to issue an informal probation to minor offenders as a substitute for serious prosecution; and he began to negotiate guilty pleas in exchange for reduced punishments with cooperative defendants. These several changes essentially replaced formal criminal proceedings with informal proceedings, and they shifted decisions that formerly had been the responsibility of either the judge or the jury to the prosecutor's office. In the process the prosecutor emerged as the principal architect of crime control in the city.

The prosecutor's authority to dismiss cases took several forms. He could dismiss by simply dropping prosecution of a case (*nolle prosequi dismissal*), by staying proceedings, or by discharging cases. All of these practices ordinarily involved the judge's cooperation, but for the most part the initiative rested with the prosecutor. For example, a *nolle prosequi* dismissal might be requested from the court if the complaint, upon investigation, lacked merit. If the complaint warranted examination but external circumstances (e.g., an unrelated prosecution) required a delay, a stay in proceedings might be sought by the prosecutor, or if, as the case developed, it became increasingly weak, the prosecutor might seek a final discharge of the defendant. Each of these methods represented long-standing practice in the criminal courts, and as the prosecutor became the strong right arm of crime control in Boston, he became less inhibited in using them.

Informal probation, as developed by the prosecutor, represented a clear expansion of his powers. Essentially, the defendant was given a stay of proceedings (technically, the case was "left-on-file") to offer evidence of good will to the court. If there was no further trouble from the defendant, the case might never be opened again, and both the prosecutor and the defendant would benefit. The broad use of informal probation by the prosecutor's office, however, did signal a break with tradition and reflected his growing willingness to handle a case according to the qualities of the defendant. A remorseful, cooperative defendant might very well receive consideration that a defiant defendant would not. Informal probation represented a swing toward particularism, and as such, departed from the stern concept of universalistic justice that guided many prosecutors and judges during the post-Revolutionary period.

Plea bargaining also marked an innovative approach to the problem of criminal prosecution. Both charge bargaining and sentence bargaining were common in the 1840s, and together they took the issue of guilt and the level of punishment out of the hands of jury and judge respectively. Moreover, plea bargaining diverted these basic questions from formal adversarial proceedings to informal negotiations in which the prosecutor and the defendant settled them privately. Such a radical redistribution of powers raised some eyebrows among the more conservative members of both the bar and the legislature.[2] In 1842 James T. Austin, the attorney general, complained in his annual report that the liquor license laws carried little authority among the public and that extraordinary measures were needed to enforce them.

> There are now standing on the docket of the Municipal Court for the city of Boston, sixty-three cases of this description, for which the past year has allowed no opportunity of trial; and there would now be eleven more, if this number of defendants had not made a voluntary compromise with the government and virtually received an equivalent to a pardon....
>
> Under a conscientious belief that the law must be executed, and in the absence of usual facilities for obtaining proof of guilt, very doubtful means of procuring evidence will be resorted to, and...what is of more consequence, the moral character of the community is more deteriorated by the trial than the offense. (Austin 1842, 7–8)

Three years later the same issue came up in Essex County north of Boston. In 1844 the district attorney of Essex County, Asahel

Huntington, was investigated by the Massachusetts House of Representatives for "taking (in fines) less than might have been required on the discharge of indictments found and not tried." Huntington's explanation amounted to a step-by-step description of how he persuaded license violators to plead *nolo-contendere* for a reduction of the charges against them. As we shall see, Samuel Parker, Suffolk County Attorney, used much the same procedure in dealing with the same class of defendants, liquor license violators, in Boston.

> Whenever a number of penalties had been demanded in different counts of the same indictment, and the defendant came forward and proposed an adjustment, his usual course had been—
> 1st. To require the party to enter a plea of nolo contendere.
> 2d. To enter into an agreement to abstain from future sales of liquor without license.
> 3d. To pay at least one penalty to the Commonwealth, and all costs which had then accrued. And
> 4th. That the indictment should then stand continued as security that the defendant would fulfill his agreement, and to be further prosecuted in case the defendant still continued in his course of a wilful [sic] violation of the laws.
>
> It was very distinctly in evidence, that this course was taken openly and publicly by the respondent, and impartially applied to all; that it was known to the Courts, the Bar, the County Commissioners, and all other persons who had occasion to take any interest in the administration of this department of the law. And it was also clearly proved, that this course was not only known but much and justly approved as tending more than any other course in the class of cases to which it was applied to attain the just end of all punishment, the prevention of the offense, the reformation of the offender....
>
> The Committee are therefore unanimously of the opinion that the charges of mal-practice in office brought against Asahel Huntington, District Attorney of the Commonwealth, for the Northern District ... are wholly unsustained by the evidence referred to for support and that no further action be had thereon by this House. (House Document No. 4: 1845, 3)

Huntington was completely exonerated by the House Committee of any wrongdoing.

The question of abuses in the prosecutor's office is not a primary issue of this study, but it is evident that as prosecutors in eastern Massachusetts, including Boston, resorted to novel methods to speed the flow of minor cases through the courts, they came under close scrutiny from several quarters. This concern about plea bargaining has continued, of course, to the present day.[3]

These several practices reflect the prosecutor's expanding powers in Boston, and they held far reaching implications for the course of justice. They meant essentially that full adversarial proceedings became a less well travelled route to justice; that the prosecutor's office assumed primary responsibility for the orderly flow of cases through the criminal courts; and that the prosecutor held enormous powers over the fate of any given defendant. Such power over defendants immensely facilitated the flow of cases through the courts and was no doubt badly needed, but it also multiplied the opportunities for abuse in the courts—particularly the reduction of punishments to smooth the course of adjudication.

Traditionally, the level of punishment had been determined by the degree of guilt, but plea bargaining reversed the equation. It prescribed that the level of punishment should be manipulated to insure a guilty plea, it meant that the punishment set the level of guilt (Mather 1973, 188). Since these negotiations were not conducted in public, it was inevitable that they occasionally resulted in punishments lower than the public could or would accept. As the prosecutor assumed responsibility for case flow through the courts, his office came increasingly under pressures that stemmed more from case management problems than from concepts of justice. It is also worth noting that a serious question today about the lower criminal courts focuses on the abuses that plea bargaining sponsors in the sentencing process.

The new policies in the criminal courts were intended primarily to divert minor cases from the full adjudication process. Many minor offenses do not require the full resources of the criminal court to reach a solution that is agreeable to everyone. It also meant that the emphasis in adjudication could shift to the pretrial phase where the prosecutor (and not the jury or the judge) frames most of the options. As the pretrial phase became more important to defendants, the center of gravity in the courts tilted sharply toward the prosecutor. He became the primary manager of the courts as well as the judge, jury, and prosecutor for most defendants. When added to his new investigatory powers, these new policies in the criminal courts meant that the prosecutor became the principal public official with responsibility for investigating, prosecuting, and punishment crime in Boston.

Dismissals

Dismissals have long been a prosecutor's tool in New England (Emery 1913), and as we have seen, they come in three distinct forms: a *nolle prosequi* dismissal, a stay in the proceedings, or a discharge of the case. The first is largely the prosecutor's decision; but the second and third may be initiated by the judge as well as the prosecutor. Unfortunately, it was not possible to differentiate the prosecutor's dismissals from those of the judge.

Dismissals offer the courts a convenient means of shedding cases that should not be adjudicated: weak cases that cannot be successfully prosecuted; cases that are overshadowed by more important ones; or cases that for a variety of reasons cannot be prosecuted further, for example, because a key witness has died. Historically, the courts have used this tool sparingly, and its use in the antebellum period represented no radical break with the past. In this context a steady expansion in the use of dismissals signals the prosecutor's growing willingness to use all of his powers for case management purposes. Technically, the prosecutor should have prosecuted every complaint for which there was a legal basis and substantial evidence, but in fact he increasingly utilized other criteria as his responsibility for pushing cases through the courts grew.

When we examine Table 2.2 in the last chapter, we see that private disputes were dismissed most frequently followed by regulatory offenses and vice. Relatively few common law crimes were dismissed. Minor offenses that, at bottom, were personal quarrels were apparently channeled out of the Municipal Court in the 1840s when its workload began to mount rapidly.

If we examine Table 3.1, it is clear that early on dismissals were used sparingly in the Municipal Court, and many of these reflected judicial and not simply prosecutorial action. At the same time, it is interesting that nearly all the dismissals reflecting prosecutorial decisions—cases that were *nolle prosequi'd* or in which the proceedings were stayed—were dismissed most frequently in the 1842–50 period when the prosecutor was beginning to expand his authority.

Cases Left-on-File

The prosecutor also offered some defendants an opportunity to avoid prosecution for the instant offense by refraining from any further misbehavior (Woodman 1945, 267). This policy reflected the prosecutor's willingness to use his authority in extralegal ways to avoid unnecessary prosecutions, and here, too, we see in Table 3.1 a steady increase during the antebellum period.

In examining Table 2.2 in chapter 2 we note that several different types of cases were especially likely to be left-on-file. Counterfeiting and felony property crimes among common law crimes, fraud among

TABLE 3.1: DISPOSITIONS IN THE MUNICIPAL COURT: 1814–1850

Year	Cases Dismissed		Proceedings Stayed		Cases Discharged		Cases Left-on-File		Guilty Pleas		Total Cases
	N	%	N	%	N	%	N	%	N	%	
1814–1820	1	0.1	0	0.0	36	4.0	34	3.8	237	26.2	904
1822–1830	2	0.2	0	0.0	12	1.2	65	6.4	217	21.3	1,017
1832–1840	0	0.0	0	0.0	19	1.3	131	9.0	285	19.5	1,458
1842–1850	15	0.4	23	0.6	100	2.4	470	11.5	1,667	40.8	4,084

private disputes, and prostitutions among vice offenses were all good candidates for this disposition.

The prosecutor's reasons, however, varied from case to case. The more serious common crimes were left on file because many of them were bound over to the Supreme Judicial Court. Others—though too serious to dismiss outright—were not sufficiently blameworthy to warrant serious prosecutions. Many fraud and prostitution cases, for example, probably represented attempts by the prosecutor to force certain minor defendants into law-abiding paths by threatening renewed prosecution if they faltered. In Table 3.2 we see the prosecutor's growing willingness to use left-on-file in handling frauds and city ordinance violations.

TABLE 3.2: CASES LEFT-ON-FILE FOR SELECTED OFFENSES IN THE MUNICIPAL COURT: 1814–1850

Year	Liquor Law Violations		Fraud		Prostitution		City Ordinance Violations	
	N	%[a]	N	%[a]	N	%[a]	N	%[a]
1814–1820	0	0.0	1	7.2	1	2.0	1	3.6
1822–1830	5	10.2	1	7.7	3	5.9	3	8.3
1832–1840	0	0.0	17	24.6	7	6.1	5	10.0
1842–1850	66	9.1	41	27.0	69	17.0	58	13.2

[a] percent of all such crimes in the years indicated

Plea Bargaining

The best evidence of the prosecutor's growing importance is his expanding use of plea bargaining in the Municipal Court during the 1840s. We note in Table 2.2 a heavy use of guilty pleas among defendants involved in common crimes, regulatory, or vice cases, but when we look at Table 3.3, we see that for the most part these guilty pleas took the form of switching not guilty pleas to guilty pleas. A straight guilty plea was relatively rare in the Municipal Court. Moreover, switched pleas seem to be restricted to vice and regulatory offenses. Very few common criminal offenders resorted to switched pleas (see Table 2.4) at any time. Switched pleas among defendants charged with prostitution, however, became common only after 1836, and regulatory defendants began to switch their pleas freely after 1842.

TABLE 3.3: THE DISTRIBUTION OF PLEAS FOR REGULATORY OFFENSES IN THE MUNICIPAL COURT: 1828–1850

Year	Prostitution							Offenses Against Religion[a]							Liquor Law Violations							City Ordinance Violations						
	Guilty or N. Cont.		Not Guilty		Not Guilty to Guilty or N. Cont.		Total	Guilty or N. Cont.		Not Guilty		Not Guilty to Guilty or N. Cont.		Total	Guilty or N. Cont.		Not Guilty		Not Guilty to Guilty or N. Cont.		Total	Guilty or N. Cont.		Not Guilty		Not Guilty to Guilty or N. Cont.		Total
	N	%	N	%	N	%		N	%	N	%	N	%		N	%	N	%	N	%		N	%	N	%	N	%	
1828	4	36.4	4	36.4	0	0.0	11	0	0.0	1	100.0	0	0.0	1	3	42.9	3	42.9	1	14.3	7	1	50.0	0	0.0	0	0.0	2
1830	0	0.0	5	33.3	1	6.7	15	0	0.0	0	0.0	0	0.0	1	0	0.0	1	20.0	0	0.0	5	0	0.0	1	100.0	0	0.0	1
1832	0	0.0	0	0.0	1	100.0	1	—	—	—	—	—	—	—	0	0.0	2	100.0	0	0.0	2	—	—	—	—	—	—	—
1834	4	14.8	11	40.7	5	18.5	27	—	—	—	—	—	—	—	0	0.0	2	100.0	0	0.0	2	0	0.0	2	100.0	0	0.0	2
1836	0	0.0	6	50.0	1	8.3	12	1	50.0	1	50.0	0	0.0	2	0	0.0	3	75.0	0	0.0	4	2	33.3	2	33.3	0	0.0	6
1838	10	26.4	19	50.0	4	10.6	38	—	—	—	—	—	—	—	0	0.0	0	0.0	1	100.0	1	0	0.0	7	36.8	0	0.0	19
1840	7	21.3	12	36.4	6	18.2	33	0	0.0	1	100.0	0	0.0	1	0	0.0	17	29.3	0	0.0	58	0	0.0	3	50.0	0	0.0	6
1842	3	8.8	16	47.1	5	14.7	34	8	12.1	26	39.4	24	36.4	66	1	11.1	3	33.3	2	22.2	9	6	24.0	7	28.0	3	12.0	25
1844	9	17.0	21	39.6	9	17.0	53	2	3.6	9	16.4	32	58.2	55	7	4.4	28	17.4	81	50.3	161	2	11.1	9	50.0	2	11.1	18
1846	25	27.5	23	25.3	22	24.2	91	6	10.6	4	7.0	38	66.7	57	2	4.5	10	22.7	20	45.5	44	4	21.1	8	42.1	4	21.1	19
1848	21	16.2	28	21.5	35	26.9	130	0	0.0	0	0.0	3	20.0	15	0	0.0	0	0.0	1	33.3	3	36	9.0	19	4.8	243	60.9	399
1850	10	9.4	13	12.3	22	20.8	106	0	0.0	2	3.7	30	55.6	54	7	1.9	9	2.5	182	50.3	362	2	13.3	8	53.3	1	6.7	15

[a] Offenses against religion consisted basically of violations of blue laws prohibiting taverns from serving alcoholic beverages on Sunday.

TABLE 3.4: THE DISTRIBUTION OF PLEAS FOR SELECTED COMMON LAW OFFENSES IN THE MUNICIPAL COURT: 1828–1850

	Felony Against the Person							Assault & Battery							Burglary							Minor Property Crimes						
	Guilty or N. Cont.		Not Guilty		Not Guilty to Guilty or N. Cont.		Total	Guilty or N. Cont.		Not Guilty		Not Guilty to Guilty or N. Cont.		Total	Guilty or N. Cont.		Not Guilty		Not Guilty to Guilty or N. Cont.		Total	Guilty or N. Cont.		Not Guilty		Not Guilty to Guilty or N. Cont.		Total
Year	N	%	N	%	N	%		N	%	N	%	N	%		N	%	N	%	N	%		N	%	N	%	N	%	
1828	1	20.0	4	80.0	0	0.0	5	3	27.3	4	36.4	0	0.0	11	1	25.0	3	75.0	0	0.0	4	42	44.2	51	53.7	0	0.0	95
1830	0	0.0	5	71.4	1	14.3	7	2	15.4	8	61.5	0	0.0	13	3	33.3	3	33.3	0	0.0	9	22	16.9	84	64.6	0	0.0	130
1832	2	14.3	11	78.6	0	0.0	14	3	27.3	5	45.5	3	27.3	11	2	40.0	2	40.0	1	20.0	5	14	21.5	44	67.7	1	1.5	65
1834	13	35.1	21	56.8	0	0.0	37	8	15.7	33	64.7	1	2.0	51	3	25.0	9	75.0	0	0.0	12	42	29.2	92	63.9	0	0.0	144
1836	8	30.8	12	46.2	5	19.2	26	5	26.3	6	31.6	1	5.3	19	5	45.5	3	27.3	1	9.1	11	34	37.0	43	46.7	2	2.2	92
1838	14	45.2	13	41.9	1	3.2	31	6	28.5	12	57.1	2	9.5	21	10	25.0	19	47.5	3	7.5	40	31	23.8	90	69.2	3	2.3	130
1840	13	30.9	28	66.7	1	2.4	42	5	33.3	9	60.0	1	6.7	15	7	18.4	13	34.2	00	0.0	38	50	28.2	59	33.3	6	3.4	177
1842	12	26.0	28	60.9	2	4.3	46	9	30.0	13	43.3	5	16.7	30	4	12.5	21	65.6	1	0.0	32	47	41.6	54	47.8	4	3.6	113
1844	21	35.6	26	44.1	5	8.5	59	4	19.1	15	71.4	0	0.0	21	9	29.0	13	41.9	5	3.2	31	73	40.1	79	43.4	5	2.7	182
1846	31	37.4	34	41.0	6	7.2	83	12	32.4	21	56.8	1	2.7	37	20	21.6	54	58.1	0	5.4	93	48	33.8	65	45.8	1	1.4	142
1848	33	30.5	61	56.5	3	2.8	108	10	22.2	20	44.4	1	2.2	45	34	40.5	29	34.5	1	0.0	84	63	34.9	102	56.4	2	1.1	181
1850	4	4.8	60	71.4	2	2.4	84	34	28.8	64	54.2	3	2.5	118	29	23.1	73	57.9	1	0.8	126	60	29.9	105	52.2	2	1.0	201

In February 1846 Peter Bent Brigham, a local tavern owner, was indicted on four charges: doing business on the Lord's day; entertaining persons on the Lord's day; selling liquor on the Lord's day; and selling liquor without a license. His case was called in March 1846, and he pleaded not guilty. The case was continued to April, when he changed his plea to guilty to one of the charges and was fined sixty-five dollars. Later that same year, in October, he was indicted again on five very similar charges, and again he pleaded not guilty. In November, however, he changed his plea to guilty to one of them and received a fine of forty dollars. He was a regular visitor to the Municipal Court in the late 1840s, and neither he nor the court varied the pattern much: a not guilty plea to an indictment containing four or five charges; a short delay followed by a guilty plea to one or two and a moderate fine. Peter Bent Brigham, however, was only one of hundreds who followed this routine.

Such abrupt changes in the proportions of vice or regulatory defendants switching their pleas suggest that plea bargaining was initiated in the Municipal Court during this period. To substantiate this inference, we must show that switched pleas were also rewarded with substantial benefits to the defendant.

If pleading guilty or switching from a not guilty to a guilty plea did in fact represent a negotiated plea, these pleas should have received milder punishments than straight not guilty pleas. In Table 3.5 we can see that defendants charged with prostitution who pleaded guilty or who switched their pleas to guilty, particularly after 1844, received less severe sentences than defendants who pleaded not guilty.

A similar benefit was *not* afforded defendants charged with minor property crimes. They received no reduction for a guilty plea. *Sentence bargaining* was common among defendants charged with prostitution after 1844, but was rare among common law offenders.

Charge bargaining was also common in the Municipal Court after 1840. When we look at defendants who faced more than one charge (see Table 3.6), those who switched their plea from not guilty to guilty or *nolo contendere* to only a portion of their charges were treated more leniently than those who pleaded not guilty—particularly after 1840. They were much more likely to receive a fine than a prison sentence.

If those who switched their pleas were more likely to receive a fine, they nevertheless received the heaviest fines. Defendants who pleaded not guilty to either prostitution or regulatory offenses (see Table 3.7), when convicted received smaller fines than those who pleaded guilty or those who switched their pleas. This finding appears, at first, to contradict earlier evidence that severity of sentence was closely related to plea. The pattern of these findings, however, suggests an explanation.

TABLE 3.5: SENTENCE IN MONTHS FOR DEFENDANTS CONVICTED OF COMMON LAW OFFENSES ACCORDING TO PLEA IN THE MUNICIPAL COURT: 1814–1850

Prostitution

	Guilty Plea Months						Not Guilty Plea Months						Not Guilty Plea Changed to Guilty Months						Not Guilty Plea To One Charge, Guilty to Another Months					
	0–3		4–8		9+		0–3		4–8		9+		0–3		4–8		9+		0–3		4–8		9+	
Year	N	%	N	%	N	%	N	%	N	%	N	%	N	%	N	%	N	%	N	%	N	%	N	%
1814–32	0	0.0	0	0.0	0	0.0	0	0.0	11	100.0	0	0.0	1	100.0	0	0.0	0	0.0	0	0.0	0	0.0	0	0.0
1834–44	3	23.1	6	46.2	4	30.8	11	26.8	13	31.7	17	41.5	2	11.1	14	77.8	2	11.1	1	33.3	2	66.7	0	0.0
1846–50	14	82.4	2	11.8	1	5.9	19	42.2	17	37.8	9	20.0	31	86.1	4	11.1	1	2.8	7	100.0	0	0.0	0	0.0

Minor Property Crimes

1814–20	58	57.4	10	9.9	33	32.7	116	51.3	21	9.3	89	39.4	4	80.0	1	20.0	0	0.0	0	0.0	2	100.0	0	0.0
1822–26	23	29.9	6	7.8	48	62.3	27	16.6	16	9.8	120	73.6	1	100.0	0	0.0	0	0.0	0	0.0	0	0.0	0	0.0
1828–32	6	8.2	9	12.3	58	79.5	24	16.4	22	15.1	100	68.5	0	0.0	0	0.0	1	100.0	0	0.0	0	0.0	0	0.0
1834–38	7	6.9	8	7.8	87	85.3	2	1.4	19	13.2	123	85.4	1	16.7	0	0.0	5	83.3	0	0.0	0	0.0	1	100.0
1840–44	15	10.6	23	16.2	104	73.2	12	10.3	20	17.2	84	72.4	3	21.4	2	14.3	9	64.3	0	0.0	0	0.0	2	100.0
1846–50	42	28.0	30	20.0	78	52.0	42	20.8	29	14.4	131	64.9	4	66.7	1	16.7	1	16.7	2	25.0	1	12.5	5	62.5

TABLE 3.6: DISPOSITION OF FIRST CHARGE ACCORDING TO PLEA AFTER SECOND CHARGE WAS DISMISSED IN THE MUNICIPAL COURT: 1830–1850

Plea to first charge:	Not Guilty								Guilty or Nolo Contendere								Not Guilty Changed to Guilty or Nolo Contendere							
Disposition:	Dismissed		Fined		Imprisoned				Dismissed		Fined		Imprisoned				Dismissed		Fined		Imprisoned			
Year	N	%	N	%	N	%	T		N	%	N	%	N	%	T		N	%	N	%	N	%	T	
1830–40	306	36.6	82	9.8	436	52.2	836		4	1.1	92	24.3	281	74.3	378		0	0.0	24	48.0	25	50.0	50	
1842–50	462	34.1	197	14.5	617	45.5	1,356		7	0.9	270	35.7	474	62.7	756		14	1.8	732	92.3	43	5.4	793	

TABLE 3.7: FINES OF DEFENDANTS CONVICTED OF SELECTED OFFENSES ACCORDING TO PLEA IN THE MUNICIPAL COURT: 1814–1850

	Nolo Contendere or Guilty Plea						Not Guilty Plea						Not Guilty Changed to Guilty or Nolo Contendere						Not Guilty Plea To One Charge Guilty to Another					
	$0–5		$6–20		$21+		$0–5		$6–20		$21+		$0–5		$6–20		$21+		$0–5		$6–20		$21+	
Year	N	%	N	%	N	%	N	%	N	%	N	%	N	%	N	%	N	%	N	%	N	%	N	%
												Prostitution												
1814–44	0	0.0	3	21.4	11	78.6	7	21.9	9	28.1	16	50.0	3	13.6	5	22.7	14	63.6	0	0.0	6	100.0	0	0.0
1846–50	4	22.2	6	33.3	8	44.4	8	28.6	11	39.3	9	32.1	8	10.3	38	48.7	32	41.0	2	12.5	3	18.8	11	68.7
							Liquor Law Violations																	
1814–42	0	0.0	3	42.9	4	57.1	8	15.7	31	60.8	12	23.5	0	0.0	5	62.5	3	37.5	0	0.0	2	66.7	1	33.3
1844–50	0	0.0	5	100.0	0	0.0	3	11.5	19	73.1	4	15.4	2	0.5	233	62.3	139	37.2	1	1.5	27	41.5	37	56.9
							City Ordinance Violations																	
1814–40	0	0.0	5	83.3	1	16.7	7	36.8	7	36.8	5	26.3	0	0.0	0	0.0	0	0.0	0	0.0	0	0.0	0	0.0
1842–50	1	2.1	26	54.2	21	43.7	34	72.3	10	21.3	3	6.4	2	0.6	147	47.1	163	52.2	0	0.0	7	70.0	3	30.0
							Assault & Battery																	
1814–20	7	26.9	15	57.7	4	15.4	16	51.6	10	32.3	5	16.1	13	81.3	1	6.2	2	12.5	0	0.0	0	0.0	0	0.0
1822–26	0	0.0	8	72.7	3	27.3	4	26.7	8	53.3	3	20.0	0	0.0	1	100.0	0	0.0	0	0.0	0	0.0	0	0.0
1828–32	1	25.0	2	50.0	1	25.0	2	40.0	1	20.0	2	40.0	0	0.0	0	0.0	1	100.0	0	0.0	0	0.0	0	0.0
1834–38	3	27.3	7	63.6	1	9.1	4	21.1	11	57.9	5	26.3	0	0.0	2	66.7	1	33.3	0	0.0	0	0.0	0	0.0
1840–44	4	25.0	11	68.8	1	6.2	7	58.3	4	33.3	1	8.3	3	50.0	0	0.0	3	50.0	0	0.0	0	0.0	0	0.0
1846–50	11	29.7	16	43.2	10	27.0	21	39.6	22	41.5	10	18.9	1	8.3	10	83.3	1	8.3	1	100.0	0	0.0	0	0.0

Defendants who were liable to a prison term but who were able to avoid it by switching their plea from not guilty to guilty probably committed a substantially more serious offense than those who, despite pleading not guilty, were given only a fine after conviction. It is to be expected that those who offended most should receive a heavier fine.

In sum, then, plea bargaining arose in the Municipal Court, where the prosecutor reigned, in the late 1830s among prostitution defendants, and then spread to regulatory defendants by the early 1840s. It took the form of offering defendants a light prison term or a fine for switching their pleas from not guilty to guilty—sentence bargaining—or of dismissing one or more charges in exchange for the defendant's guilty plea to at least one charge—charge bargaining, and it was restricted to vice or regulatory defendants. There is little evidence that common law offenders or private disputes were plea bargained. This marshaling of defendants and court personnel was necessary to facilitate case flow, but it would have been difficult, if not impossible, without a quarterback to guide the interested parties along their appointed ways. The prosecutor was the quarterback.

The Police Court

The Police Court, in contrast to the Municipal Court, did not normally utilize a prosecutor in its criminal proceedings. The complainant, usually the victim or the arresting officer, presented the case against the defendant, while the defendant, usually without counsel, rebutted the complainant's argument. The magistrates (there were three presiding serially) maintained courtroom decorum, questioned witness and defendants, handed down verdicts, gave judgments, and set sentences. In contrast to the Municipal Court, the magistrates ran the Police Court.

The magistrates' authority in the Police Court can be inferred from the facts (see Table 3.8) that few, if any, cases were dismissed by *nolle prosequi* or were stayed—though a small but steady number were discharged. Very few cases were left-on-file, but a substantial minority were left unresolved. The prosecutor's favorite options in the Municipal Court were almost never utilized in the Police Court, as we would expect, since there was no prosecutor in the Police Court. In his absence, however, the magistrate exercised considerable discretion in discharging a substantial number of defendants and in accepting a growing number of guilty pleas. The Police Court magistrates were also managing case flow as well as performing a judge's other functions.

Unlike the prosecutor in the Municipal Court, the magistrates in the Police Court showed little interest in expanding their powers. The

TABLE 3.8: SELECTED OUTCOMES IN POLICE COURT: 1826–1850

Year	Cases Dismissed		Proceedings Stayed		Cases Discharged		Left on File		No Outcome Indicated		Guilty Pleas		Total Cases
	N	%	N	%	N	%	N	%	N	%	N	%	
1826	0	0.0	0	0.0	1	0.1	0	0.0	436	23.9	0	0.0	1,825
1828	0	0.0	0	0.0	0	0.0	0	0.0	539	29.0	173	9.3	1,860
1832	0	0.0	0	0.0	50	3.3	0	0.0	488	32.1	79	5.2	1,522
1834	0	0.0	0	0.0	230	12.6	0	0.0	686	37.5	149	8.1	1,831
1836	1	0.1	0	0.0	183	10.6	0	0.0	468	27.2	274	15.9	1,720
1838	1	0.0	0	0.0	60	2.6	0	0.0	696	30.3	436	19.0	2,298
1840	0	0.0	0	0.0	160	7.3	0	0.0	629	28.9	434	19.9	2,177
1842	0	0.0	0	0.0	170	7.5	0	0.0	573	25.3	583	25.7	2,265
1844	2	0.1	0	0.0	180	7.1	0	0.0	501	19.7	894	35.1	2,547
1846	0	0.0	0	0.0	0	0.0	1	0.0	498	16.7	1,097	36.7	2,988
1848	0	0.0	0	0.0	98	2.6	0	0.0	842	22.6	1,384	37.2	3,724
1850	0	0.0	0	0.0	78	1.8	0	0.0	995	22.7	1,622	37.1	4,377

percentage of cases that were discharged or left with no outcome fell during the antebellum period. True, guilty pleas displayed a rising tendency during most of the period, and their sharpest increases came during the 1840–44 period (see Table 3.8). We shall see evidence shortly that the sharp jump in guilty pleas reflected the growth of plea bargaining in the Police Court, and there is good reason to believe that the arresting officer (and not the magistrates) managed these negotiations. The sharp increases in guilty pleas, therefore, can be laid more to the initiatives of the police than any expanding powers of the magistrates. Like the prosecutors in the Municipal Court, the Police Court magistrates controlled the flow of cases through their court, but unlike the Municipal Court prosecutor, their sway was not expanding.

Many of the cases that had been prosecuted in the Police Court in the 1820s and early 1830s began to make their way into the Municipal Court. Liquor law violations, offenses against religion, and prostitution cases, as well as counterfeiting, fraud, and minor property offenses (other than larceny) all but disappeared from the Police Court, while their numbers grew substantially in the Municipal Court. On the other hand, only one offense—larceny—was shifted from the Municipal Court to the Police Court. The jurisdiction of the Police Court was shrinking while that of the Municipal Court was expanding during the antebellum period. The prosecutor was active in the latter but not the former and was no doubt a major reason for the growing importance of the Municipal Court.

If the Police Court and its officers—the magistrates, the complaining officer, and the court clerks—were not growing in importance, it is nevertheless clear that there was a strong need to manage the Police Court's caseload. The number of cases heard in the Police Court was always substantially greater than those appearing in the Municipal Court (see Table 3.10). The caseload of the Municipal Court was growing faster than that of the Police Court, but it never came close to the volume of cases processed by the Police Court. Thus, the Police Court faced many of the same pressures that confronted the Municipal Court, and it developed essentially the same methods to limit its numbers. It diverted cases to nonlegal channels, and it negotiated guilty pleas with selected defendants.

A SHRINKING JURISDICTION

During the 1820s and early 1830s (see Table 3.10) the overall number of cases processed by both courts declined. In the Police Court declines were felt in minor crimes and most sharply among assaultive crimes. Public drunkenness, however, rose sporadically during the 1820s and 1830s, and serious crimes were essentially steady.

TABLE 3.9: THE DRIFT OF SELECTED CASES FROM THE POLICE COURT TO THE MUNICIPAL COURT: 1824–1850

Year	Liquor Law Violations		Prostitution		Offenses Against Religion		Minor Property Offenses		Counterfeiting		Fraud	
	Police Court	Municipal Court	Police Court	Municipal Court	Police Court	Municipal Court	Police Court	Municipal Court	Police Court	Municipal Court	Police Court	Municipal Court
1824	7	13	303	8	58	11	165	126	47	23	8	5
1826	11	8	227	7	16	1	134	100	15	8	7	2
1828	3	7	157	12	84	1	113	99	2	6	8	5
1832	31	2	73	1	24	0	108	68	12	10	11	0
1834	59	2	96	27	12	0	26	147	19	15	12	17
1836	106	5	58	15	7	2	14	99	17	12	11	20
1838	69	2	126	39	36	0	31	155	13	27	15	22
1840	49	99	172	33	6	2	12	179	3	12	10	10
1842	7	10	205	35	20	66	13	113	9	29	19	25
1844	1	287	62	59	25	102	28	182	27	37	12	68
1846	0	47	30	100	17	66	20	172	11	16	12	47
1848	0	6	59	161	8	53	29	201	18	28	16	30
1850	0	435	91	165	10	122	41	233	11	17	11	17

TABLE 3.10: A COMPARISON OF THE CASELOADS OF THE POLICE COURT AND THE MUNICIPAL COURT: 1824–1850

Year	Police Court N	Police Court % Annual Increase	Municipal Court N	Municipal Court % Annual Increase	Ratio: Police Court Caseload/ Municipal Court Caseload
1824	2,445	—	256	—	9.6
1826	1,875	—	204	—	9.2
1828	1,868	—	192	—	9.7
1832	1,907	2.1	169	—	11.3
1834	1,873	—	396	134.3	4.7
1836	1,750	—	247	—	7.1
1838	2,340	33.7	431	74.5	5.4
1840	2,207	—	496	15.1	4.4
1842	2,294	3.9	547	10.3	4.2
1844	2,536	10.5	935	70.9	2.7
1846	2,892	14.0	828	—	3.5
1848	3,627	25.4	1,298	56.8	2.8
1850	4,258	17.4	1,538	18.5	2.8

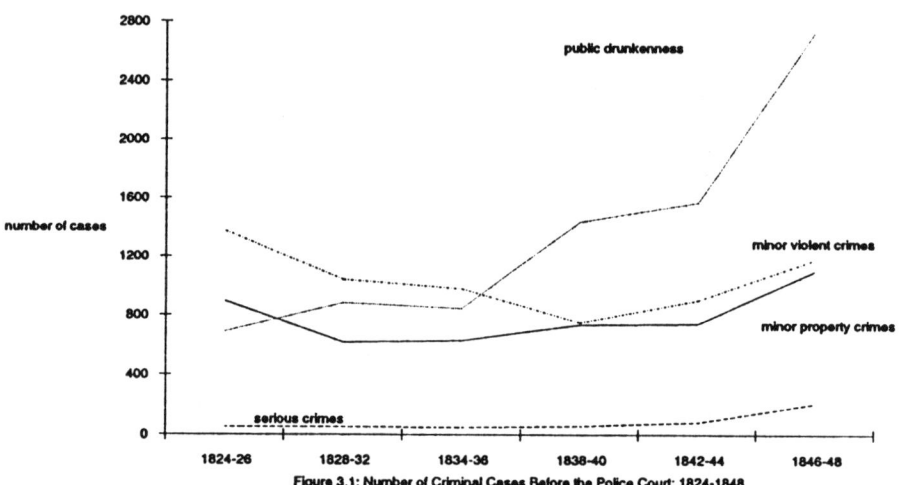

Figure 3.1: Number of Criminal Cases Before the Police Court: 1824-1848

Were the declines in minor crimes the result of an actual decline in criminality, or did they reflect a subtle policy shift in the Police Court such that minor crimes were no longer prosecuted? These declines were apparently a result of self-conscious efforts to limit the numbers of cases coming before the Police Court.

A decline in minor violations in the community without a similar change in related but more serious offenses would be unlikely. The conditions that affect minor property or assaultive crimes tend also to influence related crimes in much the same way, so that minor offenses tend to fluctuate with serious crimes of the same type. Minor theft and grand larceny tend to ebb and flow together, and so do assault and aggravated assault.

If, on the other hand, court officers were attempting to control their caseload, minor crimes would be diverted out of court and their numbers would drop, while serious crimes were still prosecuted in substantial numbers. Thus, if minor crimes were being forced out of court, fewer punishments at the light end would be encountered.

Monetary inflation would also produce much the same result. As small fines lost their sting, and as magistrates adjusted their fines upward, they would use small fines disproportionately less. But if inflation were responsible, it should affect small fines *generally* and not just certain offenses.

TABLE 3.11: PERCENTAGE OF FINED DEFENDANTS WHO RECEIVED FINES OF $2 OR LESS IN THE POLICE COURT: 1826–1850

Year	Public Drunkenness		Minor Assaultive Defendants[a]		Minor Property Defendants[b]	
	N	%	N	%	N	%
1826–32	781	95.1	746	74.5	649	88.2
1834–50	3,258	81.4	904	39.2	555	42.9

[a] Minor assaultive defendants were charged with assault and battery, assault, attempted assault, abuse, threats, fighting, disturbance and assault, disobedient assault, or pointing loaded gun.

[b] Minor property defendants were charged with larceny, fruit pilfering, stealing goods, pickpocketing, shoplifting, common pilferer, breaking glass, trespassing, destruction of property, taking clothes, eating food with intent to steal, cutting a clothes line, accessory to larceny, defacing property, or forcible entry.

Table 3.11 shows that small fines became much less common after 1832 for defendants convicted of minor property crimes or assault. The same, however, was not true of defendants involved in public drunkenness, which was rapidly becoming a serious problem in Boston during the 1840s. These declines in the early 1830s in minor crimes (see fig. 5.5) reflected basically a diversion of trivial offenses out of the courts.

Minor property and assaultive crimes rose in the 1840s, but these increases occurred primarily among the more serious cases. Since felony crimes against property and the person also rose substantially during the 1840s, these increases probably reflected changes in the level of crime in the community.

Thus, the Police Court was controlling its caseload in the 1830s and 1840s by discouraging the prosecution of minor offenses, and the proportion of such cases in its caseload shrank appreciably during this period. Despite these policy adjustments, however, general increases during the 1840s suggest an actual expansion in assaultive and property crimes in the community.

A similar reluctance to prosecute minor property crimes affected the Municipal Court about the same time. Between 1814 and 1834 property crimes that involved a small loss made up at least one-third of the total

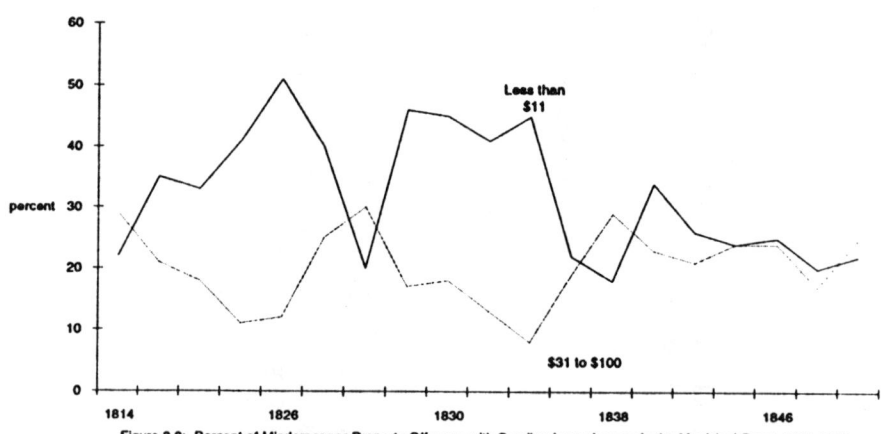

Figure 3.2: Percent of Misdemeanor Property Offenses with Small or Large Losses in the Municipal Court: 1814-1850

every year except two (see fig. 3.2), but *after* that date they constituted more than one-third just once. Serious property crimes showed no such drop, and in the 1840s they became nearly as common as minor property crimes. While minor property crimes were becoming relatively rare in the Municipal Court, serious property crimes were maintaining their levels. As with the Police Court the Municipal Court was probably diverting minor criminal complaints into nonlegal channels.

PLEA BARGAINING IN THE POLICE COURT

The use of guilty pleas in the Police Court nearly doubled between 1834 and 1836 and doubled again between 1838 and 1844 (see Table 3.8). In 1834 only 8.1 percent of Police Court cases were resolved through guilty pleas, but in 1844 the number was 35.1 percent. When we break the caseload down in terms of charge (see Table 3.12), it is apparent that the largest increase in guilty pleas was among violators of city ordinances (from 19.2 percent to 51.0 percent of such cases) between 1834 and 1836. Guilty pleas to public drunkenness nearly doubled between 1840 and 1844, and the same happened among defendants charged with prostitution. About half the cases for all three offenses were resolved via guilty pleas by 1850.

To establish that these guilty pleas were a result of plea bargaining, we must show that they were accompanied by reductions in punishments. In Table 3.13 it is clear that after 1832 smaller fines were routinely given city ordinance violators who pleaded guilty relative to those pleading not guilty, and the same is true for public drunkenness defendants after 1840 and for prostitutes after 1844.

A *not guilty* plea to other kinds of charges, however, was regularly punished *less* severely after conviction than a guilty plea to the same charges—and for city ordinance violators, public drunks, and prostitutes as well, before the beginning of plea bargaining. Police Court magistrates apparently felt that a guilty plea was a reliable indicator of guilt and deserved a severe punishment. A not guilty plea, however, left the issue in some doubt even after conviction, and the magistrates were more restrained in sentencing such defendants.

It is interesting that the benefits of pleading guilty for all three offenses—city ordinance violations, public drunkenness, and prostitution—commenced a year or two before the sharp advances in guilty pleas. In each case the percentage of defendants receiving mild punishments began to rise just before the sharp increase in the proportion of guilty pleas. It is, of course, to be expected that the cause (a mild punishment) precedes the effect (a guilty plea), and it only takes a short time for a general awareness of this relationship to develop.

TABLE 3.12: PERCENT PLEADING GUILTY OR NOT GUILTY TO SELECTED CHARGES IN THE POLICE COURT: 1826–1850

Year	Assault & Battery		Public Drunkenness		Violation of City Ordinances		Vagrancy		Prostituion		Larceny	
	Guilty %	N/Guilty %	Guilty %	N/Guilty %	Guilty %	N/Guilty %	Guilty %	N/Guilty %	Guilty %	N/Guilty %	Guilty %	N/Guilty %
1826	7.4	66.1	9.3	77.3	20.0	52.0	13.3	68.3	16.9	76.7	10.8	65.1
1828	7.1	78.5	9.7	86.4	26.2	50.1	19.0	79.3	14.8	83.2	13.6	79.1
1832	4.2	58.5	7.1	84.3	37.1	32.2	7.5	82.2	4.2	81.9	7.3	55.3
1834	3.3	62.5	8.7	81.8	19.2	29.6	12.3	82.5	20.2	77.7	5.4	34.6
1836	7.8	61.5	8.7	81.0	51.0	23.8	25.4	70.1	22.8	68.4	14.1	39.2
1838	11.9	53.8	21.7	73.1	44.2	28.5	16.0	81.5	10.5	79.0	14.9	42.5
1840	7.0	55.2	23.3	71.9	43.9	27.6	15.6	81.3	27.2	50.9	13.8	37.2
1842	10.7	61.0	36.2	59.2	44.8	32.0	28.4	69.1	25.2	51.5	23.3	35.4
1844	11.8	39.3	46.0	39.1	53.1	15.3	22.9	60.4	21.0	41.9	19.2	28.5
1846	13.8	51.0	48.7	45.2	65.1	20.8	23.9	75.0	33.3	53.3	18.6	39.6
1848	7.3	29.2	51.8	47.2	51.1	21.3	35.1	61.8	55.9	42.4	21.0	37.7
1850	6.4	18.6	51.3	47.1	65.6	23.3	29.7	66.3	48.4	33.0	22.2	33.2

TABLE 3.13: FINE FOR SELECTED OFFENSES ACCORDING TO PLEA IN THE POLICE COURT: 1826-1850

	Public Drunkenness								City Ordinance Violations							
	Guilty				Not Guilty				Guilty				Not Guilty			
	$0-2		$2+		$0-2		$2+		$0-2		$2+		$0-2		$2+	
Year	N	%	N	%	N	%	N	%	N	%	N	%	N	%	N	%
1826	29	96.4	1	3.6	220	96.0	8	4.0	16	72.7	6	27.3	34	68.0	16	32.0
1828	26	100.0	0	0.0	228	96.6	12	5.1	11	68.8	5	31.2	21	75.0	7	25.0
1832	18	90.0	2	10.0	197	91.2	19	8.8	15	75.0	5	25.0	15	75.0	5	25.0
1834	0	0.0	0	0.0	4	28.6	10	71.4	16	66.7	8	33.3	11	57.9	8	42.1
1836	1	20.0	4	80.0	17	58.6	12	41.4	57	73.1	21	26.9	13	54.2	11	45.8
1838	30	32.6	62	67.4	53	37.9	87	62.1	94	80.3	23	19.7	30	50.7	12	42.3
1840	46	51.7	43	48.3	53	52.0	49	45.0	83	81.4	19	18.6	24	64.9	13	35.1
1842	110	70.1	47	29.9	74	59.2	51	40.8	69	78.4	19	21.6	26	55.3	21	44.7
1844	246	70.0	104	30.0	101	69.0	45	31.0	148	87.0	22	13.0	26	57.7	19	42.3
1846	561	94.7	31	5.3	256	88.8	32	11.2	71	85.5	12	14.5	19	73.0	7	27.0
1848	514	95.0	27	5.0	273	85.0	48	15.0	142	53.4	124	46.6	28	40.0	42	60.0
1850	545	94.8	30	5.2	351	86.5	54	13.5	65	19.1	275	80.9	16	17.8	74	82.2

TABLE 3.14: SENTENCES IN MONTHS ACCORDING TO PLEA OF PROSTITUTES IN THE POLICE COURT: 1826–1850

	Prostitution							
	Guilty				Not Guilty			
	0–3		3+		0–3		3+	
Year	N	%	N	%	N	%	N	%
1826	14	38.9	22	61.1	103	63.2	60	36.8
1828	11	47.8	12	52.2	89	70.1	38	29.9
1832	2	66.7	1	33.3	47	83.9	9	16.1
1834	7	36.8	12	63.2	25	49.0	26	51.0
1836	4	30.8	9	69.2	13	35.1	24	64.9
1838	9	69.2	4	30.8	51	58.6	36	41.4
1840	19	48.7	20	51.3	32	43.2	42	56.8
1842	20	42.6	27	57.4	38	53.5	33	46.5
1844	2	16.7	10	83.3	10	55.6	8	44.4
1846	3	30.0	7	70.0	3	20.0	12	80.0
1848	25	75.8	8	24.2	14	63.6	8	36.4
1850	24	61.5	15	38.5	12	57.1	9	42.9

The evidence is clear: plea bargaining was begun in Boston's Police Court in the early 1830s involving charges of violating city ordinances. In the early 1840s it was utilized for public drunkenness defendants, and in the late 1840s it spread to prostitution defendants. The question now is, why?

WHY PLEA BARGAINING?

Plea bargaining was restricted in both courts to regulatory or vice offenders. There is little evidence that common law crimes or private disputes were regularly plea bargained in either court during the antebellum period. There is also little likelihood that heavy caseloads were solely responsible for the innovation. True, during the late 1830s and 1840s, sizable increases in caseload were encountered in the Police Court, but in the early 1830s when plea bargaining of city ordinance violations was begun, or in the early 1840s when it was commenced with public drunkenness defendants, the number of cases was rising only moderately (see Table 3.10)

The argument that plea bargaining is encouraged by mounting caseloads seems more appropriate for the Municipal Court. After 1836, when plea bargaining with prostitution defendants was just beginning, the caseload of the Municipal Court soared by 74.5 percent (see Table 3.10), and after 1842, when plea bargaining with regulatory defendants was getting under way, the caseload again rose sharply.

Whether plea bargaining was a response to burgeoning caseloads, however, is debatable. Although a sharp influx of vice cases (see fig. 5.12) beginning in the late 1830s followed the introduction of plea bargaining in 1836 in the Municipal Court, regulatory offenses were already rising rapidly in 1842 when plea bargaining in these offenses became common (see fig. 5.9). In both cases the sharpest increases were experienced *after* plea bargaining took hold.

It is easy to see how case management problems in the Municipal Court might encourage plea bargaining in some form, since the manager of the Municipal Court, the county attorney, was also the principal negotiator in arranging plea bargains. He may well have taken the initiative there, but there was no prosecutor in the Police Court, and little if any relationship between caseload and plea bargaining.

If caseloads made plea bargaining more attractive in the Municipal Court, it is doubtful that a growing professionalism among lawyers and judges in Boston contributed to the invention of plea bargaining, as Feeley (1982) has maintained. Their commitment to professional standards, Feeley argues, enabled them to develop just solutions privately in cases which previously had required an adversarial system and due process. As the bench and bar became more professional, plea bargaining became more acceptable as a substitute for criminal trials, particularly among the more professional lawyers and judges.

Although professional judges *did* favor plea bargaining in the Municipal Court (see chap. 4), those who pushed it hardest in the Police Court where it originated were the constables, arguably the least professional members of that court. Their lack of professionalism did not prevent their inventing the process in the Police Court.

It is also unlikely that the growing intricacy of due process was responsible for plea bargaining in Boston. True, trials were increasing in length in the Municipal Court, probably because of refinements in due process, but trials were not lengthening significantly in the Police Court. The fact that plea bargaining was introduced first in the Police Court where due process was relatively simple argues convincingly against this thesis.

The best clue we have in explaining why plea bargaining arose is the fact that both courts limited plea bargaining to regulatory and vice defendants, that is, to defendants who could only be apprehended via proactive investigations via criminal justice officials. The complainant in such cases was inevitably someone who would understand and accept a reduced punishment, but more importantly, the investigating official was someone who could also begin negotiations. If discussions of charge and punishment were based on an assumption of innocence, they led toward an ultimate trial, but if they were based on an assumption of guilt and ultimately a guilty plea, they led in an entirely different direction.

The earlier the path was determined, the fewer there were who were surprised or angered at a guilty plea and especially at a reduced punishment. Victimless crimes, such as vice or regulatory offenses, which required a proactive effort by criminal justice officials, permitted an early discussion of these issues and an effective sorting out of those defendants who could be induced to plead guilty.[4]

The condition of the defendants also predisposed them to negotiations. Regulatory defendants were often businessmen with substantial resources to contest criminal charges, but who, at the same time, recognized the waste in seriously contesting minor charges that carried little stigma. When charged with a regulatory offense, they routinely pleaded not guilty. And when promised dismissals for a portion of the charges and only a minor fine for the rest, they welcomed the bargain and pleaded guilty. Vice defendants, on the other hand, were often professional offenders with a weak defense but a familiarity with criminal justice officials and procedures. They were more inclined than regulatory offenders to cooperate with authorities even when the result could be a prison term, if the right inducement could be found. The essence of plea bargaining, of course, is negotiation, and it requires individuals on both sides with an inclination to bargain.

Why did criminal justice officials become receptive to the process? In the Municipal Court the prosecutor was in a fine position to negotiate both with vice offenders and with businessmen who had violated regulatory laws. Through his investigative responsibilities he made contact with offenders at an early stage and since he was also in control of proceedings as they advanced through the Municipal Court, he could conclude an authoritative agreement with offenders. Moreover, his responsibility for case flow in the Municipal Court made him responsive to ways whereby it might be efficiently managed. Although there is no direct evidence that Samuel D. Parker, Suffolk County attorney from 1830 to 1852, actually did participate in such negotiations, the circumstantial evidence is strong that he was the key person in the Municipal Court guiding plea negotiations.

In the Police Court, however, the constables initiated plea negotiations. If plea bargaining had been invented by Police Court magistrates or the court clerk who also had regular contact with defendants, we would not expect much variation in the percentage of plea-bargained cases among the different constables. If negotiations were commenced only after the defendant had been arraigned, different constables should have had about the same portion of their arrestees pleading guilty.

If, however, a particular constable initiated the process for, say, city ordinance violators, his suspects should display a heightened level of guilty pleas, while arrestees of other constables should show distinctly lower levels, at least until the practice became widespread in the Police Court.

Table 3.15 seems to suggest that the arrestees of different constables plea bargained at sharply different rates in the beginning. In the mid-1830s Ebenezar Shute's arrestees for city ordinance violations nearly tripled their rate of pleading guilty (from 22.0 to 65.5 percent), while the arrestees of other constables—most notably James Pierce's—pleaded guilty much less readily.

Public drunkenness defendants began to plead guilty more frequently in 1842 for all four constables, and for a few years the levels among the four remained surprisingly uniform, but by 1846, there was again a wide difference in guilty pleas among the several constables, which only narrowed in 1850. Plea bargaining commenced at about the same time for all four constables, but they made use of it at very different rates and showed little uniformity even after it had become established.

For both offenses plea bargaining ushered in much more variability in pleading, and while Shute and Reed seem to have pioneered the method among city ordinance violators, no constable stands out as the initiator among public drunkenness defendants. This variability strongly suggests that the constables (and not the magistrates) introduced plea bargaining in the Police Court.

Why did they do it? Police constables in Boston conducted regular negotiations with the underworld on a variety of issues (Lane 1967, 147–148)—to obtain information about important crimes for example, and to arrange for the unquestioned return of stolen goods—and it was only a minor step for them to suggest a guilty plea in return for a light sentence. The magistrate's guiding hand was important, but once his cooperation was assured, plea bargaining itself was relatively easily organized.

When the practice had become established in the Police Court, it was inevitable that the same would happen in the Municipal Court. The county attorney, Samuel D. Parker, could readily appreciate its many advantages, and he was in a position to implement it quickly and with discretion. He was also in a position to argue its merits persuasively to Judge Peter Thacher, the Municipal Court's sole judge from 1823 to 1843.

It is interesting that the diffusion of plea bargaining was from the Police Court to the Municipal Court—that is, from a lower court to a higher court. It is readily understandable, however, if we remember that plea bargaining depended upon an adaptable stance in the courts

TABLE 3.15: PERCENTAGE OF GUILTY PLEAS FOR SELECTED OFFENSES ACCORDING TO THE ARRESTING CONSTABLE IN THE POLICE COURT

Public Drunkenness

Year	Sam Vialle Percent G. Pleas	Sam Vialle Total Arrests	Ebenezar Shute Percent G. Pleas	Ebenezar Shute Total Arrests	Jacob Tallert Percent G. Pleas	Jacob Tallert Total Arrests	Jonas Shutter Percent G. Pleas	Jonas Shutter Total Arrests
1826–32			3.9	203				
1834			8.3	96				
1836			9.7	103				
1838	33.3	3	19.3	187	33.3	3	33.3	3
1840	26.7	60	22.0	173	21.4	98	22.3	173
1842	35.7	171	36.7	79	38.1	168	40.3	62
1844	55.3	226	45.7	151	54.4	204	63.6	44
1846	49.6	351	47.2	307	50.6	348	80.6	31
1848	54.5	330	51.9	266	53.4	313	71.0	100
1850	53.3	349	—retired—		52.7	334	52.8	362

City Ordinance Violations

Year	James Pierce Percent G. Pleas	James Pierce Total Arrests	Ebenezar Shute Percent G. Pleas	Ebenezar Shute Total Arrests	George Reed Percent G. Pleas	George Reed Total Arrests	Thomas Holden Percent G. Pleas	Thomas Holden Total Arrests
1826–32	21.1	38	15.4	52	13.6	44	7.1	56
1834	13.0	23	22.0	41	26.5	34	11.1	27
1836	26.7	15	65.5	29	51.1	47	30.3	30
1838	37.5	24	50.0	86	53.5	86	24.4	45
1840	62.1	29	55.3	47	35.3	34	20.0	5
1842	—retired—		55.9	34	—retired—		—retired—	
1844			64.6	65				
1846			64.9	37				
1848			60.2	83				
1850			—retired—					

that was responsive to conditions among defendants. The Police Court, with neither a prosecutor nor defense attorneys, was in tune with its defendants. Convenience was more easily followed there. In the Municipal Court attorneys were prominent and, perhaps, less inclined to accept such fundamental changes in pleading. It is reasonable, therefore, that plea bargaining should emerge first in the Police Court and then be adopted only somewhat later in modified form in the Municipal Court.

The Prosecutor Assumes Control

In the beginning the American colonies assumed a system of private prosecution based on an age-old practice followed in England. An attorney general, appointed by the royal governor, pursued cases of special political importance, as in England, but routine criminal cases were prosecuted by private individuals, usually the victim (Beattie 1986, 8–10). In the colonies, however, legal institutions were still rather rude and unreliable, and a better system was needed. Grand juries were swayed by local sentiment, individuals were inhibited by the expense and inconvenience of prosecution, others used the courts for private purposes, and through it all, local government was losing revenue that it might otherwise have claimed through fines. To ease these problems, public prosecutors were appointed in Connecticut and Virginia in the first decade of the eighteenth century, and by the middle of the century most of the colonies—particularly those with a Dutch heritage—had moved away from private prosecution of routine criminal cases (Goldstein 1983, 1286–87).

In the nineteenth century, as we have seen, the U.S. polity assumed a major role in fostering civic virtue, and the courts became an important instrument of its will. The police, to some extent, but especially the prosecutor flourished in this environment and began to perform an expanding role in regulating communal mores, particularly in the more novel areas of public offending such as liquor law violations and vice. As the prosecutor accepted these new responsibilities, he began also to assume some of the functions of the judge and jury.

Instead of the jury the prosecutor began to decide guilt or innocence through his ability to dismiss cases, and instead of the judge he began to set punishments through plea bargaining. By the middle of the nineteenth century, in other words, he had become the principal voice in the community defining its response to crime and vice. In earlier times community leaders—the clergy or public officials—had performed this function; but by the middle of the nineteenth century, the policing of civic virtue had become so politically delicate and technically precise that only duly appointed legal officials, that is, the public prosecutor, could perform it effectively. In this way the prosecutor took control of the crime fighting function in the community.

4
The Judges

Boston's courts were changing rapidly during the antebellum period, and the broad question here is how these changes influenced the manner in which the courts meted out justice. How did a growing caseload and the spread of plea bargaining affect the quality of their decisions? Were professional judges more sympathetic to plea bargaining, more effective, or more inclined to soften criminal sanctions than localistic judges? Did the growing activism of Massachusetts' Supreme Judicial Court encourage the more professional judges to monitor the business community closely? Did a growing antagonism toward the Irish immigrants spark a more vigorous punishment of their misdeeds? In short, how did Boston's judges react to changes in their profession and to sociopolitical turbulence before the Civil War?

The judges were not *solely* responsible for decisions reached in their courts during this period. In the Municipal Court the prosecutor and, at times, the defense attorney played an important part in these decisions, but the judges showed the greatest variation. There was only one prosecutor in the Municipal Court, Samuel D. Parker, from 1830 through 1852, and defense attorneys were not common. Thus, the only well-documented variability in the Municipal Court was to be found among the judges, and the different ways that different kinds of judges handled the court's caseload will be our focus.

In the Police Court there were no professional prosecutors and defense attorneys were rare, so that trends in that court's handling of cases reflected more clearly the decisions and policies of its judges. Unfortunately, it was not possible to determine which of the three rotating magistrates was responsible for particular cases, and linking specific judges with changes in the processing of cases was not possible.

The Course of Justice in Boston's Courts

In the early years—up to 1830—the Municipal Court behaved pretty much as a preindustrial court. Its docket was uncrowded—surpassing 300 criminal cases per year only twice; most defendants pleaded not

TABLE 4.1: THE CHANGING TREND OF PLEAS AT ARRAIGNMENT IN THE MUNICIPAL COURT

Year	Nolo Contendere or Guilty		Not Guilty		Not Guilty/Case Continued		Not Guilty changed to Guilty or Nolo Contendere		Mixed Plea[a]		Other		Total No. charged
	N	%	N	%	N	%	N	%	N	%	N	%	N
1814–20	160	13.7	697	59.5	0	0.0	30	2.6	2	0.2	282	24.1	1171
1822–30	245	21.0	656	56.3	6	0.5	7	0.6	5	0.4	247	21.2	1166
1832–40	299	17.2	762	43.8	26	1.5	36	2.1	10	0.6	606	34.8	1739
1842–50	744	14.5	1389	27.0	211	4.1	890	17.3	245	4.8	1667	32.4	5146

[a] Not guilty to some charges, guilty to others

guilty but were tried and found guilty; and since there were very few multicount indictments, virtually the only outcomes were simple guilty or not guilty verdicts. Many of the guilty defendants were sentenced to Charlestown State Prison, particularly the property offenders, while violent offenders for the most part, received minor fines.

After 1830 things began to change dramatically. The volume of minor criminal cases grew rapidly, and by 1850 the total caseload came to more than 1,500 in the Municipal Court. Moreover, as plea bargaining became common, pleading became much more complicated. A growing number of defendants pleaded not guilty initially, only to change their pleas to guilty after arranging a suitable agreement with the prosecutor; others agreed to plead guilty to only a portion of their charges in return for a dismissal or abatement of the rest. Proportionately fewer jury trials were held as growing numbers of defendants avoided trial by pleading guilty.

As judges relaxed their punishment of defendants who pleaded not guilty, the proportion of straight not guilty pleas, along with the proportion of convicted defendants receiving prison terms, dropped substantially. This moderation in sentencing in the Municipal Court, however, owed as much to a changing mix of offenses coming into the court as to the spread of plea bargaining. The growing prevalence of minor offenses led to a clear decline in the severity of sentences in the Municipal Court. Similarly, although the majority of defendants who were convincted by a jury went to prison, only a small fraction of those who plea bargained were ultimately sent to prison. Both changes resulted in a decided shift toward greater leniency in the Municipal Court.

In the 1840s the Municipal Court began to assume the character of a modern criminal court. It broadened its jurisdiction from traditional common law offenses to a wide variety of recently enacted regulatory laws and ordinances. It began to depend heavily on informal procedures for disposing of cases at the expense of the traditional jury trial. Charging issues and pleading became more crucial to the defendant than the trial, and outcomes got more complicated with informal probation, mixed pleas, and conditional sentences appearing frequently. Finally, the balance of power in the courtroom shifted sharply away from the judge and jury toward the prosecutor and his assistants.

In the Police Court, however, it was business as usual. Its jurisdiction embraced minor crimes and violations with a minimum of due process. Lawyers played little role in the proceedings, its justice was simple, and punishments were light. Bench trials were the norm, and caseloads of the Police Court were routinely four to ten times those of the Municipal Court with more than four thousand and two hundred cases being heard in 1850. Since all its cases were decided summarily, there was little

TABLE 4.2: THE CHANGING PATTERN OF JURY VERDICTS IN THE MUNICIPAL COURT

Year	Jury Verdicts				Ratio: Guilty/Not Guilty	Other		Total
	Guilty		Not Guilty					
	N	%	N	%		N	%	
1814–20	448	64.3	202	29.0	2.21	47	6.7	697
1822–30	463	70.6	163	24.8	2.84	30	4.6	656
1832–40	525	68.0	151	19.6	3.47	96	12.4	762
1842–50	739	52.9	300	21.5	2.47	359	25.7	1398

TABLE 4.3: TRENDS IN SENTENCING IN THE MUNICIPAL COURT

A. Plea: Not Guilty (Jury Verdict: Guilty)

Year	Prison N	Prison %	Surety, Fines, Costs N	Surety, Fines, Costs %	Other N	Other %	Total
1814–20	329	73.4	95	21.2	24	5.4	448
1822–30	363	78.4	84	18.1	16	3.5	463
1832–40	365	72.1	138	22.3	3	0.6	506
1842–50	485	65.6	229	31.0	25	3.8	739

B. Plea: Nolo Contendere or Guilty

Year	Prison N	Prison %	Surety, Fines, Costs N	Surety, Fines, Costs %	Other N	Other %	Total
1814–20	128	81.0	28	17.7	2	1.3	158
1822–30	187	78.2	50	20.9	2	0.8	239
1832–40	243	82.4	48	16.3	4	1.4	295
1842–50	473	65.2	231	31.8	22	3.0	726

C. Plea: Not Guilty/Continued (Outcome: Guilty)

Year	Prison N	Prison %	Surety, Fines, Costs N	Surety, Fines, Costs %	Other N	Other %	Total
1814–20	0	0	0	0.0	0	0.0	0
1822–30	2	33.3	4	66.7	0	0.0	6
1832–40	5	50.0	2	20.0	3	30.0	10
1842–50	41	55.4	33	44.6	0	0.0	74

D. Plea: Not Guilty changed to Guilty or Nolo Contender

Year	Prison N	Prison %	Surety, Fines, Costs N	Surety, Fines, Costs %	Other N	Other %	Total
1814–20	11	37.9	17	58.6	1	3.4	29
1822–30	2	28.6	4	57.1	1	14.3	7
1832–40	12	34.3	10	28.6	13	37.1	35
1842–50	35	4.0	311	35.9	520	60.0	866

E. Mixed Plea

Year	Prison N	Prison %	Surety, Fines, Costs N	Surety, Fines, Costs %	Other N	Other %	Total
1814–20	2	100.0	0	0.0	0	0.0	2
1822–30	0	0.0	5	100.0	0	0.0	5
1832–40	4	44.4	5	55.6	0	0.0	9
1842–50	11	4.8	40	17.5	177	77.6	228

opportunity for defendants to present their side, and very few (less than 7 percent in 1850) were found not guilty. In the early years (1826–34) the largest percentage was continued without a finding or simply dismissed, but with the invention of plea bargaining the major portion was found guilty and sentenced. Small fines (under three dollars) were the order of the day, although street walkers, public drunks, vagrants, and thieves were sentenced mainly to the House of Corrections for terms of up to ninety days.

The Police Court, even more than the Municipal Court, was committed to crime control and case flow. The niceties of due process carried little weight (Fenner 1856, 27), but given the volume of cases the Police Court disposed of each year, it is hard to imagine how the court and its officers could have done otherwise.

Punishment in Boston's Courts

Sentences handed down by the courts offer insights into several interesting questions. Which crimes were regarded as most serious in the community? The core values of a community are often reformulated as it undergoes the kind of far-reaching transformation that Boston experienced during this period, and the sentences that Municipal Court judges meted out give an indication as to which crimes were most abhorrent to Bostonians during this early period.

At the same time sentences provide an index of the judges' thinking, their values, and favorite doctrines regarding crime and its punishment (see Levin 1977; Clark and Trubek 1961). We know who these judges were, and we know their careers. Several were trained at Harvard Law School and were awarded honorary degrees from New England colleges after long, illustrious service as judges, professors, attorneys general, governors, or legal scholars. Others got their legal training as apprentices in law offices and confined their careers to the Municipal Court. In short some of these judges were leaders of their profession, while others did little more than hear the cases that crowded each day into the Municipal Court. Were the leaders of the legal profession also architects of legal change in Boston, or were the less exalted but thoroughly experienced jurists who knew the day-to-day problems of the court more effective in shaping the city's legal institutions? These are the issues examined in this section.

SENTENCING IN THE MUNICIPAL COURT

Which crimes were punished most severely in the Municipal Court? All cases from 1814 through 1850 were aggregated in Table 4.4, and

TABLE 4.4: JUDGMENTS ACCORDING TO CHARGE FOR SELECTED OFFENSES IN THE MUNICIPAL COURT: 1814–1850

	Felony against the Person		Assault and Battery		Felony against Property		Minor Property Crimes		Prostitution		Offense against Religion		Liquor Law Violations	
	N	%	N	%	N	%	N	%	N	%	N	%	N	%
Nolle Prosequi	26	4.1	45	7.1	6	3.9	78	2.9	117	16.1	92	20.1	421	42
Pay Surety	20	3.1	16	2.5	7	4.4	83	3.2	43	5.9	7	1.5	21	2
Incarcerated	207	31.8	99	15.5	61	39.1	1605	60.7	105	14.3	6	1.3	1	0
Discharged	83	12.8	93	14.6	39	25.0	311	11.7	64	8.8	20	4.3	33	3
Fined	90	13.8	100	15.7	4	2.6	68	2.6	126	17.2	91	19.8	118	12
Fined or Incarcerated if Defaults	48	7.4	27	4.2	4	2.6	22	0.8	72	9.8	4	0.9	9	0
Fine & Costs	81	12.5	132	20.7	4	2.6	24	0.9	52	7.3	124	27.0	225	23
Proceedings Stayed	0	0.0	0	0.0	0	0.0	0	0.0	0	0.0	0	0.0	1	0
Defendant Defaults	7	1.1	13	2.0	1	0.6	39	1.5	7	1.0	2	0.4	15	2
Satisfaction Acknowledged	14	2.2	27	4.2	0	0.0	2	0.1	10	1.4	6	1.3	2	0
Left on File	4	0.6	2	0.3	8	5.1	67	2.5	24	3.3	4	0.9	52	5
No Judgment	45	7.0	62	9.8	13	8.3	260	9.8	97	13.2	96	20.9	61	6
Total	650		638		156		2642		732		460		997	

TABLE 4.5: THE LEVELS OF FINES AND SENTENCES TO IMPRISONMENT FOR SELECTED OFFENSES IN THE MUNICIPAL COURT: 1814–1850 AGGREGATED

	Fines										
	$0–5		$6–10		$11–20		$21–30		$31–40		$41+
	N	%	N	%	N	%	N	%	N	%	N	%
Offenses Against Religion	171	46.6	50	13.7	33	9.0	83	22.6	20	5.4	10	2.7
Liquor Law Violations	70	10.3	24	3.6	352	51.9	49	7.2	136	20.1	47	6.9
City Ordinance Violations	43	9.6	27	6.0	179	40.2	15	3.4	166	37.3	15	3.3
Assault & Battery	123	40.4	63	20.7	64	21.1	33	10.9	2	0.7	19	6.2

	Sentenced to Imprisonment							
	0–3 months		4–6 months		7–10 months		11–24 months		25 + months
	N	%	N	%	N	%	N	%	N	%
Minor Property Crimes	32	71.8	8	17.8	3	6.7	2	4.4	0	0.0
Burglary	36	10.8	22	6.6	10	3.0	157	47.0	109	32.6
Counterfeiting	30	19.5	19	12.3	2	1.3	70	45.5	33	21.4

it is clear that defendants convicted of minor property crimes were sentenced to jail or prison at the highest rate—60.7 percent. Burglars were next at 55.1 percent, and counterfeiters were third with 45.2 percent being imprisoned.

At the light end those least likely to be imprisoned included liquor law violators, city ordinance violators, and offenders against religion. These three types of offenders were punished primarily with fines, as were assault and battery defendants. Among them assault and battery defendants received the smallest fines, and city ordinance violators received the heaviest. As far as imprisonment was concerned, more than two-thirds of the burglars and counterfeiters received long terms of eleven months or more, while nearly all of the minor property offenders received short sentences—six months or less.

The most severely punished defendants, then, were property offenders, while regulatory violators were punished least. Violent offenders, involving even such injuries as broken bones or gouged-out eyes, were rarely punished with prison sentences, in sharp contrast to modern practice.[1] According to Table 4.6 the majority of convicted violent offenders were fined, whereas more than 93 percent of the convicted property offenders were imprisoned.

A similar sentencing pattern was found in London courts in the early nineteenth century (Gatrell 1980; 296).[2] It could be that property was more highly valued than sight or limb by the emerging bourgeoisie in both Boston and London, but a more likely explanation (Gatrell 1980; 300–1) is that property offenders were seen by court officials as chronic offenders who pursued crime as a livelihood, whereas violent offenders were regarded as simply impulsive individuals without clear criminal tendencies. The former needed prison sentences to control their criminality, but the latter needed only fines to inhibit their more troublesome impulses.

TRENDS IN SENTENCING

The punishments of different offenses did not change over time in expected ways. We might speculate that property offenses would be punished more lightly as time passed and that violent offenses would be punished more severely, that is, they would approach the modern punishment pattern as Boston's courts modernized. But such was not the case.

It appears that serious offenses, whether property or violent, were punished more leniently, while minor offenses were punished more severely as the years went by. Thus, the sentences given *felony* violent offenders (whether fines or prison terms) grew progressively lighter after

TABLE 4.6: THE PERCENTAGE OF SENTENCED DEFENDANTS GIVEN FINES OR SENTENCED TO IMPRISONMENT IN THE MUNICIPAL COURT: 1814–1850 AGGREGATED

	Imprisonment		Fined[a]		Total
	N	%	N	%	
Felony Against the Person	207	48.6	219	51.4	426
Minor Crimes Against the Person	8	25.0	24	75.0	32
Assault & Battery	99	27.7	259	72.3	358
Felony Against Property	61	88.4	8	11.6	69
Minor Crimes Against Property	1,605	93.4	114	6.6	1,719
Counterfeiting	132	93.6	9	6.4	141
Burglary	333	97.4	9	2.6	342

[a] Includes those receiving fines, fine and costs, a fine, or incarceration if fine is defaulted.

1824, while those received by assault and battery defendants grew more severe (see Table 4.7). Similarly, while prison sentences for burglary defendants grew shorter, those received by minor property offenders were lengthening appreciably.

The key to this peculiar pattern seems to lie in the relative mix of offenders coming before the Municipal Court. As juveniles became regular defendants in the late 1830s and 1840s, the court became less willing to sentence them to lengthy prison terms. Juveniles convicted of very minor offenses were sent to the House of Reformation or the Industrial School for Boys in Westborough, but juveniles convicted of serious offenses were sent to the adult prison. Thus, the shorter prison sentences after 1836 for both burglars and felony offenders reflected the fact that many more juveniles were being convicted of these crimes in the later years and were lowering the mean sentence.

The harsher sentences for assault and battery and minor property offenders, however, are particularly interesting since juveniles were also committing these offenses in growing numbers and being punished more mildy for them after 1836. The increasingly rich mix of juveniles balanced to some extent the growing harshness of judges toward adult offenders for both offenses, and overall punishments eased after 1836 as juveniles became particularly numerous in the Municipal Court. But the flood of juveniles could not erase the overall trend toward severity for these offenses.

The sharp reduction in fines for liquor law violations after 1824 is difficult to explain, but liquor law violators and city ordinance violators were punished with increasing rigor after 1836, when plea negotiations

TABLE 4.7: FINES AND SENTENCES (IN MONTHS) TO IMPRISONMENT BY THE MUNICIPAL COURT: 1814–1850

Fines

Year	Felony Against The Person						City Ordinance Violations						Liquor Law Violations					
	$0–5		$6–20		$21+		$0–5		$6–20		$21+		$0–20		$21+			
	N	%	N	%	N	%	N	%	N	%	N	%	N	%	N	%		
1814–24	5	20.8	13	54.2	6	25.0	8	44.4	8	44.4	2	11.1	18	37.5	30	62.5		
1826–36	13	33.3	19	48.7	7	17.9	3	42.9	3	42.9	1	14.3	12	75.0	4	25.0		
1838–50	60	29.4	98	48.0	46	22.5	32	7.7	195	46.8	190	45.6	406	67.2	198	32.7		

Year	Assault & Battery					
	$0–5		$6–20		$21+	
	N	%	N	%	N	%
1814–24	58	50.9	39	34.2	17	14.9
1826–36	11	26.2	23	54.8	8	19.0
1838–50	54	34.2	75	47.5	29	18.4

Incarceration

Year	Burglary						Minor Property Crimes						Felony Against the Person				Assault & Battery			
	0–10 months		11+ months				0–3 mons.		4–10 mons.		11+ mons.		0–3 months		4+ months		0–3 months		4+ months	
	N	%	N	%			N	%	N	%	N	%	N	%	N	%	N	%	N	%
1814–24	6	11.8	45	88.2			237	44.8	37	7.0	255	48.2	13	43.3	17	56.7	45	95.7	2	4.3
1826–36	4	11.1	32	88.9			48	10.4	66	14.3	346	75.2	20	47.6	22	52.4	22	61.1	14	38.9
1838–50	58	23.5	189	76.5			153	20.8	145	19.8	436	59.4	153	60.2	101	39.8	68	73.9	24	26.1

in the form of charge bargaining became common for both offenses. Charge bargaining in these cases (Chap. 3) usually involved a reduction in the charges but a punishment at the high end for the remaining charge: hence, the increasing size of fines for liquor law violations and city ordinance violations in the Municipal Court after 1836.

SENTENCING IN THE POLICE COURT

In the Police Court the changes in sentencing were more uniform. In 1834 the punishment of every high volume offense except city ordinance violations became abruptly more severe. Assault and battery, public drunkenness, public disturbances, prostitution, vagrancy, and larceny were all given much heavier fines or much longer jail terms in the Police Court (see fig. 4.1 and 4.2). After this shift in 1834, however, there was no clear trend through 1850.

As we have seen, it is impossible to link each case with a specific judge in the records of the Police Court, but there is reason to believe that the sudden turn toward severity owed much to the appointment of a new magistrate.[3] On 19 February 1834 James C. Merrill was appointed to the Police Court bench to fill a retirement vacancy. Born in 1784 in Haverhill and educated at Phillips Exeter Academy in New Hampshire, Judge Merrill was graduated from Harvard College in 1807. After studying for the bar in a local law office, he was admitted to the Essex County bar in 1812 and to the Suffolk County bar in 1815. He was named to the Police Court bench at the age of fifty, where he served until his retirement at sixty-eight. His early life and education were in the eighteenth century, his training for the bar was in the old style, and his perspective was a traditional one.

The shift toward severity was confined to the Police Court, but in that court it touched a large portion of the defendants. The facts are certainly consistent with the conclusion that Justice Merrill's appointment was a major factor in this shift.

The punishment of city ordinance violators failed to follow the general pattern of growing severity for a very good reason. Plea negotiations had begun with city ordinance violators in 1832, and their moderating effect counterbalanced the more general trend toward harsher punishments. Public drunkenness after 1840 and prostitution after 1846 also show some moderation in their punishments for much the same reason (see Tables 4.8 and 4.9).

In contrast with the Municipal Court there is little tendency here to punish property offenders less harshly and violent offenders more severely. In this respect Boston's Police Court remained more closely attuned to the values of preindustrial Boston than to those of the modern era.

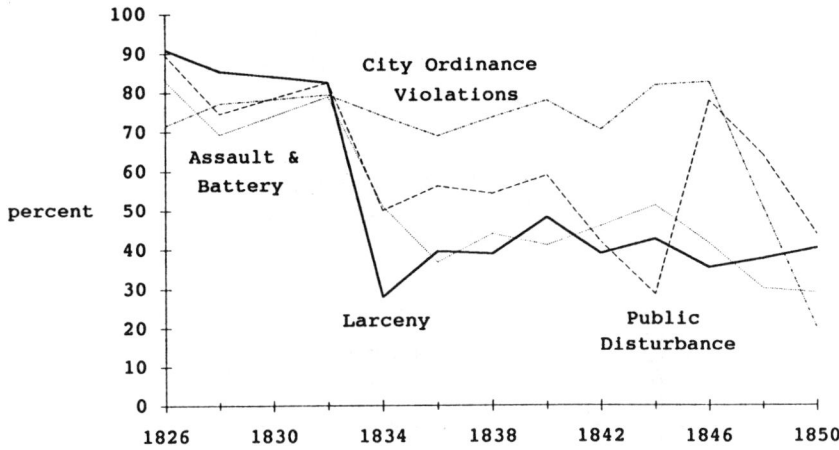

Figure 4.1: The Percentage of Fined Defendants Given Fines of $2.00 or Less in the Police Court: 1826-1850.

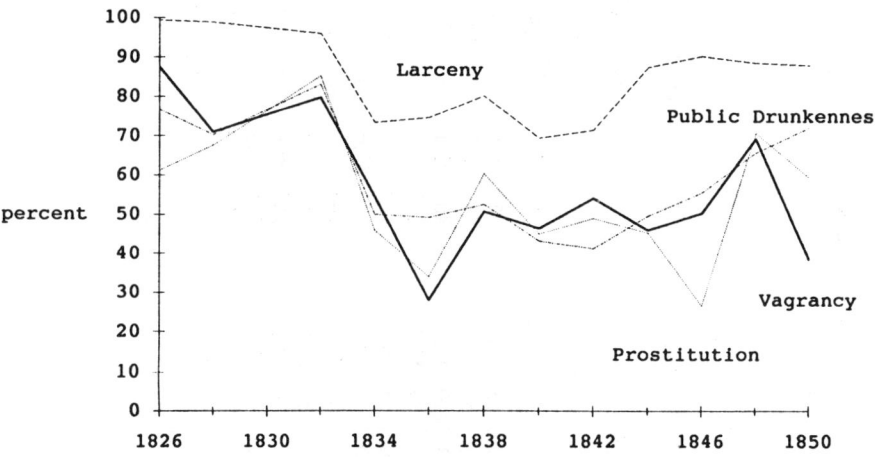

Figure 4.2: The Percentage of Imprisoned Defendants Sentenced to 0-3 Months in the Police Court: 1826-1850.

TABLE 4.8: SENTENCES IN MONTHS FOR SELECTED OFFENSES IN THE POLICE COURT: 1826–1850

Year	Prostitution				Public Drunkenness				Vagrancy				Larceny			
	0–3		4+		0–3		4+		0–3		4+		0–3		4+	
	N	%	N	%	N	%	N	%	N	%	N	%	N	%	N	%
1826	131	61.2	83	38.8	258	76.6	79	23.4	35	87.5	5	12.5	180	99.4	1	0.6
1828	104	67.5	50	32.5	221	70.2	94	29.8	71	71.0	29	29.0	170	98.8	2	1.2
1832	58	85.3	10	14.7	402	83.1	82	16.9	99	79.8	25	20.2	117	95.9	5	4.1
1834	35	45.9	39	52.7	172	50.0	172	50.0	31	59.6	21	40.4	55	73.3	20	26.7
1836	17	34.0	33	66.0	149	49.3	153	50.7	16	28.1	41	71.9	86	79.6	22	20.4
1838	3	100.0	0	0.0	242	52.6	218	47.4	33	50.8	32	49.2	97	80.3	24	19.8
1840	51	45.1	62	54.9	190	43.4	248	56.6	27	46.6	31	53.4	66	69.5	29	30.5
1842	58	49.2	60	50.8	151	41.4	214	58.7	37	54.4	31	45.6	63	71.6	25	28.4
1844	15	45.5	18	54.5	168	49.9	169	50.1	19	46.3	22	53.7	78	87.6	11	12.3
1846	7	26.9	19	73.1	311	55.8	246	44.2	41	50.6	40	49.4	86	90.5	9	9.5
1848	39	70.9	16	29.1	254	66.0	131	34.0	80	69.6	35	30.4	48	88.9	6	11.1
1850	37	59.7	25	40.3	487	72.4	186	27.6	33	38.8	52	61.2	182	88.3	24	11.7

TABLE 4.9: FINES FOR SELECTED OFFENSES IN THE POLICE COURT: 1826–1850

City

Year	Assault & Battery				Public Drunkenness				Ordinance Violations				Public Disturbance				Larceny			
	$0–2		$8+		$0–2		$8+		$0–2		$8+		$0–2		$8+		$0–2		$8+	
	N	%	N	%	N	%	N	%	N	%	N	%	N	%	N	%	N	%	N	%
1826	354	82.9	0	0.0	278	96.5	1	0.3	68	71.6	10	10.6	34	89.5	0	0.0	162	91.0	0	0.0
1828	268	69.3	4	1.0	264	98.2	0	0.0	44	77.2	2	3.5	85	74.6	0	0.0	153	85.5	2	1.1
1832	271	78.3	2	0.6	239	91.6	4	1.5	46	79.3	0	0.0	33	82.5	0	0.0	94	82.5	1	0.9
1834	99	51.0	1	0.5	4	28.6	5	35.7	54	74.0	4	5.5	3	50.0	0	0.0	14	28.0	1	2.0
1836	76	36.7	21	10.2	18	51.4	0	0.0	73	68.9	4	3.7	23	56.1	2	4.9	15	39.5	7	18.4
1838	77	44.0	18	10.3	84	35.4	3	1.3	126	73.7	4	2.4	32	54.2	2	3.4	28	38.9	20	37.8
1840	67	41.1	9	5.5	99	51.6	4	2.1	116	77.9	10	6.7	43	58.9	2	2.7	27	48.2	13	24.2
1842	108	46.0	18	7.7	186	65.3	2	0.7	100	70.4	5	3.5	18	41.9	1	2.3	30	39.0	16	20.8
1844	103	51.2	14	7.0	354	70.4	145	28.8	188	81.7	3	1.3	2	28.6	0	0.0	46	42.6	17	15.7
1846	119	41.5	17	5.9	817	92.8	3	1.2	90	82.6	2	1.8	7	77.8	0	0.0	58	35.4	39	23.8
1848	93	30.1	9	2.9	788	91.3	2	0.2	174	50.7	5	1.5	16	64.0	0	0.0	100	37.7	43	16.2
1850	129	29.1	77	17.4	908	91.4	1	0.1	88	19.8	22	4.9	28	43.8	1	1.6	133	40.3	60	18.2

Punishment and Social Position

The criminal courts strive to handle each case individually and to sentence each defendant in terms of his or her just deserts. Judges, therefore, attempt to dispense justice by adjusting each defendant's sentence to his or her degree of guilt. The question here is the extent to which the defendant's social position influenced the judges' sentencing decisions.

When judges formulate their sentences in particular cases, they usually consider the degree of threat posed by the defendant. Was the offense an aggravated crime that indicated a clear danger to the community, or was it an innocuous crime that implied little threat? In making these decisions judges often utilize a variety of cues: the defendant's appearance and demeanor in the courtroom, or the attitudes of victims, witnesses, neighbors, or relatives toward the defendant.

These factors vary according to social position, and although a judge's sentencing decisions may be more punitive toward one social or ethnic group than some others, an apparent bias may reflect more the judge's appraisal of each defendant's particular threat to the community than a broad prejudice against any particular group. Fortunately, the two types of reactions can be readily distinguished by careful analysis.

At the same time any given corps of judges can only decide the cases that come before them. If prejudice against the Irish, for example, is a factor in their being complained against, or in their being arrested, the judges may be forced to sentence Irishmen more leniently than other groups to balance out the unfairness they have already suffered.

Ideally, the pattern of complaints and arrests should be compared with the pattern of sentencing to assess carefully how judges were handling different kinds of defendants. It was not possible to make these comparisons here and the results should be regarded as only suggestive.

Nevertheless, when we look at groups likely to be targeted for discrimination, we see very little evidence that Boston's judges singled them out systematically for markedly severe punishments. Specifically, neither the Irish nor lower-class defendants received routinely harsher punishments than their counterparts, despite the fact that the Irish were suffering growing hostility and even physical violence in Boston during this period. Although there is evidence of differential sentencing, the differentials seem to be geared more to the criminal characteristics of the group in question than a prejudicial desire to harm them.

In the Police Court, for example, males regularly received distinctly shortered jail sentences than females for both public drunkenness and prostitution but heavier fines for assault and battery and public drunkenness (see figs. 4.3, 4.4, 4.5, and 4.6). Males were heavy users

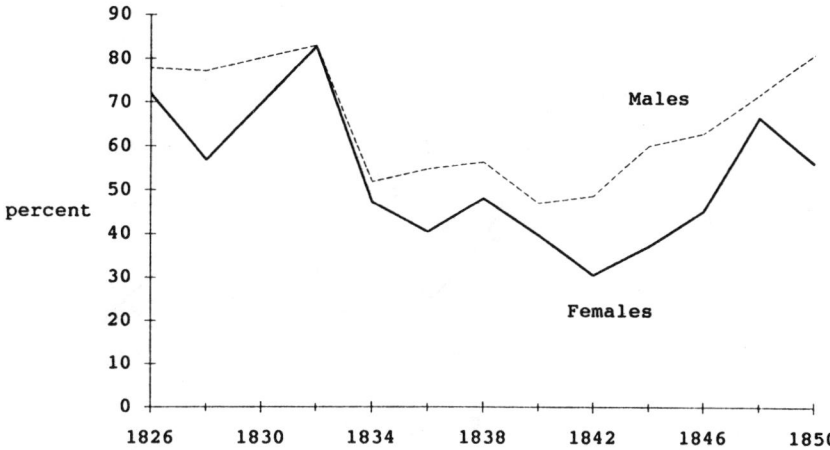

Figure 4.3: Percent Convicted of Public Drunkenness Receiving Jail Sentences of 3 Months or Less in the Police Court: 1826-1850.

Figure 4.4: Percent Convicted of Prostitution Receiving Jail Sentences of 3 Months or Less According to Sex in the Police Court: 1826-1850.

Figure 4.5: Percent Convicted of Assault and Battery Receiving Fines of $2.00 or Less According to Sex in the Police Court: 1826-1850.

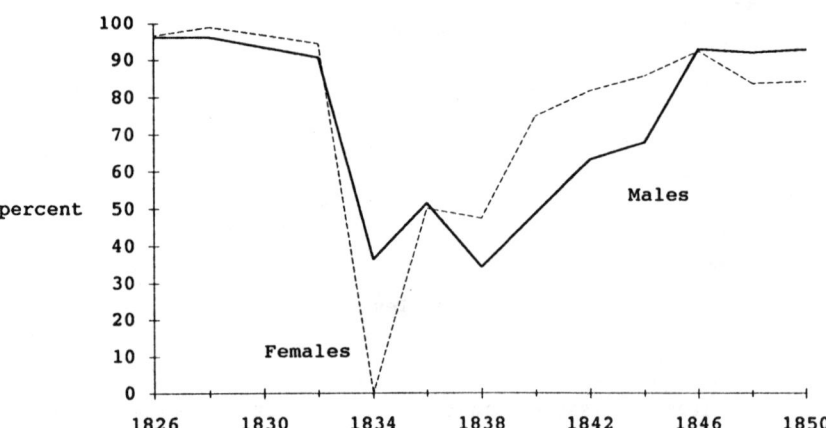

Figure 4.6: Percent Convicted of Public Drunkenness Receiving Fines of $2.00 or Less According to Sex in the Police Court: 1826-1850.

of plea bargaining during the late 1830s and early 1840s, and since prosecutors often sought heavier fines for those who were successful in avoiding jail sentences, this fact alone could explain this curious sentencing pattern.

Males, for example, were frequently charged with keeping a brothel, and after 1840 when plea bargaining became common, they pleaded guilty with great regularity (see Table 4.10). Not infrequently the wives of the men who were pleading guilty were also charged with being prostitutes, but in contrast to their husbands' cases, their cases were regularly left hanging without a disposition (cf. Figueria-McDonough 1985). The prosecutor probably felt that punishing the husband with a fine and giving his wife unofficial probation was sufficient to control the activities of both (see also Beattie 1986 414). Thus, men who plea bargained their brothel-keeping charges avoided prison but received heavy fines, whereas women charged with street-walking or lewd and lascivious conduct bargained less aggressively and received prison terms.

The lighter punishments that females received for assault and battery, and public drunkenness probably indicate that these offenses, when committed by females, were less troublesome in the community than similar offenses committed by males (cf. Engel 1971).

By the same token juveniles charged with property crimes were treated more gently, particularly in the early years, i.e., 1834–38, in the Municipal Court than adult laborers with similar charges. When charged with burglary, juveniles were especially likely to be released without a decision, and when charged with minor property crimes they were allowed to plea bargain more readily than adults. The court was content to treat juvenile cases mildly, because they were not as serious in the first place, and if convicted, juveniles faced imprisonment with adults.

Along these same lines in the earliest period eleven juveniles received lengthy prison terms for minor property crimes, while only one received a light sentence. The sentences of adult laborers were more evenly split during this early period (see Table 4.11). In the late 1830s and in the 1840s, however, juveniles were treated much more leniently than adults.

Much the same is true for burglary defendants. In the 1840s the Municipal Court began to sentence juveniles much more lightly. Although we cannot rule out humanitarian impulses here, it also is likely that the rapidly growing volume of juvenile burglars brought many more first offenders into court, who in truth deserved lighter punishments.

Nor is there any hint that social rank among adults helped to shape their punishments. When we compare the sentences of laborers, artisans, and businessmen (see Table 4.12), there is no consistent disadvantage suffered by any occupational group. Businessmen, for example, convicted of assault and battery or of minor property crimes were among

TABLE 4.10: THE OUTCOME OF PROSTITUTION CASES ACCORDING TO SOCIAL POSITION IN THE MUNICIPAL COURT: 1814–1850

Year	Guilty				Not Guilty				Released				No Decision				Guilty by Plea				No Outcome				Total	
	Men		Women		Men		Women		Men		Women		Men		Women		Men		Women		Men		Women		Men	Women
	N	%	N	%	N	%	N	%	N	%	N	%	N	%	N	%	N	%	N	%	N	%	N	%		
1814–32	6	31.6	23	37.1	5	26.3	10	16.1	1	5.3	6	9.7	2	10.5	3	4.8	1	5.3	10	16.1	4	21.0	8	12.9	19	62
1834–42	2	10.5	17	20.0	0	0.0	7	8.2	0	0.0	9	10.6	2	10.3	3	3.5	10	52.6	32	37.6	1	5.3	11	12.9	19	85
1844–50	9	10.2	26	12.1	4	4.5	19	8.9	4	4.5	7	3.3	4	4.5	34	15.9	44	50.0	79	36.9	8	9.1	45	21.0	88	214

TABLE 4.11: SENTENCES TO PRISON (IN MONTHS) FOR SELECTED PROPERTY CRIMES OF JUVENILES AND LABORERS IN THE MUNICIPAL COURT: 1824–1850

Minor Property Crimes

Year	Laborers			Juveniles		
	N <11 mos.	N >24 mos.	Ratio $\frac{<11}{>24}$	N <11 mos.	N >24 mos.	Ratio $\frac{<11}{>24}$
1824–1836[a]	80	99	0.8	1	11	0.1
1838–1844	44	17	2.6	16	7	2.3
1846–1850	77	21	3.7	73	5	14.6

Burglary

1834–1838[a]	1	8	0.1	0	3	0.0
1840–1844	10	11	0.9	12	5	2.4
1846–1850	18	20	0.9	28	18	1.6

[a] No juveniles recorded an offense before this period.

the most severely punished, but those convicted of prostitution or fraud were punished most leniently.

Nor was ethnicity a factor in sentencing. In the Municipal Court the Irish were punished with nearly the same level of severity as non-Irish defendants for assault and battery, and in the Police Court the same is true of Irish defendants charged with public drunkenness (see Table 4.13 and 4.14). They did suffer imprisonment for minor property crimes at a slightly higher rate than non-Irish defendants in the Municipal Court, and for prostitution in the Police Court as well. In neither court, however, were they punished more severely across the board than non-Irish defendants. There is very little basis for presuming that they were regular targets for judicial discrimination.

Courts can discriminate in other ways, however. They can respond to complaints from some social groups with indifference, while treating seriously the complaints of other groups. A comparison of male and female complainants, however, shows that the Municipal Court was generally fair in its handling of complaints.

Male complaints against property crimes (see Table 4.15) were more likely to produce guilty verdicts in the Municipal Court than similar complaints by females, but for violent offenses or sex crimes other than prostitution the reverse was true (see Table 4.16).

Where the women complainant may well have been an immediate

TABLE 4.12: PUNISHMENTS FOR SELECTED OFFENSES ACCORDING TO SOCIAL POSITION BY THE MUNICIPAL COURT: 1814 to 1850 AGGREGATED

	Fines of $5 of less							Sentences of 3 months or less				
	Assault & Battery		Prostitution		Fraud			Minor Property Crimes		Prostitution	
	N	%	N	%	N	%		N	%	N	%
Laborers	44	35.2	10	14.7	2	33.3		269	22.1	32	41.0
Artisans	29	45.3	0	0.0	2	50.0		25	11.6	1	25.0
Businessmen	4	22.2	11	19.3	25	86.2		3	12.0	29	59.2
Women	8	36.4	15	11.2	1	100.0		70	31.3	70	44.6
Juveniles	6	46.1	0	0.0	0	0.0		57	24.7	0	0.0

TABLE 4.13: THE PUNISHMENT OF IRISH AND NON-IRISH DEFENDANTS IN THE MUNICIPAL COURT: 1840–1850 AGGREGATED

	Nolle Prosc.		Incarceration		Discharged		Fined		No Judgment		Total[a]
	N	%	N	%	N	%	N	%	N	%	
Assault and Battery											
Irish	3	5.7	7	13.2	14	26.4	21	39.6	2	3.8	53
Non-Irish	21	8.7	35	14.5	27	11.2	91	37.6	20	8.3	242
Minor Property Crimes											
Irish	1	1.4	43	60.6	10	14.1	7	9.8	6	8.5	71
Non-Irish	30	3.9	410	53.0	74	9.6	77	10.0	94	12.2	773

[a] The figures do not equal the total because not all judgments were indicated.

TABLE 4.14: THE PUNISHMENT OF IRISH AND NON-IRISH DEFENDANTS IN THE POLICE COURT: 1840–1850 AGGREGATED

	Nolle Prosc.		Incarceration		Discharged		Fined		No Judgment		Total[a]
	N	%	N	%	N	%	N	%	N	%	
Public Drunkenness											
Irish	3	0.4	287	38.0	12	1.6	384	50.9	6	0.8	755
Non-Irish	6	0.1	2512	38.1	97	1.7	2945	52.2	90	1.6	5642
Prostitution											
Irish	1	2.2	33	71.7	3	6.5	6	13.0	1	2.2	46
Non-Irish	7	1.1	348	56.3	35	5.7	102	16.5	31	5.0	618

[a] The figures do not equal the total because not all judgments were indicated.

TABLE 4.15: THE OUTCOME OF CRIMES AGAINST PROPERTY BY COMPLAINANT'S SEX IN THE MUNICIPAL COURT: AGGREGATED DATA 1814–1850

1. Felony Crimes Against Property

	Complainants' Sex			
	M		F	
	N	%	N	%
Guilty	57	40.7	4	30.8
Not Guilty	26	18.6	4	30.8
Guilty by Plea	7	5.0	2	15.4
Total[a]	140	100.0	13	100.0

2. Misdemeanors Against Property

	Complainants' Sex			
	M		F	
	N	%	N	%
Guilty	812	40.1	47	34.1
Not Guilty	225	11.2	24	17.4
Guilty by Plea	616	30.6	36	26.1
Total[a]	2,014	100.0	138	100.0

3. Burglary

	Complainants' Sex			
	M		F	
	N	%	N	%
Guilty	148	26.6	6	22.2
Not Guilty	75	13.5	2	7.4
Guilty by Plea	152	27.3	16	59.3
Total[a]	556	100.0	27	100.0

4. Riot

	Complainants' Sex			
	M		F	
	N	%	N	%
Guilty	14	28.0	4	18.2
Not Guilty	13	26.0	9	40.9
Guilty by Plea	5	10.0	0	0.0
Total[a]	50	100.0	22	100.0

[a] The items do not sum to the total because not all items are listed.

TABLE 4.16: THE OUTCOME OF CRIMES AGAINST THE PERSON AND SEX OFFENSES BY COMPLAINANTS' SEX IN THE MUNICIPAL COURT: AGGREGATED DATA 1814–1850

1. Felony Crimes Against the Person

	Complainants' Sex			
	M		F	
	N	%	N	%
Guilty	151	28.2	42	47.7
Not Guilty	80	14.9	11	12.5
Guilty by Plea	120	22.4	11	12.5
Total[a]	536	100.0	88	100.0

2. Misdemeanors Against the Person

	Complainants' Sex			
	M		F	
	N	%	N	%
Guilty	2	28.6	4	40.0
Not Guilty	1	14.3	0	0.0
Guilty by Plea	2	28.6	2	20.0
Total[a]	7	100.0	10	100.0

3. Sex Offenses

	Complainants' Sex			
	M		F	
	N	%	N	%
Guilty	4	23.5	9	32.1
Not Guilty	3	17.6	2	7.1
Guilty by Plea	5	29.4	3	10.7
Total[a]	17	100.0	28	100.0

[a] The items do not sum to the total because not all items are listed.

victim, that is, in violent crimes or sex offenses, her complaint was taken more seriously and prosecuted vigorously by the court, but where she was less directly involved, that is, in property offenses, her complaint was less likely to produce a serious response. Married women could not own property independently of their husbands during this period, and as a result, a woman's complaint of a property offense probably had less impact than a man's. Unfortunately, it was impossible to distinguish married from unmarried complainants in these data, and we cannot know certainly whether married women received less response from the court than unmarried women.

Altogether, then, it appears that both the Municipal Court and the Police Court considered criminal cases primarily in terms of the defendant's legal characteristics and did not exercise systematic discrimination against *any* specific class or social group. Women and the Irish were especially vulnerable to discrimination during this period because of widespread social restrictions and prejudice against them, but neither group was treated more harshly in the courts (see also Hull 1987, chap. 6).

Where a particular group was sentenced differently, as for example juvenile property offenders during 1824-36 (see Table 4.11), the reason seemed to stem from a peculiarity of that group's criminality instead of an attempt to discriminate against them. Juvenile cases, for example, were much less likely to be taken to a decision in the early period because the court was reluctant to sentence them to adult prisons. Hence, those that did receive a guilty verdict were aggravated cases and probably deserved more serious punishment (cf. Beattie 1986, 437).

Nor did the defendant's occupation seem to affect his fate in the courts. Neither businessmen, artisans, nor laborers were singled out for special treatment. All in all, Boston's lower courts were using their sentencing powers in a highly responsible manner—one that would do credit to many lower courts today.

Professionalism and the Criminal Courts

This period in the history of Boston's courts was one of rapid professional development (see chap. 1). Several regional law schools were established in the early decades of the nineteenth century for the professional training of young lawyers, and the profession as a whole enjoyed a renaissance as it became a major factor in New England's growth. It is likely that well-trained and idealistic young lawyers, as they moved into the legal profession in general and on to the Municipal Court bench in particular, had a clear impact upon the cases they handled. Our task here is to identify the nature of this impact and to document it.

THREE TYPES OF JUDGES

To assess the impact of the changing nature of the judge's corps, it is necessary to identify the several different ways in which judges carried out their responsibilities (see also Galanter, Palen, and Thomas 1979). Three distinct types of judges seem to have sat on the Municipal Court bench during this period: traditional, utilitarian, and professional.[4]

Traditional judges had their roots in the eighteenth century. They were born and educated in that century; their legal training was in the old style—via apprenticeships—and their careers were relatively narrow. They shepherded the Municipal Court through its early years, and they never strayed very far from the law and Boston's legal community. They clung tenaciously to a traditional view.

Utilitarian judges were younger and less experienced than traditional judges, but like them they learned their law in law offices, not law schools, and they stayed relatively close to politics and the legal profession throughout their careers. They served faithfully on the Municipal Court bench and were generally cautious in their approach to the law.

Professional judges were born and educated in the nineteenth century, often in law schools. They earned recognition early and advanced quickly to important posts. They moved easily from the bench to leadership in academia, politics, or commerce. They were also very active in the legal profession editing reports, writing treatises, and textbooks. They were young, but they were widely known and respected and made outstanding contributions in a variety of areas. They were innovative and adaptive in the law, not cautious or hesitant.

All of the professional judges, Quincy, Washburn, Bigelow, Hoar, Merrick, Cushing, and Perkins, were prominent members of the Boston legal community and several of them held key political posts as well (see Appendix B). They served in the Municipal Court for only limited periods due to brighter opportunities elsewhere. Their average term on the Municipal Court bench was 5.9 years. Collectively, they received six honorary degrees from three colleges, four of the seven attended Harvard Law School, three were justices of the Supreme Judicial Court, three were authors of legal textbooks, and one, Emory Washburn, became a professor of law. They were, nevertheless, a younger generation. Taken together they averaged 40.4 years of age in 1840 with only 17.6 years of experience at the bar.

The traditional jurists, Dawes, Thacher, Phillips, and Allen, had served an average of 13.5 years on the Municipal Court bench by 1840, they averaged 55.3 years of age in 1840 (not including Dawes who died in 1825) and typically had accumulated 29.0 years of experience at the bar by that date (again excluding Dawes). Phillips received an honorary LL.D. degree from Harvard and wound up as president of an insurance company in Boston. None of the others was similarly recognized.

The sharp contrast between the traditional judges and the professional judges here echoes a larger competition already noted between those who favored an autonomous legal system in Massachusetts and a responsive one. The professionals, with Lemuel Shaw in the lead, ultimately prevailed in Boston and Massachusetts, but the traditionalists maintained their conservative views on the law to the end.

Most of the utilitarian judges alternated between the legislature and the bench throughout their careers. Their age in 1840 averaged 43.7; their legal experience was nineteen years; but their careers on the bench lasted just 7.2 years, mainly because the bulk of them were appointed after 1843. One received an honorary degree, an LL.D. from Brown, and another was named to an important post in industry. They included Judges Williams, Ward, Wells, Byington, Mellen, and Hopkinson.

All in all, the traditional judges, particularly Judges Dawes and Thacher, were active during the early period, that is, before 1840; the careers of the utilitarian judges and the professional judges, however, developed during the 1840s and were part of the changing legal scene. These three groups of judges form the basis for the analysis that follows.

The impact of a growing professionalism and a new, responsive philosophy upon the handling of criminal cases in the Municipal Court can be assessed in several ways. A professional bench with strong commitments to judicial effectiveness could be expected to take more cases through to a final resolution, and as the Municipal Court bench began to include a growing number of professional judges after 1842, the proportion of cases that did reach a final disposition increased.

Second, a professional, responsive bench would seek new ways to dispense justice in accord with their philosophy of judicial activism and responsiveness; they would seek to fit the punishment to the offender more precisely and would welcome new methods of speeding the course of justice. Thus, they would tolerate programmatic innovations such as plea bargaining more readily. The older, more traditional judges who were more firmly set in a philosophy of autonomous law and more jealous of their authority would sentence more harshly and resist plea bargaining, which, after all, represented a shift of judical responsibilities to the prosecutor.

Finally, as the climate of legal thinking in the Supreme Judicial Court shifted from a philosophy emphasizing the authority of precedent and the autonomy of the law to a responsive philosophy in which the value of law was weighed in terms of its social impact, such a shift would produce a growing wave of appeals and reversals as the higher court sought to bring decisions in the Municipal Court more in line with its new understanding of the proper function of the law. The fact that Lemuel Shaw, a forceful proponent of responsive philosophy, was the chief justice of the Supreme Judicial Court from 1830 to 1860, is of some relevance. Traditional judges who adhered to a very conservative view of the law should find their decisions increasingly challenged by appeals to the Supreme Judicial Court and reversed there.[5]

The Municipal Court Bench

A comparison of the outcomes displayed by our three types of judges shows many clear differences (see Table 4.17). Traditional judges consistently produced more guilty verdicts for both minor property crimes and city ordinance violations and fewer guilty pleas as well. Their terms on the bench, pre-1840 mainly, embraced only the beginning of plea bargaining in the Municipal Court, and these results can probably be explained as simply an historical accident.

The interesting comparisons are between the utilitarian and the professional judges whose careers spanned the period of greatest change—the 1840s. Professional judges were more tolerant toward plea bargaining especially with city ordinance violations, and they were much less likely than utilitarian judges to continue cases without a disposition, that is, by leaving them on file. They pushed hard to move their dockets, and they were receptive to procedural innovations where they involved only minor, victimless offenders. Property offenses were considered a serious offense, and professional judges were relatively unreceptive to plea bargaining with these defendants.

Appeals also present some interesting trends, though the results are based on small numbers and can be regarded only as suggestive. Overall, the percentage of appeals was declining from 1814 through 1850. In the decade, 1814–22, 3.0 percent of all criminal cases were appealed, but in 1844–50 only 1.1 percent were (see Table 4.18). Most of the change occurred between the first two decades: 1814–22 and 1824–32. Along with a drop in the rate of appeals, fewer were successful, and fewer were dismissed or dropped.

The overall decline of appeals speaks to the growing authority of the Municipal Court over its convicted defendants, but the drop in the percentage of sustained appeals indicates that the Municipal Court and its officers, particularly its judges and prosecutors, were increasingly in accord with the legal and philosophical views of the judges of the Supreme Judicial Court where the appeals were heard.

The percentage of sustained appeals rose sharply again in 1834–42, even though the overall percentage of appeals did not show a similar increase. These facts may indicate that the Municipal Court and its traditionalist officers (Judge Thacher and County Attorney Parker) had fallen out of step with the Supreme Judicial Court and Chief Justice Lemuel Shaw's responsive philosophy. The percentage declines in both

TABLE 4.17: OUTCOMES IN THE MUNICIPAL COURT ACCORDING TO PROFESSIONAL STATUS OF JUDGE: 1823–1850

Type of Judge	Minor Property Crimes									City Ordinance Violations								
	Guilty		Left on File		Guilty Plea		No Outcome		Total	Guilty		Left on File		Guilty Plea		No Outcome		Total
	N	%	N	%	N	%	N	%		N	%	N	%	N	%	N	%	
Traditional[a]	841	41.4	150	7.4	542	27.0	128	6.3	2030	29	8.4	16	4.7	54	15.7	133	38.7	344
Utilitarian[b]	58	26.7	28	12.9	89	41.0	11	5.1	217	7	6.3	25	22.3	27	24.1	35	31.3	112
Professional[c]	128	33.2	27	7.0	133	34.5	22	5.7	385	17	6.0	22	7.7	124	43.5	79	27.7	285

[a] Includes Judges Peter Thacher, Thomas Dawes, Jr., Willard Phillips, and Charles Allen.
[b] Includes Judges John Mason Williams, Joshua Holyoke Ward, Daniel Wells, Horatio Byington, Edward Mellen, and Thomas Hopkinson.
[c] Includes Judges Josiah Quincy, George Tyler Bigelow, Ebenezer Rockwood Hoar, Pliny Merrick, Luther Stearns Cushing, Jonathan Cogswell Perkins, and Emory Washburn.

TABLE 4.18: APPEALS OF CRIMINAL CASES FROM THE MUNICIPAL COURT TO THE SUPREME JUDICIAL COURT

Year	Appeals								Total Cases
	Sustained		Not Sustained		Dismissed or Dropped		Total		
	N	%	N	%	N	%	N	%	
1814–22	21	1.45	14	0.97	9	0.62	44	3.04	1449
1824–32	4	0.38	7	0.67	2	0.20	13	1.24	1050
1834–42	21	0.99	4	0.19	5	0.24	30	1.41	2124
1844–50	15	0.32	22	0.48	12	0.26	49	1.06	4623

the overall level of appeals, and the level of sustained appeals in 1844–50 suggests further that as the professionals began to dominate the Municipal Court in the 1840s, they were more in tune with the responsiveness of the higher court and once again were receiving its full support.[6]

The three types of judges also showed distinctive appeals patterns. Traditional judges, who sat on the Municipal Court bench during its early years, experienced the highest level of appeals, 1.7 percent of all cases, and were reversed most frequently, in 51.6 percent of all appeals. As pointed out above, their traditional legal philosophy was out of favor at the level of the Supreme Judicial Court, and their decisions were more freely challenged.

Utilitarian judges, who served for the most part after 1840, also provoked a high level of appeals, 1.5 percent of all cases, but their rate of reversal was lowest, 23.8 percent of all appeals. Professional judges had less than half the rate of appeals of either the traditional or the utilitarian judges, but only the second best level of reversals, 35.0 percent of all appeals.

The utilitarian judges were not so widely respected as the professional judges, and defendants and their attorneys were more willing to challenge their decisions. Professional judges, on the other hand, provoked far fewer appeals (see Table 4.19), and although their reversal rate was relatively high, they had fewer frivolous appeals (only 0.2 percent were ultimately dropped) and, therefore, a higher reversal ratio, that is, the ratio of sustained appeals to appeals not sustained. The level of their reversals, however, (only 0.3 percent of all cases) was the lowest of all three types. Professional judges exhibited the cleanest record both in terms of the rate of appeals and the percentage of reversals, utilitarian judges and traditional judges both experienced a high level of challenges, and traditional judges were reversed much more often than either of the other two types.

TABLE 4.19: APPEALS OF TRADITIONAL, UTILITARIAN, WORKING, AND PROFESSIONAL JUDGES IN THE MUNICIPAL COURT 1814–1850

Type of Judge	Appeals Sustained		Appeals Not Sustained		No Appeal		Appeals Withdrawn		Total
	N	%	N	%	N	%	N	%	
Traditional[a]	49	0.9	28	0.5	5496	98.3	18	0.3	5591
Utilitarian[b]	5	0.4	10	0.9	1130	98.1	6	0.5	1151
Professional[c]	7	0.3	8	0.3	2468	99.2	5	0.2	2488

[a] Includes Judges Peter Thacher, Willard Phillips, Charles Allen, and Thomas Dawes, Jr.
[b] Includes Judges John Williams, Joshua Ward, Daniel Wells, Horatio Byington, Edward Mellen, and Thomas Hopkinson.
[c] Includes Judges Josiah Quincy, George Bigelow, Ebenezer Hoar, Pliny Merrick, Luther Cushing, Jonathan Perkins, and Emory Washburn.

TABLE 4.20: JUDGMENTS BY TRADITIONAL, UTILITARIAN, AND PROFESSIONAL JUDGES FOR SELECTED OFFENSES IN THE MUNICIPAL COURT

Type of Judge	Incarcerated		Fined		Nolle Prosequi		Discharged		Total
	N	%	N	%	N	%	N	%	
Minor Property Crimes									
Traditional	1286	63.3	71	3.4	47	2.3	247	12.2	2030
Utilitarian	459	64.4	29	4.1	30	4.2	96	13.5	713
Professional	187	48.3	26	6.7	9	2.3	46	11.9	387
City Ordinance Violations									
Traditional	1	0.3	177	51.4	52	15.1	25	7.3	344
Utilitarian	0	0.0	75	52.8	16	11.3	8	5.6	142
Professional	5	1.8	204	71.8	17	6.0	8	2.8	284
Liquor Law Violations									
Traditional	1	0.4	122	48.0	93	36.6	17	6.7	254
Utilitarian	0	0.0	164	53.1	75	24.3	12	3.9	309
Professional	0	0.0	111	24.7	235	52.3	10	2.2	449
Burglary									
Traditional	202	63.7	2	0.6	20	6.3	32	10.1	317
Utilitarian	79	64.8	1	0.8	6	4.9	20	16.4	122
Professional	114	57.9	7	3.6	15	7.6	25	12.7	197

What were the attitudes of these judges toward punishment? Their sentencing patterns suggest (see Table 4.20) that professional judges were much less inclined to imprison property offenders, particularly minor property offenders, than either the traditional or the utilitarian judges. Moreover, unlike the other two types, professional judges were more punitive toward burglary defendants than minor property offenders. Professional judges were moving closer to the modern view that minor property offenders pose little threat to civil society, whereas utilitarian and traditional judges still clung to the older view that property offenders—even minor property offenders—were chronic offenders that had to be curbed with stiff punishments.

Professional judges were less consistent in sentencing regulatory violators. Traditional and utilitarian judges fined about half of the city ordinance violators and liquor law violators, but professional judges gave fines to a much higher percentage of the city ordinance violators (71.8 percent) than the liquor law violators (24.7 percent). Professional judges, however, agreed to nullify (*nolle prosequi*) more than half of the liquor law cases but only six percent of the city ordinance violations.

These trends are pronounced, and no doubt reflect the genuine misgivings that professional judges harbored toward the ways in which liquor law violations were being investigated and prosecuted. We have already seen misgivings voiced by the Commonwealth's attorney general, James T. Austin, in 1842. They probably also reflect the willingness of professional judges to participate with the prosecutor in charge bargaining in that *nolle prosequi* was becoming one of the latter's most useful tools. City ordinance violations were a less controversial offense and did not elicit quite the same proactive effort during this period of intense temperance sentiment.

The Criminal Judges of Antebellum Boston

Change was swirling through Boston, its social structure and legal institutions. At the close of the eighteenth century, Boston's criminal courts served a deeply religious, closely integrated community with little crime, no delinquency, and very little awareness of other peoples, their cultures, or religions. On the eve of the Civil War Boston was a cosmopolitan center deeply divided between those who favored the prohibition of alcoholic spirits and those who resisted it; between the Irish-Catholics and the Protestant Yankees; between those who hated slavery and those who feared secession; between those who welcomed change and those who saw it as destructive. Still, it was a progressive city with a clear vision of the future, bold plans, and immense resources.

The most important reform to affect the judges during this period was the settling of legal training into established colleges with professional legal faculties and proven curricula. Thanks to this reform, judges trained in law schools began to make their appearance in the Municipal Court. Unlike their more traditional predecessors, who, for the most part, were born in or near Boston, professional judges were drawn from all over upper New England. Most of them were marked for significant careers by their early preparation at Harvard College, but it was also their law school education that exposed them to ideas at the leading edge of the law. Upon graduation they moved easily into legal posts where they could readily realize their ambitions.

Their views on the key issues of their day can be inferred from their behavior on the bench. They were committed, first, to a careful, professional handling of criminal cases. They frowned on the common practice in the Municipal Court of leaving cases on file indefinitely without a finding; and because of the painstaking attention they gave to cases, they faced relatively few appeals of their decisions and even fewer reversals. At the same time they were closely attuned to the proactive, responsive legal climate in Massachusetts, and welcomed innovations such as plea bargaining that permitted them to monitor the business community more closely without also creating an immense backlog within the courts or hostile resistance outside. They readily adapted legal innovations to their broader purposes, and the Supreme Judicial Court demonstrated its approval through its willingness to uphold their decisions when they were challenged through an appeal.

They worked comfortably with their more utilitarian colleagues and, indeed, most notably with Samuel D. Parker, the Suffolk County prosecutor. Parker was a member of the traditional school who viewed the law as a force above men and politics. All laws, including the hated fugitive slave laws and the laws prohibiting blasphemy and workers' organizations, merited vigorous prosecution as long as they were the law of the land (Levy 1957, 185). The courts could not pick and choose the laws that deserved to be enforced. He held strong, if unpopular, positions on many issues and probably found little ground for agreement with the professional judges on most of them. Yet the pressures of his office and the flexible views of the professional judges enabled them all to combine forces in changing the face of Boston's legal institutions at a very early period in its history.

5
Crime in Antebellum Boston

In the period before the Civil War Boston underwent a sociocultural transformation that shook its foundations.[1] Traditional crafts such as ironsmiths, tailors, and cobblers became obsolete, and many new occupations connected with manufacturing and merchandising—mechanics, unskilled workers, clerks, and proprietors—doubled and redoubled. The new industrial and commercial classes emerged with a flourish, while skilled and semiskilled artisans languished (Handlin 1968, chap. 3 and 4).

As other cities on the eastern seaboard developed opportunities in manufacturing and as farmlands opened up in the west, substantial numbers of Bostonians left the city to seek their fortunes, while migrants from rural areas and from Europe flocked into Boston. By the 1840s upwards of 40 percent of the city's population was being replaced *every year* (Schnore and Knights 1969, 57)—nearly double the current rate of replacement!

Confidence in the harsh Calvinism of Puritan forefathers was being undermined, first by the Enlightment in Europe, then by the Unitarians and Transcendentalists at home, and finally by the Roman Catholicism of the Irish (Schultz 1973, 60–66). To help fill the gap, public education was launched with a vigorous mandate to impart not simply literary and vocational skills but moral values as well to children between the ages of four and fifteen. The family was reorganized as the father and the older children, including the girls, increasingly found employment away from home, and the younger children were required to attend school most of the day (Handlin 1968, chap. 3; Vinovskis 1981, 63–66).

The community was periodically wracked by riots against the Irish, proslavery, or abolitionist groups (Lane 1967, chap. 3), and the upper classes began to isolate themselves by moving first to Beacon Hill and later to Back Bay. Finally, as the values and economic interests of the citizens changed, political leadership in the city passed from the exclusive hands of aristocrats to more broadly based leaders.[2]

Those Bostonians who came of age in 1790 looked out upon a city in the 1840s that bore little semblance to the village of their youth. On 30 June 1836, the *Boston Transcript* published the following editorial:

> We have no old men now. No old mansions now. All are young. All are new. We are all young men now. Nobody wears a wig, nor a cocked hat, nor powder, nor small-clothes and silk stockings and buckles, nor white-topped boots, nor a queue, nor a gold-headed cane. We have changed all that. The "Gentlemen of the Old School," those patterns of manly elegance are fast passing way. Habits, customs, marriage, men all have changed. A bustling multitude supplies the place of a social family; and what was once a town, needing no annual director, is now a miniature world, a mighty city, where we have to ask, "who is my neighbor?"[3]

The editor's sense of loss and alienation was certainly keen.

Such a radical and pervasive transformation touched the lives of Bostonians in many ways. The family was affected as its members sought their fortunes away from home. Opportunities for women and juveniles became more plentiful as a whole host of unskilled and semiskilled occupations opened up, and substantial numbers of unattached young women and adolescents began to drift into the city.[4] The community was weakened both by the movement of families in and out of neigborhoods—particularly working class neighborhoods—so that many were filled with strangers most of the time, and by the religious and economic fissures that soon hardened into deep political divisions. The obsolescence of whole classes of occupations, together with the rapid emergence of others, further strained the social fabric by throwing large segments of the city's population into economic limbo.[5]

All this meant that as the new Boston took shape during the antebellum period, individuals were less closely bound to one another in both the family and the community. Social authority became less compelling, the Puritan heritage less relevant, and social and political unity became more problematic. The community, in other words, lost its hold on its citizens.

During this period Boston became a vibrant, rich, and ebullient city, attractive to others and confident of itself. By most measures it was a vital community. Nevertheless, several segments within the community found crime rewarding and risk-free, and others learned that conformity held little meaning. As changes in the city gathered momentum, its crime problem worsened.

The Shape of Crime in Antebellum Boston

Crime in Boston is pictured most effectively in terms of its components, that is, in terms of the criminality of such distinctive groups as juveniles, women, the Irish, and specific occupational groups (laborers, artisans, and businessmen), which we shall do in the next chapter. But let us look here at the general patterns of crime brought to the Police Court and the Municipal Court.[6] We shall break the overall pattern down into serious crime and minor crime: assaultive crime, property crime, regulative crime, and vice. When we have done that, we shall examine in Chapter 6 the criminality of specific groups and how they contributed to the patterns described below.

THE OVERALL PATTERN

During the antebellum period criminality was marked by sharp rises in both courts. In the Municipal Court the low point was reached in 1832, when one hundred sixty-nine cases were handled, but from there the number steadily rose until it reached 1,538 in 1850 for a ninefold increase (see fig. 5.1). In the Police Court the low point came in 1836, when 1,750 cases were processed, and from there the caseload increased to 4,258 in 1850 (see fig. 5.2).

Some of these increases reflected population growth in Boston since the city more than doubled in size from 61,400 in 1830 to 136,900 in 1850. When we take this fact into account for both courts, we note that the crime rates in both were clearly headed downward during the 1820s.

This early decline did not escape the notice of Mayor Josiah Quincy in 1829 who proclaimed proudly (1852: 109), after nearly six years in office, that:

> When this administration first came into power, the police had no comparative effect; the city possessed no house of correction, and the natural inmates of that establishment were on our "hills," or on our common, disgusting the delicate, offending the good, and intimidating the fearful. There were parts of the city over which no honest man dared to pass in the nighttime, so proud and uncontrolled was there the dominion of crime.
>
> ...who, at this day, sees begging in our streets...At this day, I speak it confidently, there is no part of the city through which the most timid may not walk, by day or by night, without fear of personal violence. What streets present more stillness in the night time? Where, in a city of equal population, are there fewer instances of those crimes, to which all populous places are subject?
>
> Doubtless much of this condition of things is owing to the orderly habits of our citizens; but much also, is attributed to the vigilance which...by pursuing the lawless vendor of spiritous liquors, denying licenses to the worst of the class, or revoking them, as soon as found in improper hands, has checked crime in its first stages, and introduced into these establishments a salutary fear....

Figure 5.1: Criminal Cases in the Municipal Court: 1814-1850.

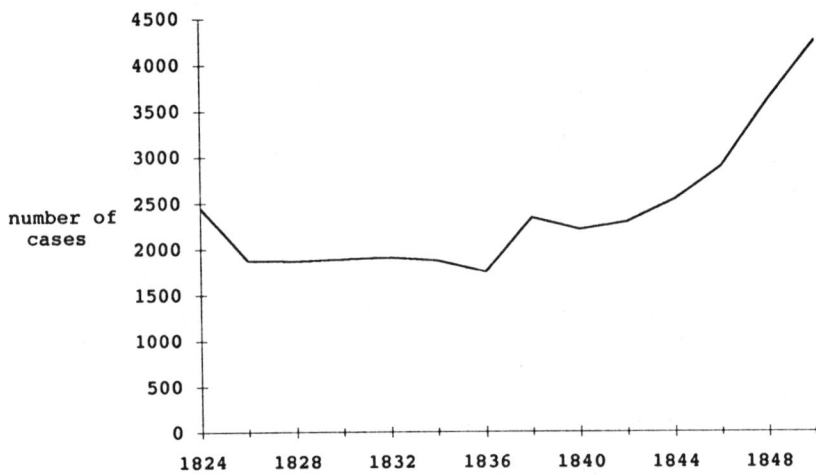

Figure 5.2: Criminal Cases in the Police Court: 1824-1850.

Figure 5.3: Criminal Cases per 1,000 in the Municipal Court: 1814-1850.

Figure 5.4: Criminal Cases per 1,000 in the Police Court: 1824-1850.

The good which has been attained, and no man can deny it is great, has been effected by directing unremittingly the force of the executive power to the haunts of vice, in its first stages, and to the favorite resorts of crime, in its last.

After Quincy left office, the prosecution rate continued downward to the mid-1830s, when it began to move sharply higher.

If we break the overall pattern down into its components, we can pinpoint some of the reasons behind these overall trends.[7] In the Police Court the minor offense rate (see fig. 5.5) starts at a very high level in 1824 and falls sharply to a low in 1846.[8] In the Municipal Court minor offenses (see fig. 5.6) start at a much lower level—about 5.0 per thousand—and after bottoming out in 1836, they begin an upward trend that nearly retraces their earlier downward curve, reaching 4.8 offenses per thousand in 1850.

Sharp declines in the minor crime rate of the 1820s and early 1830s in the Police Court owe much to that court's policy of discouraging trivial cases—namely, larceny, and assault and battery—during its early years and not simply to changes in the criminal behavior of Bostonians (see Beattie 1986, 417–19). A more complete discussion of this policy can be found in Chapters 1 and 2.

Figure 5.5: Minor and Serious Crimes per 1,000 in the Police Court: 1824-1850.

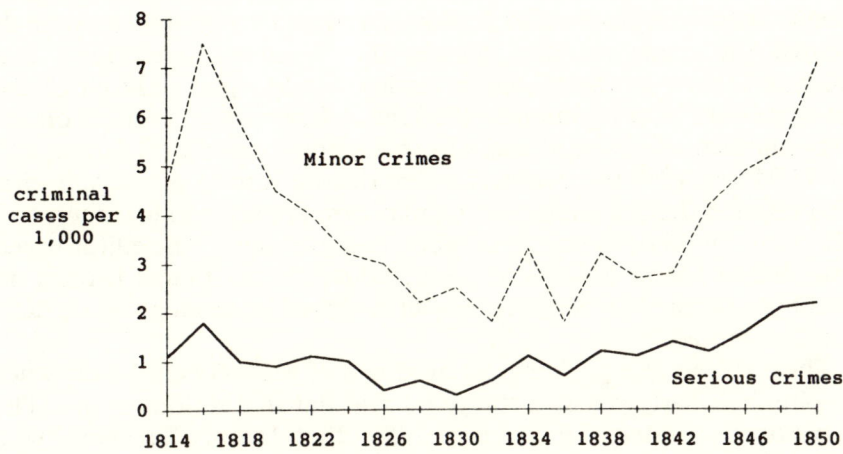

Figure 5.6: Minor and Serious Crimes per 1,000 in the Municipal Court: 1814-1850.

As far as prosecutions for serious crimes are concerned, both courts presented very similar patterns both in terms of level and direction.[9] The nadirs for both courts occurred during the 1830s from which both edged upward to highs in 1850. The clear divergence of the trend-lines of serious crime in both courts from that of minor crime in the Police Court, however, only reinforces the suggestion that the steady drop in the latter, while the others were rising, was an administered drop brought about by a Police Court policy in the 1820s and 1830s of diverting trivial disputes to noncriminal channels.

The curves for serious crime in both courts, however, paralleled closely the curve of minor offenses in the Municipal Court (see fig. 5.6). This close agreement among the three suggests that these rising trends in the late 1830s and throughout the 1840s signaled an actual climb in criminality.

The people of Boston definitely thought they were facing a crime wave. During the late 1840s, and particularly by 1850, the *Boston Evening Transcript* and the *Boston Daily Advertiser* were reporting crime stories on their local page almost every day. Many of these stories described wayward children who roamed the city looking for mischief and criminal opportunities.

On 10 March 1848, for example, the *Transcript* published an account of the growing crime problem as described before a New York City Grand Jury and proclaimed it closely relevant to Boston as well. It located the crime problem among the "pauper population" and identified "nine-tenths of our juvenile offenders [as] children of the foreign poor." On 17 January 1850 the *Advertiser* commented on the large numbers of youthful vagrants that daily pestered Bostonians, and on 12 March 1850 the *Transcript* described a throng of vagrant girls who infested the city streets selling matches, apples, and lozenges, and who were "void of shame, profligate, and profane." The editor urged that "when found at large at night, under circumstances leaving no doubt as to their character, these children should be taken up as vagrants and committed."

These stories also gave regular accounts of youthful criminals, who, despite their early years, displayed a real flair for serious crime. The *Advertiser* reported (16 January 1850) that Dennis Scanlan "who although young in years is a most notorious rogue" was arrested as a pickpocket for stealing a purse containing two hundred twenty-five dollars, and Helen Holane, "not more than 15 year of age" was arrested for pickpocketing three purses in one day (10 April 1850). The *Transcript* reported (5 January 1848) that after a previous larceny conviction Charles Smith, "a minor," was again "convicted of larceny and sentenced to two years imprisonment in the State Prison. Two other minors, John Coakley 16, and Dennis Coakley 15, [were also] sentenced to State Prison, the former for five years and the latter for three years."

Hindus reports (1980, 72) for the state as a whole that crimes against property and the person continued their rise until the eve of the Civil War and that prison commitments also rose sharply during the antebellum period. All the evidence suggests that a serious crime wave began in Boston in the 1830s and that it was halted only temporarily by the Civil War.

TYPES OF CRIME

Another approach is to look at the curves of the several different types of crime that composed Boston's crime problem: specificially, property crime, assaultive crime, regulatory offenses, and vice.[10]

Prosecutions for property crimes in the Municipal Court fell steadily from a rate of 7.0 per thousand in 1816 to their low point in 1832. From there they began a slow, irregular rise to 1850. Assaultive crimes reached their nadir in 1828 and then rose to a level in 1850 that approached, but did not reach, the high of 2.0 per thousand registered in 1816.

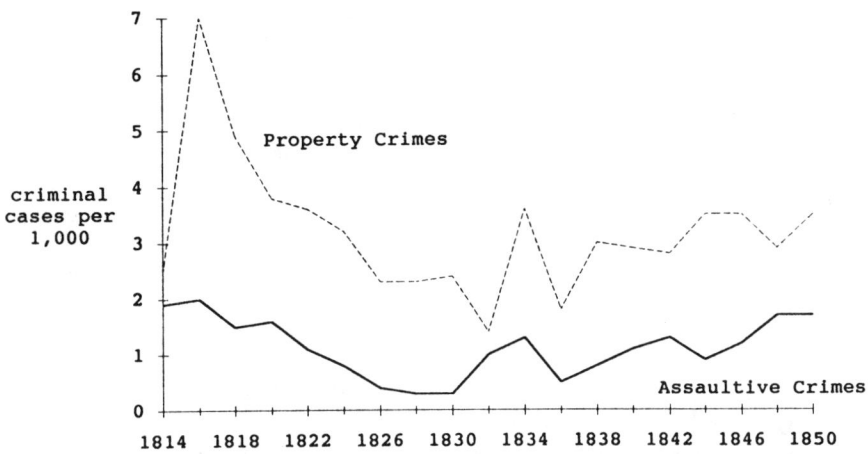

Figure 5.7: Property and Assaultive Crimes per 1,000 in the Municipal Court: 1814-1850.

In the Police Court prosecutions for property and assaultive crimes (see fig. 5.8) followed a similar pattern. From a high of 10.9 per thousand in 1824, property prosecutions fell slowly until 1842, whereupon they recovered to a level in 1850 somewhat short of their earlier high in 1824. Similarly, prosecutions for assaultive crimes fell steadily from a very high level in 1824 (17.0 per thousand) to a low in 1838. Thereafter they rose modestly through 1850.

Unlike the Municipal Court, the Police Court experienced its highest prosecution rates for both property and assaultive crimes in the early 1820s shortly after it opened its doors; and although both types rose slowly after reaching lows around 1840, they still had not reached their earlier highs by 1850. In the Municipal Court, the early years (1814–20) were also marked by relatively high rates of property and assaultive crimes, but the lows were reached in 1832 (earlier than in the Police Court), and the highs reached in 1850 came closer to the earlier highs. Thus, the early declines were sharper for both offenses in the Police Court; the lows were ten years later; and increases in the late 1840s were weaker than in the Municipal Court.

Regulatory offenses (see fig. 5.9) in the Municipal Court reached their nadir in the early 1830s and rose rapidly to a very high level in the late

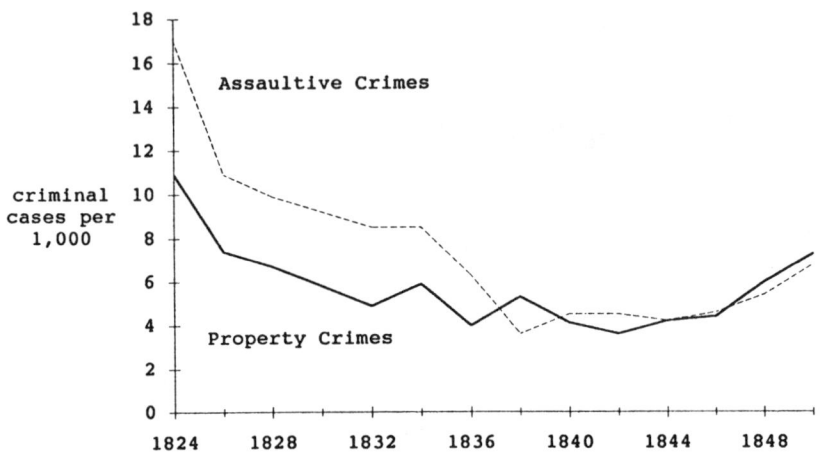

Figure 5.8: Property and Assaultive Crimes per 1,000 in the Police Court: 1824-1850.

1840s. In the Police Court, regulatory offenses (see fig. 5.10) held relatively steady between the 1820s and 1830s, but in the late 1840s they also rose to new highs. The experiences of both courts were similar in this regard; but in this case the Municipal Court exhibited the most pronounced increase in the 1840s.

Although regulatory ordinances embraced a wide range of business practices, the bulk of these offenses related to the sale of alcoholic beverages, and during the 1840s the enforcement of the liquor laws assumed major importance as the temperance movement gathered momentum in Boston during the 1830s and 1840s.

A steady increase in public drunkenness offenses was apparent throughout the antebellum period in Boston, but in the 1840s it assumed a new importance as it became the most common offense in the Police Court (see fig. 5.11), and by 1846 it constituted 40.2 percent of all cases that came before the two courts! Controlling the sale and consumption of spirits in Boston became a major public issue during this period, and the courts responded accordingly.

Another problem of considerable importance was vice, that is, gambling and prostitution. Vice offenses (see fig. 5.12) in the Municipal Court were relatively stable until 1840 when they began a very rapid

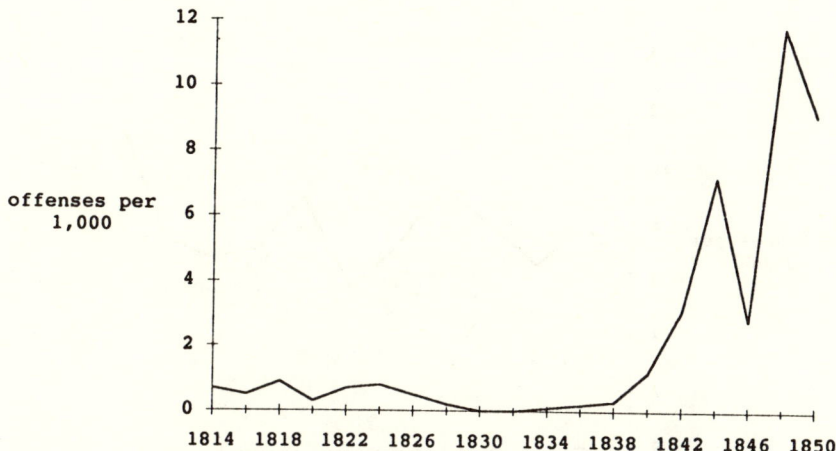

Figure 5.9: Regulatory Offenses per 1,000 in the Municipal Court: 1814-1850.

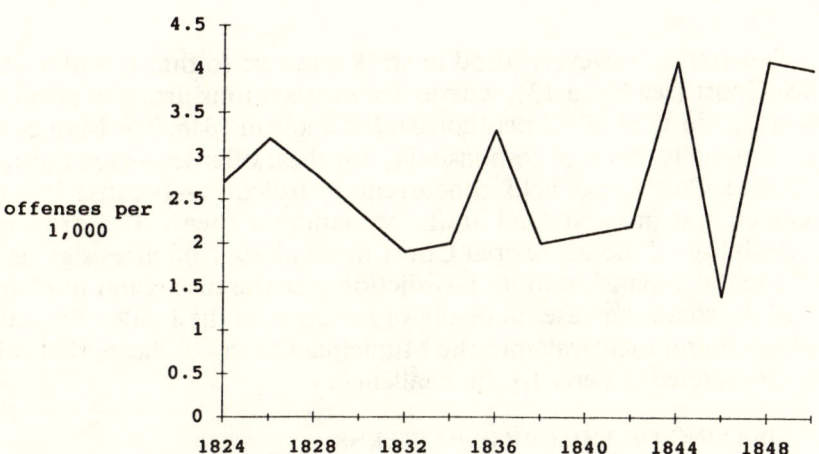

Figure 5.10: Regulatory Offenses per 1,000 in the Police Court: 1824-1850.

Figure 5.11: Pulic Drunkenness Cases per 1,000 in the Police Court: 1824-1850.

rise. This trend, however, stood in stark contrast to that found in the Police Court (see fig. 5.13), where vice prosecutions dropped steadily from a high in 1824 of 6.2 per thousand to a low in 1846. The Municipal Court gradually assumed responsibility for these offenses—even though the Police Court also held concurrent jurisdiction—because it had developed the prosecutorial staff for handling them. The growing responsibility of the Municipal Court in regulatory offenses signals a fundamental expansion in its jurisdiction (see the discussion in chap. 1), and the sharp increases in regulatory offenses in the 1840s—the bulk of which found their way into the Municipal Court—indicate that this court responded eagerly to the challenge.

THE MEANING OF THE CRIME PATTERNS

The similarities and differences in the crime patterns of the two courts tell us something about their evolving jurisdictions as well as the nature of the crime problem in Boston. The declines in virtually every form of criminality in both courts in the 1810s and 1820s strongly suggest that there was, indeed, a drop in the crime rate during Mayor Quincy's

Figure 5.12: Vice Offenses per 1,000 in the Municipal Court: 1814-1850.

Figure 5.13: Vice Offenses per 1,000 in the Police Court: 1824-1850.

administration. The fact that minor crimes declined most, especially in the Police Court, also suggests that both courts, but especially the Police Court, were simultaneously adjusting their jurisdictions to eliminate many trivial crimes.

In the 1830s and 1840s the level of traditional crimes (property and assaultive crimes) began to climb again in both courts, but the largest increases in the Police Court were felt in public drunkenness and in the Municipal Court in regulatory violations and vice. Neither of the latter offenses, however, showed comparable gains in the Police Court, suggesting that these dramatic increases in the Municipal Court signaled policy shifts in that court alone. Regulatory offenses and vice became an integral part of the Municipal Court's jurisdiction and as such virtually disappeared from the crime dockets of the Police Court.

There was certainly a growing crime problem during the late 1830s and on into the 1840s, but Boston was also modernizing its criminal justice organizations, especially the Municipal Court, and the rapid increases in regulatory offenses and vice in the 1840s bear witness to this fact.

This chapter demonstrates clearly that it is possible to infer *both* the shape of official policy and the *nature of criminality* from data drawn solely from criminal justice agencies. Such data reflect the policies of these agencies as well as the underlying incidence of the criminality being controlled. But if two independent, official estimates of the same criminal offense are available, and both indicate similar crime trends, the likelihood is strong that underlying criminality and *not* simply criminal justice policy or statutory changes were responsible. At the same time criminal justice policy can also be inferred from crime trends that diverge when similar criminal offenses reported by independent agencies are examined. Thus, an artful selection of criminal offenses and criminal justice agencies can offer a "triangulated" view of these offenses that contains much more information than a simple "linear" view.

6
The Offenders

Several types of offenders had an important bearing on Boston's crime problem. In the mid-1830s a growing parade of juveniles found their way into the courts, and in the 1840s Irish offenders, both juvenile and adult, were herded in large numbers into Boston's courtrooms. Women made a steady though small contribution, and the criminal activity of the different occupational groups—laborers, artisans, and businessman—shifted as their position in Boston's economy improved or worsened. The sociology of each of these groups has been thoroughly studied, and it is possible to suggest sound reasons why the crime pattern of each changed as it did.

Using court cases to estimate the level of crime in Boston during this period is, however, a hazardous enterprise. Not every criminal was detected, and of those who were arrested, only a portion were actually prosecuted. Court cases, in other words, even where they were free of all error, bore only a distant relationship to the true level of crime in nineteenth-century Boston. Only the foolhardy or the misguided would attempt to use official data to estimate directly the underlying crime rate of the community.

Still, much can be learned from official records like those analyzed here.[1] First, the true rate of criminality is almost certainly much larger than the rate of court cases, and court cases can at the very least provide a minimum estimate of the true rate. Even more significantly, a city's court cases can also provide an estimate of the trends in its crime rate since in most cases the rise and fall of the crime rate is the largest factor in a court's changing case load. Thus, Boston's court cases can readily yield considerable information about the changing trends in crime in the city.

But a court's case load usually reflects other things as well: that is policy changes in the mayor's office or changes in arrest or prosecution policy, and caution must be used in interpreting these trends so that policy shifts are not mistaken for changes in the crime rate. Fortunately, the impact of criminal justice policy differs sharply from the effects of changing crime rates, and differentiating the two is not difficult.

Changes in policy have an abrupt effect, and they often affect different courts differently. In Boston policy changes usually affected either the Police Court or the Municipal Court, but not both. Changes in the way the mayor viewed crime or a change in Police Court judges were widely reported and their impact was easily identified. The crime rate, however, only grew slowly, and it usually related to other broadly understood changes in the community. By comparing trends in the two courts, and by relating them to other changes in the community and region, it is possible to distinguish changes that reflect policy issues from those that derive from broader changes in the underlying crime rate.

Much has been written, for example, about the views, ideologies, and administrative styles of Boston's key mayors, judges, and police chiefs, as well as the Commonwealth's governors, attorneys general, and legal institutions. Where the trends of the two courts clearly followed initiatives taken at other levels of government, we can extrapolate how the courts were affected by these initiatives and interpret the results accordingly. Thus, it is possible by comparing trends in the two courts to identify whether the crime data represent policy or broader social changes.

For example, liquor violations and prostitution complaints both declined after 1835 in the Police Court, while larceny complaints rose. In the Municipal Court these same crimes were trending in opposite directions. Responsibility for these three offenses shifted in that the Municipal Court assumed primary jurisdiction for prostitution and liquor law violations, and the Police Court took responsibility for larceny. Similarly, in the late 1830s and early 1840s, arrests for city ordinance violations, liquor law violations, and offenses against religion began to climb sharply (see Table 5.3), suggesting that all three were part of the temperance campaign against liquor abuses. When city ordinance violations took a sharp jump in 1848, the other two declined; and when liquor law violations spurted in 1850, city ordinance violations fell back.

Variations in these three offenses were closely linked because they were used interchangeably to charge errant tavern owners. These kinds of compensating trends in court data often reflect politico-legal factors, but where the trends in two courts parallel one another, they most likely depict broad criminal trends in the community. The crime patterns of Boston offers a needed perspective on many of the changes in the courts described in earlier chapters, because crime, after all, was one of the factors that shaped the policies of the courts, the city, and the Commonwealth.

It is also important to identify the criminality of an industrializing city, Boston, early in its development for comparative purposes. The picture will fade from time to time, but it is badly needed to extend our knowledge backward yet another step. The developmental pattern of such cities will become that much clearer, and its relevance to the patterns displayed by other cities in other nations will become that much sharper.

Unless otherwise noted, the analysis that follows reflects mainly the experience of the Municipal Court since its records alone gave details about the personal characteristics of its defendants.

The Juveniles

The industrial revolution had a powerful impact on the social careers of young people in Boston. In preindustrial Boston several paths were open to middle-and lower-class youth. They could apprentice themselves to craftsmen, who, in exchange for their labor and a fee, would teach them a skilled craft; they could become common laborers; or they could move west and become homestead farmers. The first often meant remaining under the influence of their parents for an extended period, particularly if one of the parents was a master craftsman, but it also promised the most secure future. Becoming either a common laborer or a farmer often meant a life of misfortune and hardship and were chosen mainly by those who had few other opportunities. With the approach of industrialization, however, this picture improved radically.

A primary education became a prerequisite for a smooth transition into adulthood, and unskilled and semiskilled jobs in ships and factories became plentiful. Public grammar schools were established in Boston in 1789 for all children between the ages of seven and fifteen, and in 1818 a feeder system of primary schools for children between four and seven years was established. In 1821, the first public high school, the English High School for Boys aged fifteen through eighteen was established in Boston, and in 1825 a high school for girls was also opened, though it was soon closed by Mayor Quincy to reduce the city's financial burden. The Boston Latin School, a private high school, had been available to upper class children since 1635, but with the creation of a comprehensive system of public schools serving children from four to eighteen, the middle- and lower-classe children of Boston were given a similar chance to develop their talents.

Not all children took advantage of this opportunity, and the more advanced the age, the smaller the proportion, but a growing number did, and by 1847 about 75 percent of the more than 25,700 children of grammar school age in Boston were enrolled in primary or grammar schools (Schultz 1973, 279–80).

Boston's public school system was a wonder worldwide, but throughout Massachusetts similar achievements were accomplished (Vinovskis 1981, 122–29). The percentage of Massachusetts children aged five to eighteen who were enrolled in school hovered around 80 percent in the decades before the Civil War, and illiteracy retreated to less than 5 percent. Massachusetts had developed a modern public school as early as 1840, and Boston had pointed the way.

The growth of a comprehensive educational system undoubtedly paved the way for rapid industrialization, but it had other effects as well. It opened to single women a respectable career—teaching in the public schools—and about 20 percent of all Massachusetts women took advantage of this opportunity at some time in their lives (Vinovskis 1981, 64). Moreover, they quickly became the mainstay of the teaching force. In 1834 women constituted 56.3 percent of all teachers in Massachusetts, and by 1860 they made up 77.8 percent (Vinovskis 1981, 63–64). Teaching represented an expanding opportunity for women, and as such, it held important implications for their role in the family and the larger community as well.

The most significant implication of the publc school system, however, was the restructuring of social routines it forced upon large numbers of children and adolescents. Before the advent of the public school system, young people spent much of their time in or around the home, helping with the tasks of preindustrial families. In urban communities, many youths spent considerable time wandering together through the streets (Schultz 1973, 59–60; Hawes 1971, chap 4 and 5). The public schools helped to absorb the energies of these restless youths and funnel them into constructive activities. To be sure, not all children four to eighteen were enrolled in school, or if they were enrolled, attended regularly. But the consensus among close observers seems to have been that the schools provided a happy solution to the problem of idle, rootless children in Boston (Schultz 1973, chap 4).

This conclusion is curious in light of today's experience that much juvenile deviance is directly connected with the schools. Schools today represent an important and often tension-filled hurdle for youth on their way to adulthood. There are innumerable studies linking poor achievement in school with delinquency (Kornhauser 1978, 167–80), and there are some indications that juveniles who leave school early may even become for a time more conforming in their behavior (Elliott and Voss 1974, chap. 5).

As we have seen, few, if any, commentators on the antebellum schools saw any connection between juvenile crime and the advent of a public school system in Boston; indeed, quite the reverse. The truants or unenrolled children were the source of the juvenile crime problem in the eyes of most social critics (Hawes 1971, chap. 5), not the children who were enrolled in school.

There was at that time a strong moral commitment to the public schools (Barney 1987, 106–9). They were seen as the answer to profligate youth and to intractable foreign populations. The public schools were heralded along with the family and the church as key pillars to a moral, civilized society (Schultz 1973, 66–68). It is unlikely that a connection between youthful misbehavior and the public schools would have been revealed publicly, even if it had been suspected. Nevertheless, we now believe that Boston's public schools were an important factor in the growth of the city's juvenile justice system (Sutton 1988, 107—15).

The essential fact here is the emergence in Boston of a new social status among young people: the juvenile. A juvenile is semi-autonomous and closely tied socioculturally and morally to his peers. As this group appeared among Boston's youth, they began to enjoy both more latitude for misbehavior and greater sociability with young people than in the preindustrial peiod.

As Boston became, first, a beehive of commerce and, then, light manufacturing in the early 1800s, the rapidly expanding population—and particularly the expanding migrant population—offered many opportunities for young people to wander anonymously through the city in search of adventure. As these youths discovered one another during their exploits, they coalesced into small groups and became more brazen in their behavior. Not all were bent on illegal behavior, but those that were became a growing source of irritation to the city fathers.

The interesting point, however, is that many of the developing cities of the world are today encountering just the same phenomenon as they also become the focal point of streams of migrants from the hinterland. Several of the major cities of Africa and Latin America today are experiencing troops of roaming youths on the lookout for criminal opportunities in the city center (see Clifford 1976, 149–80, Clinard and Abbott 1973, chap. 5, and DeFleur 1970, 81–146). The regularity of this distinctive pattern suggests that it is implicit in the changing social structure of a developing urban society, and that juvenile misbehavior, as with so much else in the developing world, shows a distinct developmental pattern (Ferdinand 1986).

JUVENILES IN THE MUNICIPAL COURT

The fact remains that in Boston juveniles were rarely found in the Municipal Court during (see fig. 6.1) the 1820s and early 1830s. In the mid-1830s, however, their numbers began to mount, and by the mid-1840s, they were the fastest growing component in antebellum

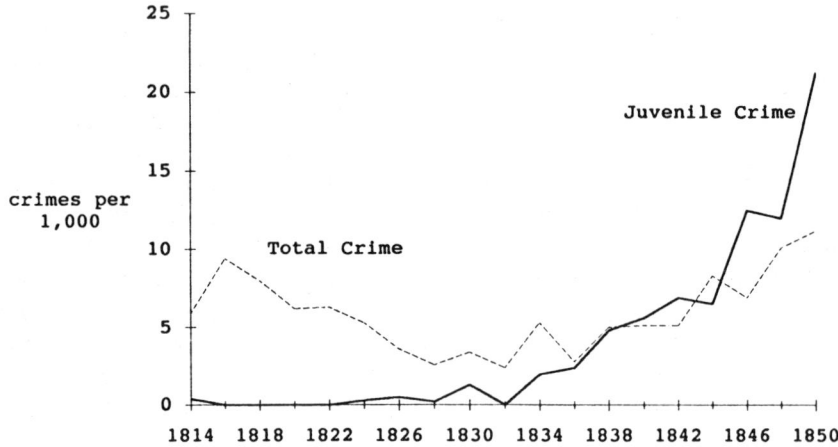

Figure 6.1: Juvenile Crimes per 1,000 (children 10-15) and Total Crimes per 1,000 in the Municipal Court: 1814-1850.

Boston's crime problem.[2] Juvenile crimes, moreover, were not concentrated simply in the minor crime category. Although juveniles had made a negligible contribution to serious crime before 1834 (see Table 6.1), by 1850 they accounted for 71.9 percent of the burglaries brought before the Municipal Court, 36.0 percent of the property offenses, and 21.6 percent of offenses against the person. In 1850 these three crime categories included the bulk, 88.2 percent, of their 270 crimes.

The contribution of females to juvenile crime, on the other hand, was slight. The total number of girls charged with crimes in the Municipal Court reached seventeen in 1850 (the figure for boys in 1850 was two hundred and fifty-three), and sixteen of the seventeen were charged with property crimes. At no time did they comprise more than 12.7 percent of the juveniles arrested and charged in the Municipal Court. Thus, the surge in juvenile offenders in the 1830s and 1840s represented basically an increase in male juvenile crime.

Several eastern cities reported similar increases in the 1840s. In New York City, for example, the chief of police, George W. Matsell, complained in 1849 of "the constantly increasing numbers of vagrant, idle and vicious children" who roamed through streets. He estimated

TABLE 6.1: PER CENT OF OFFENSES AGAINST THE PERSON, BURGLARY, AND MINOR PROPERTY OFFENSES COMMITTED BY JUVENILES IN THE MUNICIPAL COURT

Year	Offenses Against the Person[a]			Burglary			Minor Property Offenses[b]		
	Total N	Juv. N	Juv. as Per Cent of Total	Total N	Juv. N	Juv. as Per Cent of Total	Total N	Juv. N	Juv. as Per Cent of Total
1814	57	1	1.8	3	0	0.0	79	0	0.0
1816	63	0	0.0	22	0	0.0	202	0	0.0
1818	60	0	0.0	22	0	0.0	165	0	0.0
1820	36	0	0.0	6	0	0.0	125	0	0.0
1822	42	0	0.0	17	0	0.0	138	0	0.0
1824	33	0	0.0	6	0	0.0	126	2	1.6
1826	18	0	0.0	10	0	0.0	104	2	1.9
1828	17	0	0.0	4	0	0.0	99	0	0.0
1830	23	2	8.7	9	0	0.0	130	7	5.4
1832	57	0	0.0	6	0	0.0	68	0	0.0
1834	88	0	0.0	12	6	50.0	148	9	6.1
1836	46	2	4.3	12	2	16.7	101	14	13.9
1838	65	3	4.6	42	25	59.5	160	9	5.6
1840	59	3	5.1	38	28	73.7	181	20	11.0
1842	79	3	3.8	32	15	46.9	113	25	22.1
1844	83	13	15.7	31	9	29.0	186	43	23.1
1846	145	23	15.9	99	58	58.6	172	59	34.3
1848	159	18	11.3	87	57	65.5	203	59	29.1
1850	222	48	21.6	146	105	71.9	236	85	36.0

[a] Offenses against the person include assault and battery, felonies against the person, and misdemeanors against the person.
[b] Minor property offenses include larceny and misdemeanors against property.

their number at 3,000 and warned that "each year makes fearful additions to their ranks..., and from this corrupt and festering fountain flows a ceaseless stream to our lowest brothels—to the Penitentiary and to the State Prison!" (Hawes 1971, 91). In the early 1850s Charles Loring Brace, the reformer, reported while working in a mission near Five Points in Manhattan, "What soon struck us...was the immense number of boys and girls floating and drifting about our streets with hardly any assignable home or occupation, who continually swelled the multitude of criminals, prostitutes, and vagrants" (Hawes 1971, 91). And the managers of New York's House of Refuge, after surveying their wards, found the causes of juvenile crime in a child's indifference to education and religion coupled with poverty, parental depravity, and weak supervision (Pickett 1969, 109—15).

In Boston the District Attorney, Samuel D. Parker, echoed these observations in comments to a newspaper reporter:

> Mr. Parker remarked, in relation to the frightful prevalence of crime among the young that it appeared to be rapidly increasing and that more minors had been convicted within the last eighteen months than during the five or six preceding years. And he was inclined to the opinion that the employment of so many boys in peddling small articles, such as matches, soap, fruit, etc., was one cause—and the neglect of parents to keep their children at home evenings, another—of this alarming state of morals among the young. (Boston Evening Journal, 17 February, 1845:1)

Boston's mayor, John Bigelow, made much the same diagnosis in 1848 in his annual report to the city: "hundreds of children are kept from the schools by their parents, and brought up to support them in idleness and drunkenness by pilfering our wharves, and are regularly educated for the brothel and the dram-shop, the poor house, and the jail" (*Boston Evening Transcript*, 3 January 1848:2).[3]

It is impossible from this distance to verify their suspicions regarding the causes of juvenile crime, but it is easy to discount here several common explanations. First, it is clear that the increase in juvenile crime cannot be laid to a rapid rise in immigration into Boston during this period. The heavy Irish immigration did not begin until the mid–1840s—well after the rapid rise in juvenile crime had begun.

Nor can it be explained by the addition of new juvenile facilities to which judges could sentence errant young people. The House of Reformation was opened in 1826 to care for youthful offenders well before the rapid rise of juvenile crime in the 1830s, and the State Reform School for Boys was not established until 1847 as a training school for boys. The girls' reformatory was established in 1856 at Lancaster.

It is true that the Asylum and Farm School for Indigent Boys was opened in 1832 on Thompson's Island in Boston Harbor—just on the threshold of the surge in juvenile crime, and the Boylston School for Children of Tender Years was founded in the late 1830s (Pickett 1969, 94–96). Both institutions were intended only for "morally exposed" boys who needed a "reformatory discipline" but who had not yet been convicted of serious crimes. Since neither school served juvenile criminals, they could not have been an important factor in the juvenile crime rate.

It should be remembered that the Municipal Court received only the more serious criminal cases. The Police Court undoubtedly received a much larger number of juveniles, although they were not identified as such in the Police Court records. Thus, the volume of juvenile crime in the late 1840s was certainly much higher than the levels indicated here. Indeed, police arrest figures for the 1850s show that the arrest rate for juveniles in 1849—51 was nearly twice their case rate in the Municipal Court in 1850, that is, 506.0 arrests per 10,000 juveniles to 212.7 cases per 10,000 (Ferdinand 1985, fig. 2). The experience of the Municipal Court, though giving some indication of a rapidly escalating problem in Boston, offers only a dim suggestion as to its scope.

It is probably true that the Municipal Court data also underestimated the amount of juvenile crime during the 1820s and early 1830s. It may well be that the opening of the House of Reformation in 1826 as well as the Asylum and Farm School in 1832 were responses to a growing problem of minor juvenile behavior, but we cannot know for certain from these data.

It is worth noting that during this period the law made no distinction between adults and juvenile criminals. Juveniles convicted of felonies were sent to the State Prison at Charlestown just as adults. The destructiveness of this policy, however, rapidly became intolerable as growing numbers of children began to appear in the ranks of convicts at Charlestown. This fact was a major argument on behalf of the efforts to establish a state reform school for boys in the 1840s.

The Irish

The sad history of Ireland and its English overlords recedes at least to the twelfth century and the Norman King Henry II. It is a story of subjugation and exploitation that, over centuries, systematically reduced the Irish to a miserable and hopeless existence in Ireland (Handlin 1968, 37–47). The potato crop failure, in the mid-1840s in Ireland, pushed many of her sons and daughters to new places, including Boston, but it was only the final chapter in a long history of hopeless poverty.

A steady trickle of Irish immigrants had landed in Boston before the 1840s, but the introduction of steamships to trans-Atlantic commerce and the decision of the Cunard Line to establish its North American terminus in Boston opened up cheap trans-Atlantic travel to the desperately poor. A one-way ticket from Liverpool to Boston cost as little as seventeen dollars in the 1850s (Handlin 1968, 48–49). In 1840, 3,936 immigrants landed in Boston, and by 1849 this number had swollen sevenfold to nearly 29,000. In 1850 about 35,000 Irishmen lived in Boston when altogether the city held only 137,000 souls, and by 1855 the number of Irish had increased to 50,000 (Handlin 1968, 51–52).

The poverty of the Irish immigrants when they arrived was profound. They often had barely enough money to cover the price of their ticket and when they landed, they had little with which to start their new life. Their occupations were unskilled—more than 64 percent followed just two pursuits: laborers and domestic servants—and their wages were minimal (Handlin 1968, 250–57). As their numbers grew, poverty mounted to serious proportions in the city. In 1845 the Irish constituted 39 percent of the city's 4,810 paupers, and just five years later, they included fully 63 percent of Boston's 11,294 paupers (Handlin 1968, 256). The Irish and poverty became synonymous, and their neighborhoods were slums.

The Irish and their ever-growing ranks constituted a mounting threat to the tranquility and complacency of Bostonians. Their persistent poverty not only posed an expense and an embarrassment to the city's comfortable middle and upper classes, it also bred crime. The Irish were soon socially isolated and ultimately shunned by the larger share of Bostonians for the problems they created.

Anti-Irish fights and riots were commonplace. On the night of 11 August 1834, a mob of several thousand sacked, and burned the Ursuline Convent in Charlestown.

The trouble began on July 23rd when a young lady from the Convent appeared at the door of Edward Cutter, who lived nearby, and begged him to take her to a west Cambridge address. Next day when Cutter inquired about her in Cambridge, he was told that she had returned to the Convent with Bishop Fenwick on the condition that she could receive an honorable discharge in two or three weeks if she completed her work. Later, on August 9th when Cutter attempted to see her at the Convent, she was nowhere to be found. Soon rumors were flying in Charlestown regarding her mistreatment and disappearance.

On August 11th, Monday night, around eleven o'clock in the evening, several barrels of tar were set afire near the Convent as a signal, and by midnight several hundred had gathered, fifty to one hundred of whom were disguised with painted faces and outlandish costumes. The nuns, aware of the danger, fled with their young students from the rear of the convent, while the mob broke in the front door and carried off valuable musical instruments and furnishings. Around twelve thirty in the morning candles were used to ignite the second floor and the building was quickly engulfed. It burned to the ground. Several other buildings were also put to the torch: the chapel, the bishops's lodge, the stable, and the Old Nunnery.

No constables made an appearance during the entire time, and the fire companies that made their way to the conflagration were prevented from doing their duty. Within a week eight suspects were arrested (*Daily Advertiser and Patriot*, 13 and 18 August 1834: 2, 2).

Three years later the shoe was on the other foot when a riot broke out between several volunteer fire companies and an Irish funeral procession. A large crowd of several hundred Irish mourners had gathered in Broad Street on 11 June 1837 in the late afternoon. A fire wagon returning to a nearby firehouse passed an Irishman, his wife, and children, and after a flurry of insults a fight broke out in which the Irishman was severely beaten. His compatriots, who were gathering for the funeral, began to threaten the engine company, but the company sounded a general fire alarm to summon additional companies, and the Irish mourners backed off. The procession got underway along Broad Street, but soon another engine company dashed up. The funeral party, seeing the new company as antagonists, set upon them with an extraordinary frenzy. As additional companies arrived, they jumped into the fray, and soon a full-scale riot was underway, raging back and forth as reinforcements on both sides made themselves felt. The fury of the fighting overwhelmed the funeral and soon spilled over into the neighborhood. After several hours of bitter hand to hand conflict with stones, heavy timbers, and other makeshift weapons, a military contingent arrived and by nightfall all was quiet.

Severe damage was done to several Irish houses, many homes were ransacked, and a large number of rioters on both sides received painful injuries. Dozens were arrested and processed through the courts. Though it is difficult to prove, it seems that Irish sensitivities were deeply affected by the burning of the Ursuline Convent and that their belligerence in Broad Street was one result (*Daily Advertiser and Patriot*, 12 and 24 June 1837: 2, 2).

There were other less violent confrontations, but these testify to the intensity of feeling on both sides that prevailed in Boston during the antebellum period.

THE IRISH AND CRIME

The Irish were widely blamed for the city's rising crime problem (Schultz 1973, 237–51), and as we can see from fig. 6.2, their contribution *was* increasing.[4] Both the numbers of Irish defendants and their percentage share of the total rose steadily through the 1830s and 1840s. Between 1832 and 1850, the percentage of Irish defendants nearly doubled in both courts.

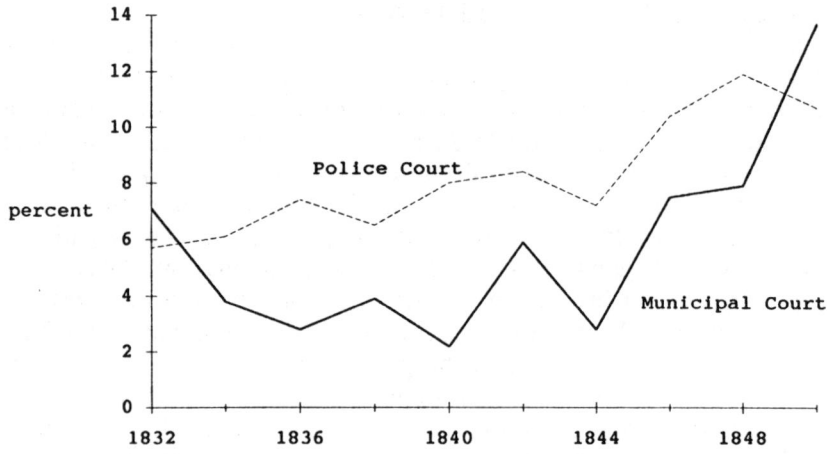

Figure 6.2: The Percentage of Irish Defendants Among All Defendants Appearing Before the Police and Municipal Courts: 1832–1850.

The sharpest increase came in burglary, and among burglars juveniles were easily the most prominent group. By the late 1840s they were responsible for 85.4 percent of the burglaries charged against Irish defendants in the Municipal Court. Another area of growing Irish activity was assaultive crimes. The number of assault and battery complaints against Irish defendants rose more than fivefold between 1832 and 1850 in the Police Court, and during the same period in the Municipal Court, the number of assaultive indictments (assault and battery, felonious and misdemeanor crimes against the person) grew elevenfold. It is interesting, however, that the percentage highs in Irish assaultive offenses occurred in the 1834–36 period in both courts—a period of most intense anti-Irish feeling in Boston—and not in the late 1840s when other crime was also escalating sharply.

The fact that non-Irish assaultive crimes also bulged in the 1830s in both courts suggests that ethnic conflict was, indeed an important factor.

We have already noted that juveniles were largely responsible for the sharp increase in Irish burglaries. As we can see (fig. 6.4), the contribution of Irish juveniles to Boston's overall crime problem was also growing, particularly in the late 1840s.

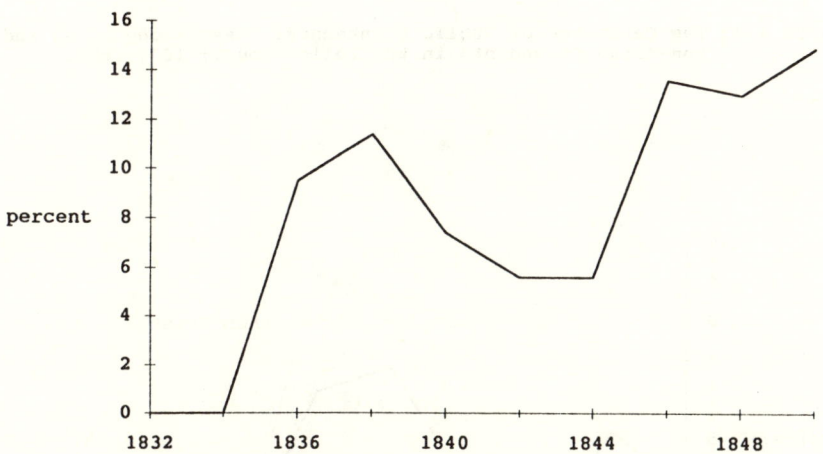

Figure 6.3: The Percentage of Irish Defendants Among Juvenile Defendants in the Municipal Court: 1832-1850.

Irish adults were also active—but in public drunkenness. Prosecutions of Irish public drunkenness fluctuated around 40 percent of their total offenses in the Police Court (see fig. 6.4) and stood regularly at least 10 percent higher than the comparable non-Irish figure. Prostitution, on the other hand, was relatively rare among Irish defendants in the Police Court (fig. 6.5).

These data suggest that the Irish were, indeed, an important factor in antebellum Boston's growing crime problem. In particular, they

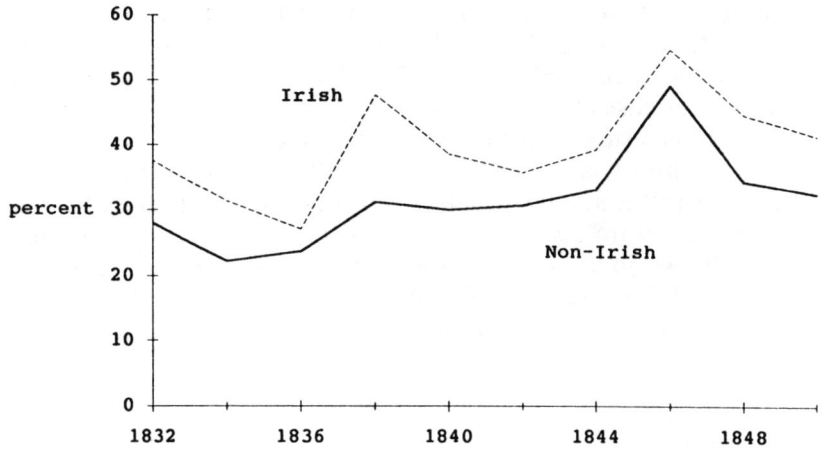

Figure 6.4: The Percetage of Public Drunkenness Cases Among Irish and Non-Irish Defendants in the Police Court; 1832-1850.

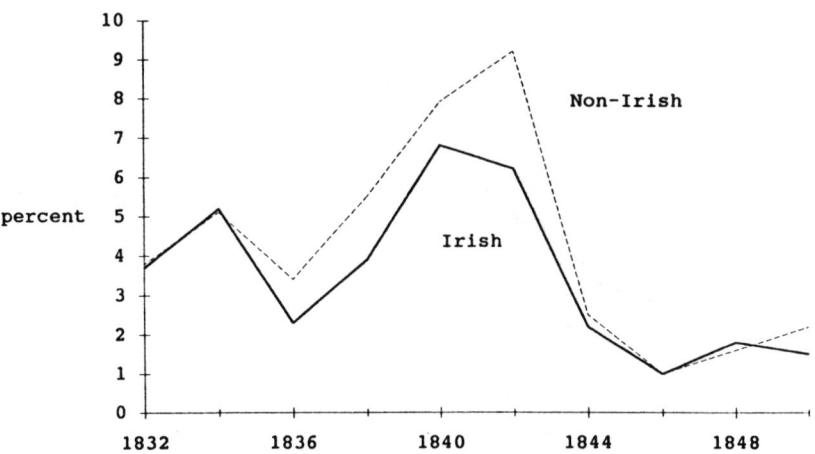

Figure 6.5: The Percentage of Prostitution Cases Among Irish and Non-Irish Defendants in the Police Court: 1832-1850.

contributed to the level of property crime through the activities of Irish juveniles, and ethnic conflict seems to have involved them in assaultive behavior to a heightened degree during the 1830s and probably beyond as well. At the same time their proverbial fondness for spirits led to an elevated level of public drunkenness.

Nevertheless, it is worth noting that the Irish only became a major ethnic group in Boston after 1844. The sharp upturn in antebellum Boston's crime problem occurred *before* 1844 (see fig. 5.1 and 5.2). Although the Irish were a factor, they were obviously not the only factor. Even without the massive Irish immigration of the late 1840s, Boston's crime wave would still have grown to major proportions during the last years of the decade.

Women

The antebellum period in Boston was a time of some significance for the status of women. During the colonial period married women had been regarded as their husbands' partners with equal but separate responsibilities in the family. They were crucial to the welfare of the family and enjoyed some authority, particularly in domestic matters (Demos 1970).

Nevertheless, a woman's decisions were still largely shaped by the men in her life. She often married a man of her father's choosing. Once married, she was subjected to her husband's authority and was often severely abused if she deviated from his wishes. As a wife she could own little property in her own right; she could not occupy important public offices; nor could she vote. In short, she was largely controlled by the man nearest her.[5]

After the Revolution the position of women in Boston began to change. As public education took hold in the 1820s and as industrialization gathered momentum in the 1830s, women found a variety of careers beyond the traditional domestic ones (Barney 1987, 38–40). The demand for school teachers grew rapidly in the early nineteenth century, as already noted, and women also played an increasingly important role as employees of textile mills in New England (Cott 1977, chap. 1). As economic opportunities developed, young women moved more readily beyond the family and experienced both the freedoms and the difficulties of independence.

During this period the feminists began their campaign to emancipate women in much the same way the abolitionists fought to eliminate black slavery. To be sure, many still believed that women's place was in the home, and the cult of domesticity was still firmly rooted in the minds of most women (Cott 1977, chap. 2), but the door to greater self-direction had been opened.

No one knows for certain how these broad changes affected women, but there are, at least, some strong probabilities. Economic growth in Boston drew many single women from the countryside and from abroad. Many became school teachers, some went to work in the shops, and others became domestics. But as unattached women became common in Boston, some must have been vulnerable to alienation and exploitation, and their criminality, and the city's, must have been affected. A contemporary survey of New York's prostitutes in 1858, for example, found that well over half were recent migrants from upstate farms or from Europe (Sanger 1858, 452, 456).

WOMEN IN COURT

The overall crime rate of women—as with men—varied according to the court. In the Police Court the rise in female crime after 1844 reflected an increase in public drunkenness brought on by the growing presence of Irish women in Boston (see Diner 1983, 112–13). During the 1830s public drunkenness never included more than 50 percent of the charges against women in the Police Court, but during the 1840s this percentage ranged as high as 64 percent (see Table 6.2). In the Municipal Court the increase in women's criminality after 1832 was led by a rise in prostitution cases.

These changes, however, must be viewed in the context of the evolving jurisdictions of the two courts. In chapters 2 and 3 the shift of regulatory cases and prostitution from the Police Court to the Municipal Court is discussed in relation to the prosecutor's growing role in crime control in Boston. This shift, as it unfolded, contributed directly to the rise in women's criminal cases in the Municipal Court in the late 1830s (see fig. 6.7) by adding a large number of prostitution cases to the court's caseload. By the same token, it also contributed to the decline of the Police Court's case load (see fig. 6.6) into the early 1840s.

Rapid urbanization and heavy Irish immigration must also be taken into account. Single women were becoming especially prominent in sex offenses (adultery and fornication) and prostitution in the Municipal Court, particularly in the late 1840s, while married women were focusing more on assaultive crimes and crimes against property (see Table 6.3).

The involvement of single women in sexual offenses and prostitution is readily understandable as more and more young people were drawn from the New England countryside into the shops and industries of Boston. At the same time as growing numbers of Irish wives immigrated with their impoverished husbands to the city, property and assaultive crimes became relatively common among married women.

TABLE 6.2: PERCENTAGE DISTRIBUTION OF FEMALE OFFENSES AMONG FIVE MAJOR CATEGORIES IN THE MUNICIPAL AND POLICE COURTS

	Municipal Court				Police Court				
Year	Assault & Battery	Minor Property Crimes	Prostitution	Total	Assault & Battery	Prostitution	Drunkenness	Larceny	Total
1814	6.9	44.8	24.1	29					
1816	19.2	42.3	7.7	26					
1818	16.0	50.0	6.0	50					
1820	5.9	67.6	14.7	34					
1822	12.9	51.6	3.2	31					
1824	2.3	75.0	11.4	44					
1826	0.0	62.5	25.0	8	13.1	41.4	28.8	5.8	396
1828	0.0	40.0	46.7	15	12.2	31.8	27.7	4.8	393
1830	3.6	57.1	28.6	28	—	—	—	—	—
1832	0.0	86.7	0.0	15	17.8	13.1	40.8	6.2	321
1834	2.8	27.8	41.7	36	13.2	20.5	40.4	11.5	356
1836	3.4	48.3	31.0	29	11.4	15.1	43.4	15.1	325
1838	0.0	46.2	38.5	52	8.1	18.6	49.5	14.9	484
1840	1.3	67.8	22.5	80	4.7	23.6	50.0	10.9	512
1842	0.0	14.6	29.3	41	7.9	28.9	39.7	9.3	471
1844	6.1	31.7	35.4	82	12.1	11.6	54.7	9.6	406
1846	6.3	20.7	44.1	111	11.3	5.9	64.3	10.2	460
1848	4.1	16.3	54.7	172	13.1	9.8	48.2	17.4	564
1850	11.6	22.7	27.3	172	14.6	12.6	51.8	22.6	643

Figure 6.6: Women's Criminal Cases per 1,000 in the Police Court: 1826-1850.

Figure 6.7: Women's Criminal Cases per 1,000 in the Municipal Court: 1814-1850.

TABLE 6.3: PERCENTAGE DISTRIBUTION OF SELECTED CRIMES BY WOMEN IN THE MUNICIPAL COURT ACCORDING TO SOCIAL POSITION: 1814–1850

Year	Crimes Felony & Misdemeanor/Against the Person, Assault and Battery								Felony and Minor Property Crimes								Sex Offenses & Prostitution							
	Single Women		Widows		Married Women		Total		Single Women		Widows		Married Women		Total		Single Women		Widows		Married Women		Total	
	N	%	N	%	N	%	N		N	%	N	%	N	%	N		N	%	N	%	N	%	N	
1814–26	11	73.3	0	0	4	26.7	15		114	89.1	2	1.6	12	9.4	128		17	45.9	5	13.5	15	40.5	37	
1828–34	10	52.6	0	0	9	47.4	19		31	70.5	3	6.8	10	22.7	44		18	56.3	5	15.6	9	28.1	32	
1836–42									62	66.7	6	6.5	25	26.9	93		24	45.3	4	7.5	25	47.2	53	
1844–50	24	37.5	1	1.6	39	60.9	64		56	52.3	5	4.7	46	43.0	107		155	65.7	5	2.1	76	32.2	236	

Single women, particularly those involved in prostitution, were likely to engage in other types of crime from time to time, but married women and particularly Irish women were not easily drawn into prostitution (see Diner 1983, 114). Thus, two independent streams helped to shape female criminality during this period: young, single people from surrounding states and the Irish from Europe. Their crime patterns were distinctive and their imprints on the historical record readily identifiable.

Economic Change

Boston's shift from a preindustrial to an industrial economy during the antebellum period transformed not only the occupational structure but the basic rhythm of the community as well. As industrialization proceeded, laborers were needed in growing numbers to run the factories and to serve the expanding city, and merchants prospered as inexpensive goods became increasingly abundant. But as manufactured goods from textiles to shoes to rifles flooded the markets, artisans found it increasingly difficult to survive. Moreover, as some merchants served their markets well and prospered handsomely, others found it difficult to compete. As the economy developed, rewards flowed generously to certain occupations, and young people shifted their sights from more traditional occupations to those that had a promising future (Barney 1987, 33–35).

These changes were often difficult for the people involved because it forced them out of routines that had been etched in their lives by long usage. An artisan, for example, performed his work in a shop in his home, and his sons often became apprentices as they approached adulthood. An artisan was accessible to his family, and especially to his older sons, but when the artisan became a laborer, he was forced to work away from home, and he could no longer assure his sons of respected careers in adulthood. He also found that he and his family were treated differently in the neighborhood, as a result of his diminished status in the community.

The economic changes that Boston actually underwent during this period were painstakingly documented by Peter Knights in a recent study of the city. Table 6.4 shows that the number of unskilled laborers grew more than sevenfold, and their share of the total work force moved up from 14.6 percent to 25.4 percent between 1830 and 1860. During this same period large merchants (proprietors, managers, and officials in Table 6.4) grew from 1,385 in 1830 to 5,420 in 1860, although their percentage share of the work force remained relatively stable, and clerical and sales workers spurted from 3.0 percent of the work force in 1830

TABLE 6.4: THE OCCUPATIONAL STRUCTURE OF ANTEBELLUM BOSTON: 1830–1860

Occupations	1830 N	1830 %	1840 N	1840 %	1850 N	1850 %	1860 N	1860 %
1. Unskilled & Menial	1,085	14.6	2,010	17.0	6,660	30.9	7,430	25.4
2. Semiskilled & Service	790	10.6	875	7.4	1,350	6.3	3,230	11.0
3. Petty Proprietors, Managers & Officials	1,580	21.2	2,330	19.7	2,450	11.4	2,880	9.8
4. Skilled	1,875	25.2	2,560	21.6	6,260	29.1	6,820	23.3
5. Clerical & Sales	220	3.0	290	2.5	960	4.5	2,620	8.9
6. Semiprofessional	170	2.3	225	1.9	190	0.9	175	0.6
7. Proprietors, Managers & Officials	1,385	18.6	3,245	27.4	2,820	13.1	5,420	18.5
8. Professional	340	4.6	290	2.5	830	3.9	700	2.4
Total	7,445	100.1	11,825	100.0	21,520	100.1	29,275	99.9

Source: Adapted from Peter R. Knights, *The Plain People of Boston, 1830–1860*. New York: Oxford University Press, 1971, Table V–1, p. 84.

TABLE 6.5: THE ASSESSED WEALTH OF EIGHT OCCUPATIONS IN ANTEBELLUM BOSTON: 1830–1860

1830

	Under $200		$200–$1,000		$1,001–$10,000		$10,000+		Total
	N	%	N	%	N	%	N	%	
1. Unskilled & Menial	30	96.8	1	3.2	—	—	—	—	31
2. Semiskilled & Service	27	96.4	1	3.6	—	—	—	—	28
3. Petty Proprietors, Managers & Officials	8	16.7	40	83.3	—	—	—	—	48
4. Skilled	57	98.3	1	1.7	—	—	—	—	58
5. Clerical & Sales	3	33.3	6	66.7	—	—	—	—	9
6. Semiprofessional	—	—	5	100.0	—	—	—	—	5
7. Large Proprietors, Managers & Officials	—	—	1	1.8	42	76.4	12	21.8	55
8. Professional	—	—	2	16.7	7	58.3	3	25.0	12

1840

	Under $200		$200–$1,000		$1,001–$10,000		$10,000+		Total
	N	%	N	%	N	%	N	%	
1. Unskilled & Menial	36	94.7	2	5.3	—	—	—	—	38
2. Semiskilled & Service	18	90.0	2	10.0	—	—	—	—	20
3. Petty Proprietors, Managers & Officials	3	5.5	51	92.7	1	1.8	—	—	55
4. Skilled	58	100.0	—	—	—	—	—	—	58
5. Clerical & Sales	1	12.5	6	75.0	1	12.5	—	—	8
6. Semiprofessional	1	20.0	4	80.0	—	—	—	—	5
7. Large Proprietors, Managers & Officials	1	1.1	4	4.5	66	74.2	18	20.2	89
8. Professional	1	12.5	3	37.5	3	37.5	1	12.5	8

	1850									1860								
	Under $200		$200–$1,000		$1,001–$10,000		$10,000+		Total	Under $200		$200–$1,000		$1,001–$10,000		$10,000+		Total
	N	%	N	%	N	%	N	%		N	%	N	%	N	%	N	%	
1. Unskilled & Menial	38	86.4	5	11.4	1	2.2	—	—	44	33	84.6	5	12.8	1	2.6	—	—	39
2. Semiskilled & Service	16	100.0	—	—	—	—	—	—	16	22	100.0	—	—	—	—	—	—	22
3. Petty Proprietors, Managers & Officials	5	15.6	26	81.3	1	3.1	—	—	32	6	25.0	17	70.8	1	4.2	—	—	24
4. Skilled	67	95.7	1	1.4	2	2.9	—	—	70	57	98.3	—	—	1	1.7	—	—	58
5. Clerical & Sales	12	85.7	1	7.1	—	—	1	7.2	14	18	72.0	1	4.0	5	20.0	1	4.0	25
6. Semiprofessional	2	100.0	—	—	—	—	—	—	2	1	100.0	—	—	—	—	—	—	1
7. Large Proprietors, Managers & Officials	1	2.4	—	—	29	69.0	12	28.6	42	1	1.7	—	—	39	66.1	19	32.2	59
8. Professional	1	9.1	—	—	2	18.2	8	72.7	11	2	25.0	2	25.0	1	12.5	3	37.5	8

Source: Adapted from Peter R. Knights, *The Plain People of Boston, 1830–1860*. New York: Oxford University Press, 1971, Table V-3, pp. 92–93.

to 8.9 percent in 1860 in response to the spreading commercial industrial economy. At the same time the percentage of artisans in the work force (skilled workers in Table 6.4) fell slightly, and small retailers (petty proprietors in Table 6.4) fell substantially. Great forces were at work realigning work and community in nineteenth-century Boston.

Along with these changes, a shuffling of social rank also took place. The levels of wealth of different occupations are given in Table 6.5, and we can see that between 1830 and 1860 the extremes of the occupational structure—that is, unskilled and menial laborers, on the one hand, and large proprietors on the other—improved their net worth considerably, whereas skilled (Table 6.5 here) workers showed little gain and the wealth of petty proprietors and semiskilled workers actually deteriorated. The occupations that were helped the most—unskilled laborers and large proprietors—were all directly connected with a growing industrial economy, and those that were hurt the most—skilled workers, and small proprietors—were closely connected with the preindustrial handicraft economy.

OCCUPATIONS AND CRIME

How were these socioeconomic changes reflected in the crime patterns

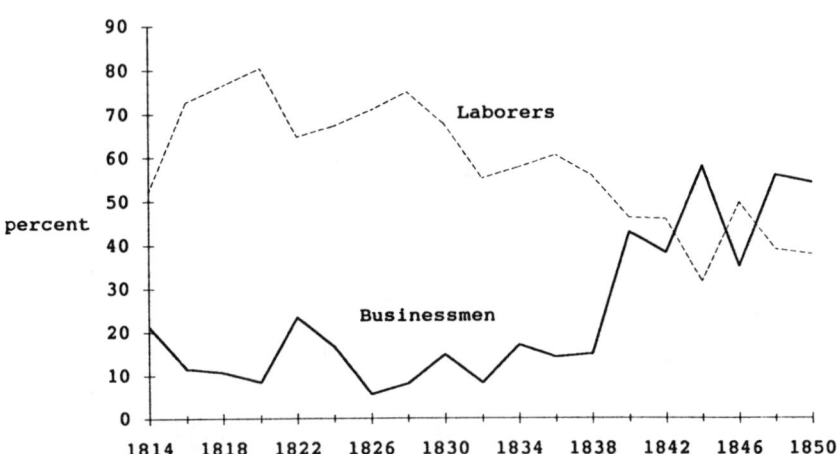

Figure 6.8: The Percentage of Laborers and Businessmen Among All Defendants Before the Municipal Court: 1814-1850.

of Boston? This question can be answered most readily by considering figs. 6.8 through 6.11.[6] Until 1838 laborers were unrivaled in their share of the Municipal Court's caseload. They constituted more than 50 percent of the defendants from 1814 through 1838, and in the early 1840s they were still dominant, though closely followed by businessmen. In 1844, however, businessmen outstripped laborers as defendants and became the largest group in the late 1840s, accounting for more than half of the defendants in the Municipal Court.

Artisans and professionals were never very common in the Municipal Court. The artisans rarely constituted more than one-fifth of the caseload, and after 1832 their share fell steadily to around 5 percent of the total in the late 1840s (see fig. 6.9). Although professionals were slowly increasing their share, their percentage of the total exceeded 5 percent only twice, and by 1850, it still hovered around the 2 percent level.

The number of defendants in all groups was increasing, as might be expected in a rapidly growing city like Boston. But businessmen were increasing both in numbers and in criminality, and by the late 1840s their offending rate had far outstripped all the rest. The number of laborers in the Municipal Court was also increasing in the late 1840s— helped considerably by the Irish immigration—but not so rapidly as

Figure 6.9: The Percentage of Artisans and Professionals Among All Defendants Before the Municipal Court: 1814-1850.

TABLE 6.6: NUMBER AND PERCENTAGE OF SELECTED OFFENSES OF LABORERS, ARTISANS, BUSINESSMEN, AND PROFESSIONALS IN THE MUNICIPAL COURT, 1814 THROUGH 1850 AGGREGATED

	Laborers		Artisans		Businessmen		Professionals	
	N	%	N	%	N	%	N	%
Felony Against the Person	386	10.9	96	11.4	35	1.4	6	4.2
Misdemeanor Against the Person	29	0.8	6	0.7	3	0.1	9	6.3
Assault & Battery	308	8.7	117	13.9	32	1.3	27	18.8
Total	723	20.4	219	26.0	70	2.8	42	29.3
Felony Against Property	59	1.7	13	1.5	34	1.4	1	0.7
Misdemeanor Against Property	1,545	43.7	299	35.6	71	2.9	4	2.8
Burglary	257	7.3	30	3.6	4	0.2	—	—
Larceny	76	2.1	4	0.5	—	—	—	—
Total	1,878	54.8	346	41.2	109	4.5	5	3.5

	No.	%	No.	%	No.	%	No.	%
Offenses Against Religion	20	0.6	1	0.1	327	13.5	—	—
Liquor Ordinance Violations	8	0.2	3	0.4	917	37.9	1	0.7
Violations of City Ordinances	44	1.2	51	6.1	560	23.1	33	22.9
Total	72	2.0	55	6.6	1,804	74.5	34	23.6
Prostitution	198	5.6	23	2.7	121	5.0	5	3.5
Sex Offenses	29	0.8	15	1.8	5	0.2	3	2.1
Fraud	55	1.6	23	2.7	159	6.6	17	11.8
Counterfeiting	169	4.8	45	5.4	27	1.1	6	4.2
Riot	147	4.2	7	0.8	—	—	1	0.7
TOTAL[a]	3,537	100.0	841	100.0	2,422	100.0	144	100.0

[a] Only the most common offenses are included in this table. The figures in the total reflect *all* offenses brought to the Municipal Court.

the businessmen, and as a result their percentage fell. Since artisans were declining in the city at large, their weak numerical growth in the Municipal Court reflected basically an increase in criminal complaints.

The crime patterns of these occupational groups present some interesting contrasts (see Table 6.6). Both laborers and artisans concentrated a large percentage of their offenses in just two categories: property and assaultive crimes. Businessmen committed mostly regulatory offenses, and the crimes of professionals fell primarily in the regulatory and assaultive categories. Relatively speaking, neither of these latter two groups committed many property crimes, although both were high in fraud, a result of their regular commercial involvement with the public, and professionals were unusually active in sex offenses.

These patterns suggest two distinct explanations for the criminality of antebellum Bostonians. A substantial number of their crimes were directly implied by the opportunities inherent in their work (Cohen *et al.* 1981). Businessmen and professionals were involved in regulatory offenses and frauds because they were engaging in commerce and service that carried contractual obligations, and artisans were relatively high on counterfeiting because some of them were skilled printers and engravers.

At the same time there is an apparant association between economic status and property crime. The lower the assessed wealth of an occupational group, the more intensive its involvement in property crimes. Laborers and artisans far surpassed businessmen and professionals in property crimes, and fell far below them in assessed wealth (see Table 6.5). On closer examination, however, we note that the artisans have a *lower* assessed wealth in Table 6.5 than laborers and that their wealth relative to that of laborers actually deteriorated during the antebellum period.

Even though artisans were poor and becoming poorer than laborers, their involvement in property crimes did not rise; indeed, it even declined along with that of laborers. This fact, together with the fact that property crimes in both groups were hardly affected by the severe depression of 1837–42 (see below), suggests that economic conditions alone were not responsible for the high levels of property crimes among laborers and artisans.

Property crime among these groups probably owes as much to a tradition of theft as to relative poverty. Such a tradition among a segment of the laboring or artisan classes might explain why their involvement in property crime was almost unaffected by shifting economic conditions. It might also explain why their involvement in property crimes was so much greater than that of businessmen or professionals. The relative poverty of laborers and artisans may have

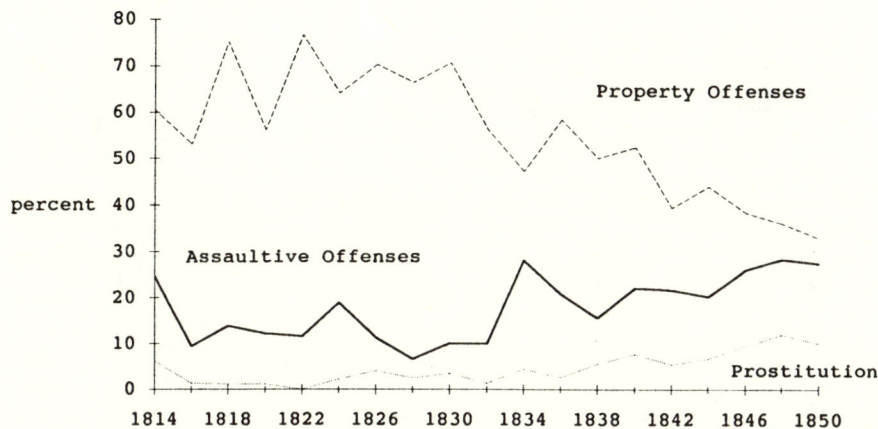

Figure 6.10: The Percentage of Assaultive, Property, and Prostitution Crimes Among Laborers in the Municipal Court: 1814-1850.

made property crime attractive to some, but once the skills and rationalization of theft had been acquired (Matza 1964), opportunity, not poverty, became the primary stimulus. There was widespread anxiety regarding the dangerous classes during this period, and a portion of the lower class that pursued criminal as well as legitimate opportunities would have given some point to these fears.

When we turn to the crime trends of these several groups (professionals were not included because their annual numbers were too small), we gain another perspective on the relationship between occupation and crime.

HISTORICAL TRENDS

During the early 1830s the bulk of the crimes committed by laborers and artisans were property offenses, but in the 1840s assaultive offenses and prostitution began to climb while property offenses fell sharply (see fig. 6.10).

Businessmen, on the other hand, displayed a very different pattern, having never committed more than a handful of assaultive or property crimes. Regulatory offenses, which were their specialty, became common

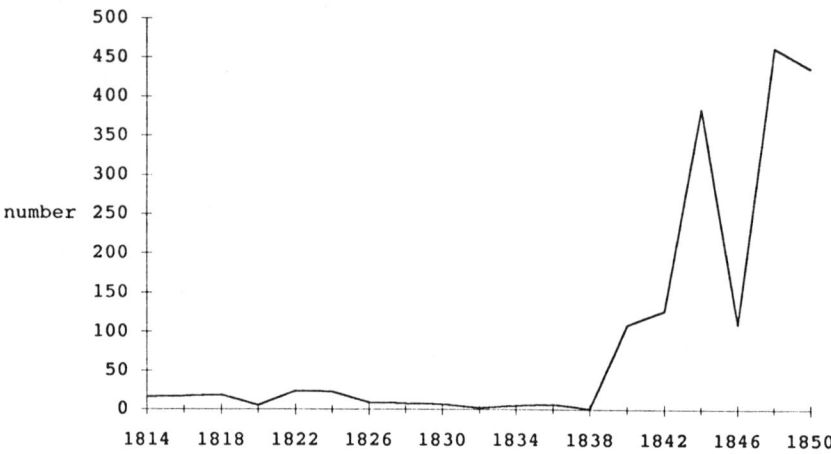

Figure 6.11: The Number of Regulatory Offenses Among Businessmen in the Municipal Court: 1814-1850.

only after 1838 (see fig. 6.11). Before that date regulatory offenses were slowly declining.

The sudden, sharp increase in regulatory complaints after 1838 speaks clearly to a shift in prosecution policy in the Municipal Court following passage by the legislature of the "Fifteen-gallon Law" in 1838 (chap. 1: pp. 10-13). As temperance forces gathered strength in Boston during the 1830s, they finally succeeded in gaining prohibitory legislation, and the Municipal Court enforced these prohibitive laws aggressively. Most of the regulatory violations recorded during the 1840s were violations of laws controlling the sale of alcoholic beverages.

The disproportionate jump in cases involving property crimes among both laborers and artisans during the 1820s and 1830s is more difficult to explain. The early 1830s, when property complaints against them were increasing most rapidly, were prosperous years in Boston, nor was the severe depression of 1837-42 accompanied by any sustained increase in either property or assaultive complaints. The improving economic condition of laborers (see Table 6.5) during the late 1840s might explain a decline in property crimes for this group, but the economic decline of the artisans during the 1840s was not followed by any noticeable surge in their property crimes. Clearly changes in their economic fortunes had little affect on the criminality of laborers or artisans during this period.

The increases in assaultive complaints in the early 1830s for both groups, on the other hand, probably reflected the bitter feelings between the Irish and Yankees that marked this period. We have already noted several anti-Irish riots that occurred in the 1830s, and the continuing rise in assaultive crimes in the 1840s among laborers and artisans seems to reflect this legacy of hostility as well as the sharp upturn in Irish immigration after 1844.

The Anatomy of Crime in Boston

We can begin to see now the main outline of antebellum Boston's crime problem, as well as some of its basic causes. The level of crime in both the Police Court and the Municipal Court drifted downward during the 1820s, when Mayor Quincy spearheaded a major campaign to eliminate prostitution and other minor crimes. The effort was apparently successful, and crime of all types sank to antebellum lows in both courts during the 1830s.

Some of this early decline in crime resulted from a growing reluctance in the Police Court to prosecute private disputes involving minor violence. This slight jurisdictional change, however, produced a precipitous drop in minor assaultive offenses recorded in the Police Court, which, in turn, resulted in serious distortions in the trends of minor crime and total crime in that court.

In the 1830s juvenile crime—particularly juvenile property crime— began a sharp rise, and female crime shifted its focus such that married women began to commit property and assaultive crimes more frequently, while single women turned more often to sex offenses and prostitution. During the late 1830s vice and regulatory offenses involving the sale of alcoholc beverages soared in the Municipal Court, and in the Police Court public drunkenness also began to climb.

The dislocations of industrialization were beginning to make themselves felt in the family and community by 1830, and these broad changes undoubtedly contributed to the sudden rise in juvenile offenses during the 1830s and to the changing trends in female crimes. Moreover, a growing public clamor in the late 1830s for the control of vice and public drunkenness resulted in more aggressive policing of these two problems and mountainous increases in regulatory and vice arrests in the Municipal Court. Public drunkenness arrests also rose in the Police

Court during the 1840s, but they showed none of the sharp increases displayed by regulatory offenses in the Municipal Court. The influx of poverty-stricken Irish immigrants during this period served to magnify each of these several problems.

These broad changes in criminality seemed to establish the jurisdictions of the two courts in two distinct areas. The Police Court focused on minor crimes that involved neither serious punishments nor difficulties of prosecution. The Municipal Court handled crimes that involved major punishments as well as defendants who were likely to insist on a jury trial. Vice operators and tavern owners, along with major felons, found their way into the Municipal Court, whereas public drunks and misdemeanants were left to the Police Court.

The Municipal Court was the higher court with capable judges and a professional bar. It was well equipped to contain the intense passions and to adminster the severe punishments that serious criminality triggers. At the same time it was sufficiently authoritative to adjudicate complaints against well-established businessmen who were regularly summoned to answer charges involving regulatory offenses. The Police Court could do neither, and by default (as well as by design), it handled everything else.

The confusion of the first two decades of the nineteenth century when four courts (in addition to the Supreme Judicial Court) handled criminal cases was finally resolved. By 1850 the Police Court and the Municipal Court had effected a clear division of labor that had continued in many respects through their successor courts to the present day.

7
Modernizing Boston's Lower Courts

The criminal courts of Boston crossed an important threshold during the antebellum years. Their clientele, their structure, their rules and policies, their informal practices, and the results of their deliberations all began to look like those used commonly today in many lower criminal courts. At bottom were not only a mounting case load, an evolving due process, and a maturing adversarial system, but also a fundamental shift in the courts' links with the surrounding sociopolitical world.

To understand how Boston's early courts came to resemble ours today, we need a picture—idealized to be sure—of what the present-day courts look like. With this picture as our base, Boston's courts before 1830 can be compared with today's courts and their modernizing path traced.

The Modern Criminal Courts

The lower courts today are multipurposed institutions serving a broad cross-section of the American people (Sarat 1979). Primarily they administer justice to those who violate the fundamental mores and prohibitions of the community, but they also mediate disputes between private citizens, they act as social welfare agencies for citizens whose derelictions owe more to social or psychological deficiencies than criminal tendencies, and they monitor the business and politico-governmental sectors for their compliance with state and local laws. Each of these functions serves a distinctive clientele, and taken together their clientele reflect the wide diversity of American society.

The lower courts are also highly specialized and tightly focused both in jurisdiction and in processing. Juvenile courts, family courts, felony courts, and misdemeanor courts today handle the criminal jurisdiction that was covered all alone by the Court of General Sessions in the eighteenth century and by the Municipal and Police Courts through much of the nineteenth. Cases that formerly were funneled into a single court served by a single staff are today, in Boston, distributed among nine city and county courts.

The modern criminal courts are congested with minor cases in which relatively little is at stake either for the defendant or for the victim and that are resolved quickly through plea bargaining virtually to the exclusion of trials altogether. Their defendants range from petty, chronic offenders well-known to courtroom regulars to youthful criminals, with long juvenile records, who are eager to graduate to the big time. They send their serious criminals to the higher trial courts (Mather 1973), their white collar criminals to the felony or civil courts, and their organized criminals on to the U.S. district courts.

In the nineteenth century Boston's criminal courts had a much broader jurisdiction. They handled not only the petty offenders that make-up the bulk of the caseload of these courts the world over, but they also arraigned and tried a goodly number of the serious criminals, nearly all of the business defendants, and a very large number of quarrels involving private citizens that today probably would not qualify as criminal matters at all. Early on, they also assumed welfare responsibilities (thanks to the pioneering efforts of John Augustus) to supervise and uplift indigent, petty offenders. If anything, the early courts displayed a more varied clientele and a more versatile corps of officers than today's highly specialized lower courts with their limited jurisdictions.

Courtroom Workgroups

Today a criminal case encounters several different teams of assistant district attorneys and magistrates as it winds its way from the preliminary hearing, through the grand jury hearing, to arraignment and trial. These specialists assume responsibility for only a brief phase of the overall processing of the case, and when they have completed their task, they hand it over to the next team, which tackles a different phase. During the early decades of the nineteenth century, criminal cases were handled with much more dispatch than today and by a single county attorney in the Municipal Court without assistants. After the grand jury issued an indictment, the arraignment and trial followed in short order.

Today with such fragmentation there is considerable room for organizational breakdown in which files are misplaced and defendants are overlooked. In early Boston, when a single prosecutor handled all phases of the case, such breakdowns were undoubtedly rare.

This fragmentation of case processing, moreover, tends to structure the ways in which court officers organize themselves. The assistant district attorneys who handle preliminary hearings develop working relationships with arresting officers, jail personnel, public defenders, defendants, and bail bondsmen; the assistant district attorneys who specialize in grand jury hearings see sheriffs, police detectives, and private citizens all day; the assistant district attorneys who take care of arraignments work closely with defense attorney regulars and defendants; and assistant district attorneys who conduct trials develop special relationships with the local criminal bar. Some assistant district attorneys participate in all phases of a case, but most spend their time at a single level.

On this basis distinctive work groups tend to emerge in many courtrooms in which the cooperative efforts of all the members, including particularly the defense attorney and the assistant prosecutor, are united in disposing of the case as smoothly, quickly, and conveniently as possible (Nardulli 1978, chap. 5). Different work groups have distinctive goals: the preliminary hearing team seeks to determine the validity of the defendant's arrest; the work group handling grand jury indictments considers the merit of prosecuting the defendant; the arraignment group sets the stage for the trial by formally charging the defendant; and the trial work group seeks to uncover the defendant's guilt or innocence (Eisenstein and Jacob 1977, chap. 4 and 5).

Each member of each work group has specific goals that may conflict with those of the rest. Serious conflicts, however, are rare, because each member knows that over time the specific goals of each will be achieved most effectively, if moderation is the rule. If a defense attorney vigorously contests an arrest on a valid but minor point during a preliminary hearing, she may find later that the prosecutor just as vigorously contests a continuance that she badly needs. A cooperative attitude works to the benefit of all, and those who obstruct the team sooner or later find that others can also be uncooperative.

In the nineteenth-century courtroom, work groups developed in a similar fashion around the significant tasks that required the cooperation of parties with distinctive viewpoints. There is considerable anecdotal evidence indicating a spirit of cooperation in the Police Court among the constables and regular defendants on a variety of issues: a reward for the return of stolen goods (Lane 1969, 56–57); the dismissal of a charge in return for evidence against a more important offender (Savage 1873, 250–51); or a reduced sentence for a guilty plea. Similarly, in the Municipal Court, the prosecutor and his investigators regularly worked out a reduction in charges in return for a guilty plea with minor offenders where there were no victims and the punishments were minimal. There is no record of defense attorneys participating extensively in these negotiations in either court, but it is entirely likely that they did.

On the basis of these informal work groups the modern lower courts have evolved their own characteristic pattern of outcomes. Not only do they punish most offenses (particularly property offenses) with less severity than nineteenth-century courts, but they also take very few cases to a jury trial.[1] These work groups have become, in effect, informal tribunals for reviewing charges and arranging dispositions. The stiffly formal proceedings of early nineteenth-century trial courts have largely disappeared in favor of private negotiations at nearly every phase of the process.

As a result the dignity and authority of the early nineteenth-century courts have today been severely eroded. Our modern lower courts process many more cases than their nineteenth-century counterparts, but their moral authority in the community is much less, and the significance of case outcomes beyond the immediate participants is usually slight.

Today's courts are disorganized hives in which private discussions regarding a hundred different cases often drown out the formal proceedings, which, in any case, have usually been resolved earlier via informal negotiations. Scarcely anyone in the courtroom pays attention to the formal hearing because the pretrial informal phase wherein matters of consequence are decided without judge or jury (Feeley 1979, chap. 7) has assumed primary importance, and the formal court hearing merely ratifies and records what has already been decided informally.

The presumption of guilt has replaced the presumption of innocence in these courts (Packer 1968, 144), and the primary focus has switched to the defendant's sentence. The defendant's guilt is assumed by all parties including the defense counsel, who devotes much of his energies to persuading the assistant prosecutor to soften the sentence. The lower courts today, therefore, have come to resemble the inquisitorial courts of continental Europe except that they lack their dignity and moral authority.

Finally, today's courts are closely attuned to the social and political climate of the community. Judges and prosecutors are cognizant of the sensibilities of the people, and though not required by law or formal rule, they often reflect local sentiments in their rulings. The modern lower courts are tied closely to the local community through a hundred formal and informal links, and their deliberations regularly reflect this fact (Neubauer 1974, chap. 1; Levin 1977, chap. 8).

Boston's Premodern Courts

The early lower courts in Boston were trial courts. The Police Court held bench trials sometimes presided over informally by the Court Clerk (Fenner 1856, 101–3), and the Municipal Court held jury trials. Both courts disposed of their caseloads quickly. In 1824 the Police Court handled 2,445 defendants, or about forty-seven cases per week, and the Municipal Court dealt with 256 cases, or about five cases per week. Defendants were permitted lawyers in both courts, but most often they were unrepresented, and the hearings themselves were one-sided with the hapless defendant raising few objections to the proceedings, calling few witnesses, or presenting little evidence in his own behalf. The adversary system was unbalanced with rather loose rules of evidence and few appeals. Despite the one-sided nature of the trials (or perhaps because of it), the judges in the Police Court enjoyed unrivaled authority. They often questioned the defendants pointedly about their crimes, dismissed large numbers, and found most of the rest guilty. In the Municipal Court the judge and jury together determined the fate of defendants (Van Dyke 1983, 939–40; Nelson 1975, chap. 9). The jury interpreted the law and evaluated the evidence to render a verdict, and the judge advised the jury on the relevant law and formulated the sentence. The sentences themselves were determinate, that is, the defendant was given a fixed sentence determined by statute, and severe by our standards today, particularly for property crimes.

There was ample room, nevertheless, for defendants to avoid the full weight of the law. Dismissals were common in both courts–particularly for private quarrels that found their way into the courts, and many cases were simply held open (left-on-file) with the option of reinstating the prosecution if the defendant's behavior worsened. In addition in the Municipal Court, the county attorney could and did quash criminal cases that did not warrant prosecution. The law was harsh in grinding out justice, but there was ample opportunity for defendants who deserved mercy to escape punishment. These several techniques for stopping or suspending cases, however, conferred unusual powers on the officers of the court. In the Police Court the judges enjoyed wide latitude in shaping the outcomes of cases, and in the Municipal Court the judge and the prosecutor exercised broad control over the fate of defendants. When law is rigid, process must be flexible.

The Early Modern Courts

The first step toward modernity came when the early courts began to sponsor work groups that linked them informally with their agents (police detectives) and their clientele (defendants). As these work groups established themselves in the organization of both courts, discretionary power flowed downward from the judge to the most active members. These informal teams helped primarily to align the formal decisions in both courts more closely with practical realities. In the Police Court constables and defendants handled a variety of issues much more quickly and conveniently through informal negotiations than court officers could in formal court hearings, and the prosecutor did much the same in the Municipal Court.

Since its cooperative teams were already in place at a very early date, the Police Court worked out many of these informal arrangements first and particularly the most important one, plea bargaining. In the 1830s, as we have seen, constables were negotiating with thieves to return stolen goods in return for a reward or with suspects for information about more serious offenders in return for impunity in a pending case. It was only a small step from these kinds of arrangements to negotiations for guilty pleas, and it was only a matter of time before members of these teams took that step. When informal work groups assumed responsibility for the resolution of certain minor criminal justice problems, their discretion expanded, and their ability to tackle more important problems grew as well.

In the Municipal Court the prosecutor was also expanding his powers under the mandate of the newly enacted liquor laws of the 1830s and 1840s. The proactive posture these regulatory laws forced upon the prosecutor paved the way for cooperative teams much like those in the Police Court. These work groups were the mechanism whereby Boston's premodern courts adapted to their changing environment and they played a key role in modernizing Boston's courts.

As trial procedures became more complex during the early decades of the nineteenth century and as trials began to lengthen, informal shortcuts became increasingly attractive (Langbein 1979, 265), and the cooperative work groups that were playing a key role in this process consolidated their powers and became fully legitimate in both courts. As these work groups exercised greater discretion in resolving the troublesome problems of both courts, some judical authority slipped downward to the constables and police in the Police Court and to the county attorney and his team in the Municipal Court.

In other words, the structure of Boston's premodern courts was being refashioned to resemble that of the modern lower courts. The two major centers of discretionary power today are lodged in the police department and in the prosecutor's office where informal work groups supervise the pretrial phase of each criminal case and more often than not settle it extralegally to nearly everyone's satifaction.

Since these work groups unfold in both settings in terms of their own immanent logic, they are not constrained in the first instance by rules of law. Work groups can and do evolve techniques and policies that conflict with the spirit if not the letter of the law. The police sometimes devise intricate traps for suspects (John De Lorean, for example) involving cooperative informants that nevertheless produce only an acquittal because of entrapment. Similarly, the prosecutor's office often develops working policies governing charge bargaining so that serious charges–burglary, for example–are reduced to minor charges such as criminal trespass or even larceny in order to insure guilty pleas. The methods or policies reflect more the cooperative arrangements of the work groups than limitations of the law because the work groups are themselves informal and extralegal (see, for example, Nardulli *et al.* 1985).

Their methods and policies, moreover, are rarely examined for their legal significance. Until recently defendants who had negotiated a guilty plea with the prosecutor were routinely required by the judge to swear in open court that they had not been pressured nor given any inducement to plead guilty, and of course, entrapment is still a rather novel defense in criminal trials. Informal work groups, therefore, exert pressure on both the police and the courts to change in ways that are expedient and convenient, and the results are examined only belatedly, if at all, for their legality. Plea bargaining was first reviewed in Massachusetts in *Commonwealth v. Clark Greene* (13 Allen 251, 1866), more than three decades after its inception in the Police Court. Work groups, therefore, can and do foster policies that are effective in solving troublesome practical issues but that go largely unexamined for their legal import.

They are a force for change, change that is not coordinated with formal legal change. As due process became more complex, the professionalization of the bar continued, and the rights of defendants expanded during the nineteenth century, plea bargaining was invented to balance these processes and, indeed, contributed to the concentration of even greater power and discretion in the hands of the prosecutor and his assistants. The effort to provide full due process protections for defendants led indirectly to a redistribution of powers within the lower criminal courts such that prosecutors gained almost unchecked discretionary powers to define the fates of defendants. In the end, due process was largely circumvented by the faceless work groups that took charge of the minor cases that were flooding the courts.

Professionalization also played a role in the modernizing of Boston's lower courts, not so much by way of improving the quality of its bar (although it did that, too), but through its affect on the bench—particularly the Municipal Court bench. As professional judges came onto the Municipal Court bench during the 1840s, they brought with them a new sympathy for responsive, proactive legal institutions and innovations such as plea bargaining. From the support these judges offered the prosecutor and his work groups in this area, plea bargaining was established in the repertory of most Municipal Court regulars, and it became the preferred method of disposing of minor, victimless crimes in that court.

This endorsement by professional judges of plea bargaining is particularly interesting, since their counterparts today often take just the opposite view. Silberman (1973) reports that modern professional judges are more committed to due process and less sympathetic to a pretrial resolution of criminal cases than localistic judges, and Levin (1977, 68–73) found that professional judges who adhere to formalistic rules were hostile to plea bargaining in Minneapolis. Professional judges seem to endorse the dominant legal views of their era and to act accordingly. Through them the leading law schools exert a guiding influence on legal institutions.

Law Schools, Work Groups, and Legal Change

Just as work groups helped to coordinate the activities of Boston's courts with the changing character of defendants, professional judges in Boston served to coordinate the lower courts with the broader legal profession. Before the Revolution, American lawyers had trained in England at the Inns of Court. As apprentices they learned the perspectives and techniques of practicing lawyers and prepared themselves for the profession. After the Revolution, the Inns of Court were no longer the proper step toward a legal career in the United States, and the lawyers began to train in law offices scattered throughout the thirteen states.

The apprenticeship method of training lawyers, however, was inadequate. As the profession evolved and new legal doctrines took shape, there were no effective means for diffusing them to practicing lawyers. Appeals and written opinions were rare, and embraced only a small number of cases. Law journals were becoming more common, but they were at best a weak means of forging widely scattered lawyers into a unified profession. As the courts entered the nineteenth century, they depended upon a bench and bar guided more by eccentricity and prejudice than by established legal doctrines.

The founding of law schools in four-year colleges helped to correct this problem. First, the better students were drawn to these schools where they were taught an authoritative respect for the law. From there they filtered into the profession and carried with them the prevailing ideas of their profession. These early law centers became sponsors of legal evolution, and their graduates were their agents. They conferred a common perspective and purpose on their students that was largely lacking in lawyers who had apprenticed in law offices just after the Revolution.

Several of these early law schools were established in New England colleges, and the dominant perspective among Massachusetts judges during this period was swinging sharply toward an activist, responsive view of the law. The primary responsibility of the law, in their eyes, was to shape social and economic forces according to the welfare of the community. This view was adopted by many graduates of these law schools and used for years in their careers, and as their numbers grew, they began to chart the direction of their profession. In short, the new law schools provided an efficient mechanism whereby a significant portion of the legal profession could be united behind a distinctive sociolegal perspective, and the activities of professional judges in Boston's antebellum courts illustrate this process very nicely.

They were opinion leaders in business, politics, and education as well as in the legal profession itself. Within the criminal courts they were receptive to innovation and worked effectively with others as they reshaped the courts.[2] The prosecutor expanded his domain, and the professional judges were especially responsive to these developments as well as to the informal arrangements such as plea bargaining that work groups were developing to dispose of the court's business.

The work groups helped the courts adapt to the changing criminological environment, and the professional judges helped to align the lower courts with the responsive legal doctrines that were taking shape in the minds of Judges Shaw, Washburn, and other leading legal personalities. By these mechanisms Boston's courts were bound tightly to the social and legal institutions of the community and rendered responsive to its needs.

Binding the courts to the community in this fashion helped to open them up to emerging social and political movements within the community. Boston's courts in the early nineteenth century had been isolated by the absence of such ties, but as they slowly developed during the antebellum period, the courts were transformed from autonomous institutions that administered the law with little regard for its social or economic consequences to responsive institutions that attempted to meld together the diverse elements of the community so that a commonwealth for all could be achieved.

The modern courts are closely attuned to currents within their communities, and this process was set in motion shortly after the Revolution but something has been lost in the process. Boston's criminal courts in the years before the Civil War were an integral part of a grand effort to build a New England commonwealth in the ultimate sense of that term. They worked closely with leaders in both the Massachusetts

State House and Boston City Hall to fashion a society that was guided by elevated purpose but that was also democratic and responsive to the vision and aspirations of the people. Not all the public figures in Boston's courts understood this vision, but some did (Josiah Quincy, Emory Washburn, and Lemuel Shaw, for example), and they worked hard to shape their community to that end. The lower criminal courts were definitely legal institutions, but they were also part of a larger movement to make Boston and its citizens into an effective self-governing body that pursued a wholesome and humane path.

The leading figures of the court system, particulary in the antebellum years, were committed to the larger purpose of the courts and focused their own action accordingly. It softened and sensitized their applications of the law and informed their responsiveness.

Something Has Been Lost

Today, the sense of a larger mission has largely disappeared from the courts. Though they remain deeply responsive, the modern courts and their officers are responsive, almost indiscriminantly, less governed by a sense of what is wholesome for the community than by a sense of what can be justified. Responsiveness without a broader vision of political and social purpose tends to be eclectic and diffuses its authority as it embraces disparate and occasionally peripheral issues.

This development can be most readily seen in the effort to develop a sound juvenile justice system. As delinquency develops, the juvenile's troubles with the family, neighborhood, and school become apparent. To control delinquency it is not enough to punish the delinquent. The courts must also reach out to the family, neighborhood, and school. But as the juvenile courts attempt to reform these groups, they move beyond the realm of law toward a set of problems that are more social psychological. They also begin handling adolescents whose offending has only been trivial. Can adolescents whose delinquency has not yet ripened be dealt with authoritatively via the court and its social programs?

The juvenile court has been drawn into a whole range of activities to which legal skills are only remotely relevant. When a responsive court attempts to prevent delinquency without a clear concept of what kind of community it wants to create, it often gets bogged down in debates regarding ends, means, and relative worth. Responsiveness without a sense of ultimate purpose is likely to spread itself thin, to be arbitrary, and ultimately to become oppressive.

We left Boston's criminal courts in 1850 while they were still struggling to install a new commonwealth. Today, they have largely lost that ideal and along with it any sense of a broad, humane mission. As Boston's criminal courts moved into the twentieth century, the earlier vision of a commonwealth was lost; and with all their legal professionalism, the lower courts lost their sense of mission. They devolved from a highminded responsiveness to a curious type of superficial responsiveness—a kind of autonomy that is unpredictable, eccentric, and controversial. They need a social philosophy growing out of the New England's heritage that can steer the courts through today's thickets of secularism and fragmented politics to a justice that unites more than it divides.

A Burgeoning Caseload

Another factor in the modernizing of Boston's lower courts was the growing case loads of both courts. In response to these pressures the Police Court added two court clerks in the 1840s, and the Municipal Court added an assistant prosecutor in 1852. The structures of both courts were becoming more open and diverse, providing more opportunity for specialization and fragmentation, but even more important, the growing case load forced both courts to shed their trivial cases. As the truly minor cases were eliminated, a new tier of minor cases became "trivialized" and the normal crimes of the modern era began to appear (Sudnow 1965). Instead of assault and battery, snowballing, smoking cigars in public, or spitting on the sidewalk, the lower courts today are trivializing larceny, purse snatching, and auto theft.

The burgeoning case load, moreover, forced the courts to specialize their functions. In 1855 the Municipal Court became the Superior Court, and in 1866 the Police Court was reorganized as the Municipal Court. The new Superior Court assumed the felony jurisdiction of the old Municipal Court, and the new Municipal Court took the misdemeanor jurisdictions of both the old Municipal Court and the Police Court. In addition, seven district courts today handle the same criminal jurisdiction as the new Municipal Court outside of Boston's downtown district. Thus, the two lower courts of preindustrial Boston have today become nine.

These changes in Boston's courts were part of a worldwide drift in which routine cases were differentiated from extraordinary cases, channelled into distinctive courts, and handled via very different procedures. Routine cases consisted for the most part of minor, "normal" crimes about which very little was in dispute. The defendant's case was weak, and the most important issue was not guilt or innocence but the level of punishment. Extraordinary cases included those rare disputes that raised a new legal issue about which there was as yet very little agreement. These cases focused on novel types of crime (liquor law violations in the 1830s, for example) or upon novel legal defenses such as Hinckley's insanity defense or De Lorean's claim of entrapment.

Routine cases are usually handled outside the courtroom via extralegal negotiations, for example, plea bargaining, while extraordinary cases are handled via lengthy jury trials using a full range of legal procedures and strategies. The first stream is usually dealt with in the lowest criminal court, while the second is tried in an intermediate trial court. In Boston today the Municipal Court handles most of the routine cases, though it also holds jury trials, while the Superior Court deals with the more important, contested cases.

This bifurcation of the criminal courts' case load is a general phenomenon found not only in many foreign countries but also in the civil courts as well (Friedman 1983, 18–40). Throughout the world there is a clear tendency for the routine cases to drift out of the courts into arbitration or even mediation. Just as routine criminal cases are disposed of via plea bargaining, routine divorce, auto accident, and work place injuries are today often handled via mediation or arbitration.

When a new kind of case makes its appearance in the courts, the trial courts determine the guidelines of its resolution, and once these have been firmly established in case law, the need for a trial diminishes and extralegal methods of resolution take over.

The courts concern themselves primarily with novel, important cases that reflect the shifting social and legal currents of society. When these cases are no longer controversial, they often no longer require the ceremonial authority of the courts, and they drift into extralegal channels. Since "normal" cases make-up the bulk of the case load in most courts, the case loads of the lowest criminal courts usually grow at a slower pace than the population. Normal cases are constantly sifted out of the lowest court into extralegal channels. The case loads of the intermediate courts that handle the extraordinary flow will wax and wane depending on the volume of new cases that are generated by the changing community or changing legal system. This process of bifurcation and maturation is clearly evident in the development of Boston's modern legal system.

All in all we have traced here the transformation of Boston's lower courts during the first half of the nineteenth century as the city around them changed. It was the changing social fabric and the city's evolving crime pattern that prompted the modernization of Boston's courts in the first place, but it was also the courtroom work groups and the activist judges that enabled them to evolve hand-in-hand with their changing sociopolitical environment. They brought in their wake the innovation of plea bargaining and the vast expansion of the prosecutor's powers, streamlining of the court's jurisdiction, the easing of sentences, and above all, the emergence of the courts and law schools as the conscience of American life.

When the courts were more isolated in the early part of the nineteenth century, they were peripheral institutions in which change was slow and hesitant. With the activist judges guiding the way and the work groups quietly arranging things, the pace of legal development picked up noticeably during the antebellum period.

Relative to that time our lower criminal courts today still deal with an enormous variety of minor offenders, but they have narrowed their jurisdiction to routine crimes for which the appropriate outcome is well-established. As they have targeted these offenders, they have abandoned jury trials almost entirely, and due process is rarely heeded in their deliberations. Worst of all, however, they have lost most of their ties with the higher courts that keep the common law tradition alive.

Today's lower courts have developed a kind of legal and moral isolation, a kind of autonomy, such that the legal rules and doctrines of the higher courts, the sentencing policies of the state, or even the sentiments of the community play little part in framing their methods or dispositions (Feeley 1979). Work groups, with the prosecutor at their center, have become dominant. Moreover, these work groups are largely self-contained, paying little heed to the standards of the larger profession. They are guided by just two priorities: the timely, efficient processing of cases, and responsibility to one's professional colleagues. If these goals are achieved, the lower courts have little to fear from the rest of the legal profession or even from society at large. Though they have become basically a private forum for sentencing minor offenders, no one except for a few stodgy academicians who feel a certain nostalgia for the authority, formality, and legality of premodern criminal courts will complain as long as they discharge this responsibility effectively.

8
The Future of America's Responsive Courts

Boston's court system began to assume a modern form during the early decades of the nineteenth century when the city's leadership was visionary, and the people's confidence was high. Americans were committed to building a new nation based on the ideals of justice and liberty for all, and Bostonians were blest by a steady succession of strong leaders—John Adams, Josiah Quincy, Emory Washburn, and Lemuel Shaw, for example—who were wise in statecraft. It was a good time to chart a new path in government, and the politico-legal system that emerged in the early years of the nineteenth century was committed not simply to individual rights and justice but to social and economic advance as well. It was a responsive politico-legal system that turned the best offices of the state to the community and its needs.

The legal system that emerged in Boston, however, had hardly been launched before it began to founder on the rocks of social conflict and factionalism. It had been organized in the decades after the Revolution on a solid foundation of Calvinism and the social contract. But early in the nineteenth century the sharp divisions of the Jacksonian and antebellum eras made a commonwealth based on a broad moral consensus difficult if not impossible. Frictions among ethnic, religious, and political groups made firm agreements on broad goals and policies difficult if not impossible.

In addition most forms of crime were headed toward Civil War era highs, and to make matters worse, pockets of citizenry—the Catholic Irish, and proslavery groups—were losing confidence in the city's political institutions. For the first time alienation, deviance, and crime were becoming urgent issues for city government to deal with.

To meet these several challenges Boston's criminal justice system began to assume a distinctly modern form. A proactive police force was assembled, not simply to quell riots, but also to assert the courts' responsive rulings in the community. A public school system was inaugurated to insure a competent, responsible body politic, and a whole host of institutions and programs were established to supervise adolescents who resisted the regimen of their schools. Plea bargaining was invented as a convenient method of paring down the volume of minor offenses in both the Police Court and the Municipal Court. The police swept the streets free of vagrants, prostitutes, and drunks, while the courts pursued a regulatory policy toward the city's brothel keepers and tavern owners. Boston urgently needed a new criminal justice system to reinforce civil order, because growing numbers of its citizens were unfamiliar with their responsibilities in the Commonwealth.

The state courts focused upon business activities to insure that they remained properly aligned with the ideals and purposes of the Commonwealth. Boston's police grew rapidly during the 1850s to a force of nearly two hundred to insure compliance with court initiatives, and the prosecutor with his case load mounting skyward emerged as a key figure in crime control policy. All this was accomplished in the twenty-five years between 1830 and 1854, and in quick order a legal system in close coordination with Boston's governing institutions assumed major responsibility for justice and the common good.

The roots of these changes in the city's government were to be found ultimately in its emerging social structure. Adolescents were facing a new regimen in the public school system, and those youngsters who rejected its demands could not be allowed to roam freely in the neighborhoods. The self-discipline of the whole hinged upon the punishment of the few (Foucault 1977, part 1).

Massive dislocations in the adult sphere were also at work. New forms of manufacturing offered broad opportunity to those with innovative but risky ideas. Some prospered, and many failed. It was a dangerous time frought with opportunity, but either way growing numbers of adults and children found themselves with little income and few obligations to occupy their time. These vagrants and their wayward activities also needed to be disciplined.

A well-ordered community, in which nearly everyone plays an integral part in a finely woven social fabric, such as prerevolutionary Boston, has little need for a formal legal system that can catch and punish minor offenders. Such a community can do all this effectively via informal social structures already in place. But a rapidly changing community in which many anonymous people attempt to navigate within a porous, permissive social structure, such as Boston was becoming, needs not only self-disciplined and purposeful citizens to do its work but also a *pervasive* criminal justice system for apprehending and redirecting the many who are still relatively undisciplined and without sound goals.

In Boston an aggressive police force and the diligent county prosecutor, Samuel Parker, faced an immense work load during this period and sought legitimate ways of making it manageable. Houses of Industry and Correction and Charlestown Prison were available for rootless adults, and a wide variety of new juvenile agencies provided supervision for truants and wayward adolescents who roamed Boston's streets and alleys. This emerging criminal justice system was needed to reinforce the evolving social structure by punishing and correcting those who had not yet learned to accommodate themselves to its structure.

In all likelihood it also contributed to the evolution of Boston's deviant subculture as well (see Cohen 1985; Ferdinand, 1989). As the criminal justice system collected a broad selection of Boston's growing deviant population into tightly packed custodial institutions, it enabled their inmates to socialize one another into the byways of crime and delinquency. In addition the newer, rehabilitative reforms undermined older institutions by diverting many of their more tractable inmates to newer programs, leaving only the most difficult and antisocial offenders for them to deal with.

As populations of these older institutions became more antisocial, their programs calcified, and they became more punitive. Thus, as Boston's criminal justice system was assembled in the antebellum period and brought an expanding deviant population under control, it also contributed to a hardening of both its older institutions and the most antisocial segment of its deviant population. Its new criminal justice system helped to create a more antisocial and sophisticated deviant population.

For a time after the Civil War the city's Yankee leadership was still exercising control on behalf of the ideals of the founding fathers, but they were intensely aware of the differences between themselves and the common people and were becoming pessimistic about their ability to guide the community toward these goals. By 1880 at least one hundred Irish-born officers were members of Boston's Police Department (Lane 1967, 197), by the mid-1880s the Irish had taken control of the Democratic Party in the state, and in 1884 Hugh O'Brien, Democrat, was elected mayor of the city. The legislature reacted in 1885 by giving control of the police to the governor who was still reliably Yankee (Lane 1967, chap. 11).

The handwriting was on the wall. Many Yankees lost interest in city government and focused instead on protecting their cultural niche. As Baltzell (1964, 112–13) indicates:

> Many members of this class, of old-stock prestige and waning power, eventually allied themselves with the Progressive movement. Many also like Henry Adams, withdrew almost entirely from the world of power. The "decent people," as Edith Wharton once put it, increasingly "fell back on sport and culture." And this sport and culture was now to be reinforced by a series of fashionable and patrician protective associations.

Boston's social elite began to build private schools for their children, summer resorts in Maine, private men's clubs in the city, private golf clubs in the suburbs, and to think about moving from Boston's Back Bay to Brookline. Some persisted in their commitment to the commonwealth ideal (see Baltzell 1964, 144–49). Charles W. Eliot as Harvard's President, for example, guided the university to national stature during this period, but most gave up on Boston and retreated to the nearby suburbs.

Their commitment to a commonwealth based on a body politic united in pursuit of justice, liberty, and the common good had nearly dissolved. Other nations, for example, Israel most recently, but much earlier revolutionary France as well, after an early phase of self-confidence and idealism, have also faltered on the destructive shoals of factionalism.

Ironically, just as its Yankee leadership began to lose heart, the criminal justice system in Boston managed to gain control over its wayward juveniles and rootless adults. Crime and delinquency declined after the turmoil of the Civil War was past and continued downward until the early 1960s (Ferdinand 1967, 1989), despite a massive new flood of immigrants from eastern Europe and Italy. The extaordinary growth of New England's economy after the Civil War played a large part in this decline by easing the integration of the newcomers into the Boston community, although the growing effectiveness of the city's criminal justice system was probably also a factor.

Nevertheless, the loss of moral consensus in Boston meant that its political leaders could no longer muster support for the idea of a commonwealth. Where consensus was weak and the body politic suspicious, the leaders' symbolism fell on deaf ears. Policies had to be short range, and they had to answer directly the practical needs of the masses. Class and ethnic politics replaced the idea of a commonwealth, and city government took an entirely different tact. Machine politics became the order of the day, culminating with the election of James Michael Curley as Mayor in 1913.

Some Yankees still found their way into politics at the state level, where they continued to pursue the idea of the commonwealth, and Boston's courts were still attended by Yankee lawyers (but rarely by Yankee judges) pursuing responsive paths within the community. The rules had changed, and broad support for a government devoted to high-minded ideals and institutional improvement had largely disappeared from the city.

Responsive Courts in Twentieth Century America

In the late nineteenth century those Calvinists in New England, the midwest, and the far west, who, consciously or unconsciously, still followed the philosophy of John Locke, formed themselves into a Progressive Party to keep their vision alive (see Hofstadter 1955: part IV). They favored close restrictions on immigration, a determined acculturation of the immigrant classes to bourgeois values, honesty and efficiency in government, a reining in of corporate power, a professional police, conservation of the wilderness, and a strong stance in foreign affairs. They were confident in the ability of government to guide the people toward a better society, but they no longer believed that the people were a vital, inventive resource. The people needed more than ever sound, enlightened government.

But the solution, as it often does, became the problem. Leadership in the courts and in government at both the state and federal level had become estranged from the common people. A progressive (but elitist, mean-spirited) government could still pursue the welfare of the community, but without a good sense of exactly what was needed. Political elites in government and the courts sometimes viewed the public as alien and even intractable, and antisemitism and social Darwinism found broad support among the Brahmins of New England (Baltzell 1964, 90–93). During the post-Civil War period and on into the twentieth century, state and local governments settled into a kind of apathy, while the federal government dealt in quick succession with Reconstruction, the dislocations of rapid industrialization, World War I, and then the Great Depression and World War II.

Whenever government strayed from such purely legal issues as antitrust laws, tariffs, the federal reserve system, or tax policy, into Prohibition, low-income housing, aid to mothers of dependent children, Lyndon Johnson's War on Poverty, or abortion it encountered serious difficulties. State and federal leaders knew very well how to fashion laws and programs to accomplish specific legal or political goals, but they often had severe blindspots when it came to social reform. A government of professionals and scientists is not especially skillful at social engineering, we now know, and broad-gauged programs that deal with people and their needs often cause as many problems as they solve (see Glazer 1988, chap. 8).

The specialists often follow a different set of values than the population targeted for reform; they often do not know practically the problems they are reforming; they view the problems narrowly; and the reforms usually have little impact on *their* (the reformer's) own lives. Thus social reforms authored by governmental experts tend to be surgical, brash, and experimental (Posten 1971).

Responsive government was founded initially on the concept of a commonwealth in which an innovative, self-reliant body politic proposed programs to its government primarily for the common good. To be effective the ministers of government must appreciate the needs of the body politic and understand the goals of the people. When social and political elites are isolated from the people, and when society becomes so fragmented that there are few points of consensus, government can no longer be broadly responsive. Its major programs often become controversial and imbalanced.

The federal courts encountered much the same problem in the post World War II period as they sought to respond to social needs. The courts took the lead in the 1950s in confronting racial discrimination. Legally sanctioned discrimination was contrary to the equal protection clause of the Fourteenth Amendment, and though school desegregation aroused fierce resistance in many white communities, ultimately all sections embraced it, and today legally based racial discrimination is discredited.

Court ordered busing on behalf of racial integration, however, encountered stiff resistance, particularly in Boston where it bypassed middle-class schools in favor of schools in working class districts. Bostonians wondered out loud (Logue 1983) why the Irish working class (and not the middle class) had to bear the brunt of school integration? A city that had had a long history of support for oppressed blacks was transformed in a few months into a caldron of ugly race hatred.

Much the same happened when the courts sought to protect due process from police excess. Nearly everyone outside of policing endorsed the Supreme Court's decisions culminating in the exclusionary rule, based as they were on a clear constitutional mandate, but here, too, specialists (constitutional lawyers and criminologists) in the courts were attempting to deal with issues that were very broad and for which their legal expertise alone was not sufficient. The courts viewed both of these issues (racial discrimination and police abuse of a suspect's rights) in narrow legal or scientific terms and were unmindful of their broader social implications (see Horowitz 1977). To some extent these difficulties stemmed from an inherent problem courts have in evaluating multifaceted social issues.

Legal due process is effective in sifting the truth from sharply differing accounts of specific events, but in focusing narrowly on immediate, specific events, the courts severely limit their ability to find the meaning of events that carry wide ramifications beyond an immediate web (see particularly Horowitz 1977, chap. 2). For example, they like to deal with "ripe" or sharply defined issues. They need witnesses that have exact information regarding an issue, focused protagonists, and issues with an immediate legal remedy. Courts usually will not consider vague problems with no clear offender, victim, or plaintiff, or evidence that deals only indirectly with the issue at hand. Hearsay evidence and conjecture about the broad implications of events are rejected. This means in practice that many social problems with broad significance cannot be dealt with comprehensively via the courts.

Furthermore, even though benchmark cases that have spearheaded reforms, for example, *In re Gault* (1967), are typically the most extreme of their class, their outcomes apply to all relevant cases including those where the legal texture is vastly different. In *Lau v. Nichols* (1973) the Supreme Court ruled that school districts must provide bilingual instruction when a substantial number of students in the school do not understand English. Although the Civil Rights Act of 1964 intended that lessons in English should be provided where needed, in practice it came to mean that students would receive instruction in their own language if they did not understand English. Furthermore, although the students in *Lau v. Nichols* were Chinese, and the school had done almost nothing to meet their needs, those affected were primarily Spanish speaking, and the schools they attended often had a much better record in providing instructional needs. Thus, *Lau v. Nichols* designated the curriculum for a broad range of ethnic groups far removed from the original case (see Horowitz 1977, 16–17, 41).

Legal remedies tend to be balanced in favor of the complainant, sometimes punishing violators out of proportion to the offense. In the criminal courts the Miranda rulings force all police officers, not just those who have routinely violated suspects' constitutional rights, to repeat precisely the Miranda incantation. Similarly, the exclusionary rule (until recent reforms) released guilty defendants who were the victim of inadvertent missteps by officers sincerely attempting to follow its requirements.

Finally, court-mandated reforms are difficult to correct, even when they clearly have unwanted consequences, because they are part of a broad web of rulings that are difficult, it not impossible, to extricate from the law (Horowitz 1977, 51–56). The Mirauda decision has by this time inspired such a large number of auxiliary decisions that taken together they constitute a substantial doctrine in our criminal procedure. It would be difficult to uproot the Mirauda ruling for any reason.

In sum court-based reforms are narrowly framed, blind to important implications, and cumbersome to change. However important court based reforms may be, they contain significant drawbacks as a way of achieving social reform.

As the civil rights revolution took hold in the 1960s and 70s, for example, talented blacks and others enjoyed new opportunities to live, be educated, or employed wherever they saw fit. These new guarantees, however, also meant that those already mired in poverty sank into even more desperate misery (Wilson 1987). As middle-class blacks moved from the inner city, they left behind those who were profoundly impoverished, and the lingering problems of minority neighborhoods were thereby concentrated and intensified. Inner city schools became jungles, drug-financed gangs took over the streets, and life in the inner city became unbearable.

Each of these problems in the inner city predated the Civil Rights revolution of the 1950s and 1960s, and other factors, for example, the shift in the broader economy from manufacturing to service jobs were also a factor. The flight of talent and leadership from the inner city, which the Civil Rights revolution fostered, weakened the inner city to such an extent that these other problems were compounded and all but overwhelmed the weakened inner city.

Civil rights guarantees to all Americans are paramount, for they are the very core of our society. Hopefully the misery of the inner city ghetto will be only temporary, but that is not the point.

The point is that the likely impact of Civil Rights decisions on the *inner city* was never considered in the court hearings, because it could not become part of the legal argument. Nevertheless, the desperate condition of lower class Blacks is of social significance, and a society that ignores such facts in designing social reform does so at its own peril. A bias toward court-based reform, as opposed to legislative reform, makes narrowly framed, short-range solutions almost inevitable.

In this case, however, there was no alternative. In the United States racial segregation was much too controversial in the 1950s for the Congress to deal with alone. If the legislature *can* find a way to act, however, the debating process permits a more balanced review and greater opportunity for subsequent refinements than due process in the court.

Deeply divisive issues are avoided by legislatures because compromise is intensely unpopular on both sides of the debate. An acceptable outcome is unlikely, and protracted, destructive debates can engulf less intense issues that can and should be resolved. If, however, difficult problems bear upon basic rights and contain a clear legal dimension, they can be quickly resolved by appealing directly to the relevant law through the courts. Thus, some difficult issues that would be impossible to handle in the legislature may be readily dealt with in a legal forum (Horowitz 1978, 11).

In addition to the fact that such cases afford court officers an opportunity to develop new legal doctrines and find new threads of meaning in earlier decisions, they also promise an enduring settlement of gnawing social issues. Where the legitimacy of the law is unquestioned and its meaning inescapable, the need for change can be awakened in the body politic. In such cases the courts perform an invaluable educational function, pointing out the meaning of the law and gaining through their authority a broad shift in public behavior.

Broad social changes that attended the *Brown v. Topeka Board of Education*, 1954 illustrate this point. These social changes eased a difficult racial issue and pointed to broad reforms that could ease it even further. At first the decision was controversial and stirred bitter opposition, but ultimately its wisdom was accepted, and deep-seated racial tensions that polarized the nation subsided to some extent. Only the Supreme Court could have taken the lead here, because the state legislatures and the Congress were too divided to act. The authority of the Supreme Court was needed to change engrained social habits, and by finding a constitutional basis for *Brown v. Topeka Board of Education*, the Supreme Court was able to persuade virtually all Americans that racial integration was the best course in the long run. The courts can play a broad educational role in society by resolving intractable conflicts, if the issue and the relevant law are clear. Some issues that cannot be resolved via political debate in the legislatures may yield readily to a legal decision.

Some court decisions, however, can lead down an opposite path. Since key court decisions often repudiate the claims of at least part of the body politic, if the court's legal basis is not well founded, the court's decisions may only enflame the body politic and entrench the divided factions even further. In 1856 the Supreme Court handed down a narrowly framed decision, *Dred Scott v. Sanford*, that seemed to question some of the fundamental civil rights of the Constitution. It enraged the North and strengthened demands for the abolition of slavery. The Civil War became inevitable. If the Supreme Court frames key decisions that are based weakly on a narrow interpretation of the law, resistance will grow in a divided legislature, and pressures will build to correct the court's biases. Responsive legal systems, then, may contain the seeds of their own evolution, especially when the larger society becomes fragmented. Under these conditions legal institutions tend to alternate between responsive and autonomous phases.

Responsive government works best within a cohesive, purposeful body politic, but in fragmented, highly stratified societies autonomous courts and interest group politics are probably more successful. During wartime or other national crises such as economic depressions, the body politic often unites behind national goals; but during peacetime and prosperity, factions tend to become more strident. Structural change as well as national issues can trigger fluctuations between responsive and autonomous legal systems.

Robert Bork and Responsive Courts

Robert H. Bork, the 1987 unsuccessful Supreme Court nominee, has an alternative explanation for the attenuation of legitimacy that responsive courts experience. Although Bork writes with a definite agenda in mind, his ideas are the outcome of a careful analysis and bear directly on the problems of responsive courts.

According to Bork (1990, 69–73) the legal realists, a school of thought that sought to demystify legal institutions in the 1930s, laid the foundation for social activism in the Warren court in the 1950s. They taught that the awesome majesty of the legal system was little more than a convenient myth. The law, the judges, and the legal system were human institutions performed by human beings and deserved no more respect than many other less exalted institutions. Some judges were better than others, but all were human and committed all too human errors. Science, logic, and consistency in the law were evident more often in the ideal than in practice.

This view (see Gilmore 1977, 87–91; Bechtler 1978) was championed by Karl Llewellyn at Columbia University's Law School, and by the 1940s it had a wide following, including at least two Supreme Court Justices, Hugo Black and William O. Douglas.[1] Black and Douglas, by contemporary account (Schlesinger 1947, 201–2), were governed in their courtroom deliberations more by political intuition and values than legal doctrine. The proper course, Bork says (1990, 71), is as follows:

> Any lawyer who is honest with himself knows that he often intuits a conclusion and then goes to work to see if legal reasoning supports it.... A judge will have such intuitions [even] in cases where he has not the remotest personal preference about the outcome.... But the honest ... lawyer or ... judge, also changes his mind when the materials with which he works press him away from his first tenative conclusion.

Black and Douglas followed a different path. They forced their legal reasoning to reflect their intuitions, and their opinions, says Bork (1990, 70), regularly shredded the fabric of legal logic. Such disregard for the rule of law showed the way for an activist Warren Supreme Court ten years later.

If (as the legal realists claimed) the law is not simply a science that yields logical conclusions, but more basically an institution governed by judicial predilections, those who are straightforward in their subjectivity are at least as honorable as those who hide behind mysticism to disguise their human fallibility. Legal realism, by demystifying the law, provides an excuse for political activism in the courts.

Bork's complaint, however, is not that Black and Douglas flaunted their subjectivity. Rather, they used the constitution as a cloak for their personal preferences. They maintained an appearance of legal objectivity while pursuing a more personal agenda. Such deception is difficult for the public to detect and very difficult to correct.

The very first case of the Warren court, *Brown v. Board of Education* (1954), was also its greatest triumph. Although the Warren court failed to give a sound legal argument for its ruling against the Topeka Board of Education, such an argument was, nevertheless, available in the equal protection clause of the Fourteenth Amendment, says Bork (1990, 75).

Based on social scientific studies, the court argued that school segregation fostered a sense of inferiority among black children. Forcing children by law into psychologically damaging environments favors some over others, and thereby violates the equal protection clause of the Fourteenth Amendment according to the Warren court. In other words, since racial segregation in the public schools is psychologically damaging, it is unconstitutional.

But the Fourteenth Amendment was originally focused on the states and their legal codes, not on racial segregation and its harmful results (Bork 1990, 74–83). Nevertheless, it did intend equality before the law. Legal codes that affect races unequally are unconstitutional whatever their psychological impact, and this was the clear intention of the framers of the Fourteenth Amendment. The framers were not concerned with racial segregation as such because, after all, it was practiced widely in the north at the time and could easily have been addressed had the framers' wished to do so. It was not clear in 1868 when the Fourteenth Amendment was written that segregation meant unequal public facilities. Racial segregation in that era posed no special problem to the Fourteenth Amendment.

By the 1950s, however, it was indisputable that segregated facilities meant unequal facilities, and this is the argument that should have been used, according to Bork (1990, 75–77). In focusing on the psychological impact of segregation, the Warren court gave the wrong signal to the legal profession. It did not condemn unequal facilities as such, which would have been more consistent with the Fourteenth Amendment, and it showed that much can be achieved in constitutional cases, even via decisions that are not carefully grounded in constitutional law, if the conclusions coincide closely with prevailing legal opinion.

In this vein, according to Bork, the Supreme Court proceeded to eliminate racial segregation in a variety of settings, and incidentally set the stage for similar loose performances from the Burger and Rehnquist courts in other areas. In *Bolling v. Sharpe* (1954) in which school segregation laws in the District of Columbia were challenged, the Warren court confronted the troublesome fact that the equal protection clause of the Fourteenth Amendment focused mainly on the states and, therefore, held no jurisdiction in this case. It deftly sidestepped this problem, however, by proclaiming that the Fifth Amendment, which *was* applicable to the District of Columbia, contained (by analogy with the Fourteenth Amendment) an equal protection intent. This decision had no precedent nor historical basis and was little more than judicial fiat, says Bork (1990, 83).

In a series of cases involving the election districts of several states—*Baker v. Carr* (1962), *Reynolds v. Sims* (1964), *Lucas v. Forty-Fourth General Assembly* (1964)—the Warren court ruled again in all three that the equal protection clause of the Fourteenth Amendment governed. Equal protection under the law meant that each person's vote was to be equal to every other person's vote, that is, that election districts had to contain the same number of voters. No matter that the Congress, which was defined by the constitution, does not follow such a rule in the Senate, nor that a majority of the states at the time did not follow such a rule in their legislatures, nor that a variety of other electoral methods could also ensure equal protection under the law. Bork (1990, 78–79) suggests that this willingness of the Warren court to base its arguments on questionable reasoning not only amounted to a judicial power grab but also encouraged subsequent courts to follow the same path.

Predictably, then, the Burger court ruled unanimously in *Griggs v. Duke Power Co.* (1971) that the Civil Rights Act of 1964 prohibited the use of unvalidated ability tests in screening job applicants where only disproportionately small numbers of minorities were retained in the applicant pool. The Burger court interpreted the language of the act to mean that inadvertent discrimination against minorities was also forbidden, even though the Congress clearly did not intend to prohibit discriminatory tests as long as they were not designed consciously to screen-out minorities (see Horowitz 1977, 14).

Original Intent

To avoid courts and justices that are ruled more by a personal agenda than legal doctrine, the courts must be bound by *original intent*, by neutral principles interpreted and applied neutrally (Bork 1990, 143-60). Since the circumstances at the time a law is passed defined its meaning and since that is usually the only time any law is ratified by democratic process, the original intent of the law's framers determines its authority. To assess accurately its legal authority, therefore, it is necessary to go back to the framers' explanation of the law. If that proves impossible, the only alternative is to reconsider the issue in the legislature via public debate.

Moreover, where the issue has changed substantially, as in the Second Amendment's guarantee of the right to bear arms, a new debate is all the more necessary. It is not sufficient, says Bork, to reinterpret the constitution or early legislation to fit modern circumstances, however convenient that might be. If the Supreme Court is to frame new law, it must first find a bonafide precedent or a sound constitutional basis.

Using original intention wherever feasible insures that any given case will be judged by rules derived independently of the case, that is, by neutral principles interpreted and applied neutrally. Judges in arriving at legal decisions are forced to select the appropriate doctrines and then to show their connection with the case at hand. Both steps must be carried out without bias.

The real problem lies in defining the meaning of legal doctrine. A judge's bias in selecting or applying legal doctrines is more easily detected and overturned than a subtle distortion of the meaning of legal doctrine, particularly when it is done by a Supreme Court justice.

Bork (1990, chap. 7) argues that although judges must use legal doctrines according to their framers' intentions, they must also exercise skill and discretion in applying just the right doctrines to the case at hand. Judges are free to extend existing doctrine to novel cases, but Bork would restrict their ability to redefine legal doctrine.

The distinction between extending doctrine to novel cases as opposed to reinterpreting doctrine to fit new cases, though clear in principle, is by no means clear in practice. For some, the rights of privacy are very clearly implied in the constitution in its guarantees of freedom of speech, freedom from unwarranted search or seizure, and freedom of religion. If government is permitted to regulate private discussions regarding these questions, the freedoms themselves will be seriously impaired. For Bork, however, the failure of the constitution to mention specifically the right of privacy in broader questions such as abortion can only be remedied by a forthright constitutional amendment on that subject.

Bork insists that *new* doctrines should only be derived via democratic process, that is, through duely endorsed new constitutional amendments or by appropriate legislative process. Judge-made doctrine, which enjoys a long tradition in the common law, should only be a synthesis or clarification of meanings unmistakably implicit within existing doctrine. Judicial interpretations that distort or change the meaning of doctrine are illegitimate. The best judges show ingenuity and skill in linking old doctrine to new cases, while keeping the sense of old doctrine intact.

Problems arise when judges distort the meaning of old doctrine. Not only is it egoistic, but it endangers the law. Novel *doctrines* that have never been ratified by a legislative vote (as Supreme Court justices' predilections have not) are likely sooner or later to become controversial. To avoid politically motivated attacks on the Supreme Court and a redefinition of its purpose in more political terms, it must hew strictly to a legal and not a political agenda.[2]

The grey area wherein it is difficult to say *whether* a novel legal solution is a judge's skillful use of old doctrine or a judicial power grab is where Bork and his critics part.

Still, Bork has a point. It is easy to see how responsive judges in their zeal to resolve troublesome social problems could be beguiled by their own legal dexterity to fashion new doctrines out of old that are more art than substance. Such temptations would be particularly common among judges and lawyers in a responsive legal system.

Thus, as a responsive legal system begins to deal with difficult modern issues in ways that are less legal than social—with such issues as affirmative action or abortion, for example—factions become intransigent in their respective beliefs, and the hoped for legal "solution" simply spurs both sides to greater fanaticism. In this way the ideal of responsive legal systems helping the people to fulfill their sociocultural potential becomes untenable.

As their responsive decisions come under attack, the courts will pull in their horns and concentrate on noncontroversial cases that can be readily decided by noncontroversial legal doctrines and unimpeachable reasoning. In short they will become autonomous courts that draw a sharp distinction between legal and political questions. They will make full use of legal science in settling bonafide legal issues, and they will avoid troublesome social or political issues, leaving them to the legislature.

Legislatures must remain in close contact with a multifaceted public and therefore, are probably better suited, other things being equal, than the courts for dealing with difficult political problems at the local level. If there is a common ground, the legislature will find it and fashion a compromise that is acceptable. The resultant legislation will necessarily be focused, because support dwindles and opposition grows as it becomes far reaching. Within this restriction, the legislature is likely to take the lead in whatever social development is pursued.[3]

When responsive courts drift from a solid constitutional basis into sociolegal jurisprudence where their rulings may become controversial and broadly unwelcome, the legislature is likely to assume greater authority, the courts are likely to retreat to their legal preserve, and a responsive legal system will become more autonomous.

The Decline of Responsiveness in the United States

In Boston, to be sure, the courts have traced a more even path. The immigrants that Boston's nineteenth-century Brahmins so despised have now fashioned a new vision of the commonwealth, and in 1990 Boston had a Greek-American governor (Michael Dukakis) and an Irish-American mayor (Raymond Flynn) who would have, except for their names, been indistinguishable from their progressive, nineteenth-century Yankee antecedents in the State House and City Hall. They still feel a responsibility to govern well for the benefit of all, and the area's educational institutions still provide a body politic devoted to the development of enlightened initiatives.

The fact remains that Boston today includes large numbers of working- and lower-class Irish, Italian, and black people for whom the idea of a commonwealth is remote. Populist politicians pressing for limitations on minorities find a willing audience there, as do strident black nationalists.[4]

For these reasons it seems likely that Massachusetts government and law will continue along a responsive path, but that responsive initiatives will increasingly strike sour notes, particularly with ethnic, working-class groups. Conservative leaders will denounce these policies, and support for them will weaken. The credibility of responsive leaders will decline, and populist pressures to move back to autonomous law will build, that is, to a legal system in which the law governs within its narrow domain but is cautious outside.

Conservative government and law are returning to California, and progressive initiatives on a variety of fronts, for example, capital punishment, auto insurance, torts and contracts, and state taxes, have already been reversed. Even though the commonwealth tradition is probably stronger in Massachusetts, it is likely that a similar reversal will occur there as well.

If this analysis is correct, it carries broad implications for the courts and the United States as a whole. The era of social reform and renewal that began in the 1930s with Franklin D. Roosevelt's initiatives and continued in the 1950s under Chief Justice Earl Warren and in the 1960s by Presidents John Kennedy and Lyndon Johnson is over. The Congress will play a larger role in charting the course of government, leaving the Supreme Court and the president to move in less controversial directions.

The activism of the Supreme Court under Rehnquist has already slackened significantly, and recently President George Bush has become noticeably more cautious on domestic issues. In this conservative climate the Congress as well will be hesitant to pursue bold initiatives. Thus, the very young, the poor, minorities, the very old, social deviants, and the handicapped, the focus of much recent governmental attention, will be left more to their own resources, and innovative, ameliorative programs will become largely the responsibility of private groups and foundations.

The courts and the rest of criminal justice still face a major task in developing the doctrinal basis of many of the legal reforms of the last half century. To what extent does the Civil Rights Revolution of the 1960s affect the civil rights of nonminorities? Does affirmative action, for example, conform to the equal protection clause of the Fourteenth Amendment with regard to nonminorities? If so, what is the doctrinal basis for such a conclusion?

If our personal ideals and the law don't coincide here, changes in the law may be in order. These changes, however, will be more lasting and more effective if they reflect the will of the majority and have passed the test of public debate and democratic vote. They will also be more nearly neutral in their interpretation and application.

The place of the Miranda limitations and the exclusionary rule also provoke some uneasiness, and not simply among law enforcement spokesmen. How might they be modified in light of the large number of Supreme Court decisions that define these two doctrines? Could both the cause of justice and the rights of suspects be served better through penalties administered to law enforcement offenders by their supervisors, as is the case in much of western Europe, or by court invalidation of tainted evidence. And if the former, how can police supervisors be persuaded to adopt a constitutional perspective in defining administrative guidelines?

More broadly, what are the limits of legal reform? Even though some issues seem slated for a legal remedy by the ready availability of prominent legal precedent, other issues are better resolved by political debate. How can we tell which is which?

Much depends upon the state of the body politic. Fundamental issues that would be impossible to resolve in a deeply divided legislature but that contain a clear legal mandate may yield readily to a sound court decision, for example, *Brown v. Board of Education*, 1954, especially where the law already enjoys the allegiance of all responsible parties.

Where the body politic is unified, a responsive legal system provides a convenient avenue for resolving basic issues in society, especially where the law is directly relevant. Under these conditions the legal system should work closely with the legislature, undertaking basic reform authoritatively and promptly but leaving basic political issues to the legislature.

As reforms become institutionalized and less controversial, as for example, collective bargaining did in the 1930s, refining them becomes the responsibility of the legislature. When the political elite are in full sympathy with the people and know intimately how to shape social and political institutions so that nearly everyone can see the benefits of basic initiatives, responsive courts work well.

A temptation, however, arises within such legal systems for judges and attorneys to undertake social engineering in resolving a variety of issues including some quite peripheral to the law. Responsive legal systems then become the focus of political pressure and are likely to revert to an autonomous form. In the long run political realities dictate the format of the law, and insofar as responsive courts tread on political ground, they will be drawn into the political process. Where their legal foundation is not strong, they will be politically vulnerable.

Where the body politic is deeply divided and the law fails to address key issues clearly, responsive law is apt to be controversial and ultimately ineffective. Under these conditions the legislature is in a better position to surmount divisive issues and arrange compromises that will allow government to move ahead with other problems. Whether an issue is dealt with via political debate in the legislature or by legal argument in the courts depends to some extent upon the nature of the issue and its politico-legal context.

Responsive legal institutions are most effective in coherent societies where the political process is relatively harmonious. In the United States responsive courts have tended to use their influence widely and in so doing they have become increasingly controversial. Activism in the courts seems to be in decline in the 1990s. At some future date responsive courts will no doubt rekindle their mandate, but for now their flame seems to be dimming.

Autonomous legal institutions are most effective where politics is adversarial. Their legal authority can be decisive in settling basic conflicts in society, but they must use their authority in social issues only sparingly. If they are not mindful of their inherent limitations, they too can come under attack. The Anglo-American political tradition has emphasized the virtue of limiting the use of legal authority in basic political conflicts with the result that today common law courts still enjoy an independence and a public confidence second to none in the world.

Appendix A: The Method

This research proceeded along a series of discrete steps. First, it was essential to determine both the suitability of the data for the purposes of this research and its availability. Second, it was important to develop the specific methods to be used in collecting these data. Third, the staff had to be recruited and trained. Fourth, the data needed to be collected and prepared for analysis; and fifth, the analysis of the data had to be carried out. Each of these steps was a major project in its own right.

Gaining Access to the Data

The dockets of the Boston Police Court, which were the principal data source for that court, are kept in the Social Law Library of the Suffolk County Court House in Boston and are readily available to users of that library. The library itself is intended for the use of attorneys who practice within the Suffolk County Courthouse and have a legitimate need for its services. Others, however, can readily obtain permission to use the library by appealing to the staff. Thus, access to the dockets of the Police Court is not difficult to obtain.

The dockets themselves are in varying states of preservation. The paper on which they are written is tough, but the books themselves are frail and dusty, and the handwriting is faint and often difficult to read. Moreover, not all the docket books for all years are available. Specifically, the books for the even years, 1826 through 1850 (with the exception of 1830), were available for this research. The books for 1824 were utilized in an earlier research project (Ferdinand 1980) but have since disappeared. The odd years, 1831 through 1868, are also available but were not utilized here. Although there are minor inconveniences in using these materials, they can be readily adapted to the purposes of historical research.

The record books of the Municipal Court are under the control of the clerk of the criminal section, Superior Court of Suffolk County. Permission to use these files from both the clerk and the Massachusetts Criminal History Systems Board is necessary prior to any application of them to research purposes. The records of the Municipal Court cannot be removed from their general storage area, and although the staff of the Superior Court is very cooperative, the conditions for collecting the data are not ideal. Space is limited, the lighting is dim, and the air is stagnant. Nevertheless, all the dockets of the Municipal Court from 1800 through 1859 are available to those who receive permission to use them.

The Data Sample

The years of this research were the even years from 1814 through 1850 for the Municipal Court, and the even years from 1824 through 1850 (except 1830) for the Police Court. This sample of the antebellum period was dictated by the limited funds available for the project.

It was important to cover the early years, that is, the years immediately preceding the antebellum period, so that social and legal conditions in the town could be fully described and a proper baseline established. It was also important to gather full information during the antebellum years themselves to permit a careful description of the city and its courts as both changed. It was also important to cover as much of the antebellum period as possible.

Since the early years, that is, 1814–30, are, perhaps, least understood, it was decided to begin the research as early as possible for the Police Court—that is, in 1824, the first year with a complete series of docket books. Data collection for the Municipal Court was begun with 1814, well before the town was reorganized as a city in 1822. Since there were insufficient funds to gather data on every year, it was necessary to limit the research to every other year. Only a partial set of docket books of the Police Court for 1830 was available, and accordingly this year was excluded. It was decided to gather *all* the cases for each even year, because the scope of the analysis required as large samples as possible for each year. The complexity of the analysis is improved with sample size, and the same is true of the reliability of the results. For these reasons, it was necessary to collect all cases for the available even years. The study, therefore, continued from the earliest years as long as funds remained for both courts, and at 1850 the funds were exhausted. Altogether data on approximately forty-five thousand three hundred cases were collected for both courts.

Statistical Analyses

Since all the cases described in the records of both courts were gathered for each year, the data do not represent a sample. They include the entire universe of cases for each year, and consequently, statistical analyses to determine the likelihood of two samples deriving from a single universe are not necessary. It is possible to assume that two different years are distinct samples of a single universe—that is, that the two years themselves constitute a single universe, and in this fashion derive an estimate of the reliability of a historical trend. By the same token it is possible to assume that two distinct groups within a single year, e.g., males and females, are not statistically different on some characteristics and to test this possibility for illustrative purposes. For the most part statistical analyses comparing two populations in the same year are not meaningful, since the groups represent entire populations and any differences between them are actual differences and not simply sampling biases.

The Adequacy of the Data

The docket books of the Police Court provide only the barest outline of the case under consideration. A brief description of the offense, the examination, the judgment, the result, the officer, the process whereby the defendant was brought into court, the defendant, and the complainant is provided. The record books of the Municipal Court, on the other hand, provide much more information. They give the presiding judge, some details of the charge, and specific information regarding the details of the case in court. A good sense of the specific offense, the verdict, and the disposition of the case can be gotten from these record books, as well as a glimpse into the social background of the offender: his occupation, the sex, the relationship, if any, to the complainant.

The validity of these records, that is, their accuracy in describing the actual events of each case, cannot be determined from this distance, but there is no reason to suspect any systematic bias in the manner in which they were transcribed. It is probably safe to conclude that their validity is respectably high. Moreover, the accuracy with which the events of the case in turn describe what actually happened in the community is probably as precise as any data available to social scientists anywhere. The events of a criminal court case are part of a legal record that is open to careful scrutiny and systematic rebuttal from the opposition. The accuracy of criminal evidence, therefore, is subjected to the closest kind of examination and probably achieves a very high level of validity. Once again, however, from this distance its actual validity cannot be determined.

The reader should also bear in mind that criminal courts only try cases that come before them. A certain, unknown portion of all criminal offenses is never the focus of a criminal complaint, and an additional portion is never taken beyond the initial stage of a complaint. Since the records utilized here give no indication of these offenses, the level of criminality reported here can only be an estimate of the underlying volume of crime in the community. Moreover, since the court itself selects certain offenses for especially careful prosecution and ignores others, the estimates developed here are also clouded by the changing policies of the courts. The validity of information in these records as a measure of total criminality, therefore, is probably rather low—although again it is unmeasurable, but when used with skill these data can still yield important insights into both the quality of criminal procedure and the nature of criminality characterizing a community and its courts during key historical periods.

The Codebook and the Coders

Since this research grew out of an earlier project that focused on the dockets of the 1824 Police Court, it was important to use the classifying system that was used for that project. Accordingly, the offense, the process, the examination, the outcome, and the judgment were all coded precisely as in the earlier study. For each category the precise wording in the docket books was used in the code. Thus, two hundred ninety different offenses were coded, one hundred eight arresting officers, forty-five different pleas on examination, and ninety different judgments—all in the language actually used by the courts.

Keeping the initial coding as close as possible to the court's language relieved the coders of difficult coding decisions, but more importantly made it possible to reconstruct exactly what the court did in each particular case. It is usually difficult to foresee how such information might be used in an analysis, but as focused issues surface, they often demand a precise answer that is only possible when the original language is closely preserved. Such a policy permits a careful answer to very pointed questions.

The same codebook was used for the Municipal Court records, except that more information was available there and required several additional codes. In particular the defendant's occupation (more than one hundred twenty occupations were listed), the dates when the offense was committed, when it was brought to court, and when completed, and the type and value of stolen property were all coded with minute precision. The codes were constructed by the coders as they encountered new categories, and close coordination among the several coders was maintained.

The coders themselves were recruited from Boston area universities, and all but one of them had had training in social science research. Two of them had had experience in historical research with court records. The coders were trained both in reading and interpreting the records, and although there was no ultimate authority for the meaning of a particular entry in the records, it was regularly possible to decipher even the most difficult scrawl. Experienced coders, when scrutinizing the same piece of evidence, can almost always develop an interpretation to which all can agree. In the beginning the work of the coders was compared with the records, and in no case was sloppy or inadequate work detected. At the close of the research those coders who had remained with the project had developed into highly skilled and efficient researchers. Their investment in the research was considerable, and it is recognized in the forward of this report.

Collecting and Analyzing the Data

The data collection team began their work in May 1979 and continued as a team through September 1979. During these five months eight coders coded approximately 30,000 cases from Police Court docket books and 9,200 cases from the record books of the Municipal Court. Several of the coders continued to code part-time through July 1980 and added another 2,100 cases to the pool. A research assistant was hired in September 1980, and she carried forward the coding until an additional 4,000 cases were coded. All in all about 36,100 cases were coded for the Police Court including the even years from 1826 through 1850, except 1830. Approximately 9,200 cases formed the data pool for the Municipal Court drawn from the even years 1814 through 1850.

A mark sense data sheet was developed specifically for this project, and using the data sheet each coder recorded the coded information directly onto a machine readable form. Although there was some difficulty with this method, it avoided the necessity of punching and verifying the data cards. The difficulties that arose included several episodes of misreading the sheets and broken readers, and ultimately a loss of the reader altogether. It is possible for the machine to misread the data sheets, but whenever this happened, it was a simple matter to reread them. The data sheets must all be fed into the reader with the same orientation, and occasionally this cardinal rule was violated. These mistakes were easily identified, and the sheets affected were then reread. The electronic reader also occasionally broke down and reading then was halted for weeks at a time. When the author changed teaching positions near the end of the project, the reader was no longer available. But all in all, the advantages of eliminating the need to punch and verify data cards saved considerable expense and time and were well worth it.

Appendix B: Judges of the Municipal Court

Among the more celebrated legal minds to serve on the Municipal Court bench during this period, i.e., 1814–50, were Emory Washburn, Josiah Quincy, Luther S. Cushing, Jonathan C. Perkins, Ebenezer R. Hoar, George T. Bigelow, and Pliny Merrick. Emory Washburn was born in Leicester, thirty miles west of Boston, in 1800. He graduated from Williams College in 1817 and studied at Harvard Law School shortly after it opened in 1817. He was admitted to the bar in 1821 and served several terms in both the Massachusetts House and Senate between 1826 and 1842. He was appointed to the benches of the Municipal Court and the Court of Common Pleas in 1842 where he served until 1847. After practicing law for several years, he was elected governor in 1854, and when his term expired, he joined the faculty of Dana Law School in Cambridge. He authored several important legal textbooks, and in 1854 he was awarded honorary degrees by both Harvard and Williams College. He died in 1877.

Josiah Quincy was born in Boston in 1772 and studied at Phillips Andover Academy. He graduated from Harvard in 1790 and studied law in Boston where he was admitted to the bar in 1793. He served both in the Massachusetts Senate and the United States House, and was appointed to the Municipal Court bench in 1822. He resigned in 1823 to become second mayor of Boston. Although his administration was controversial, he is now regarded as one of the finest mayors Boston has ever had. He became president of Harvard College in 1829 and remained there until 1845. In addition to writing several respected books, he received two honorary degrees from Harvard and Yale, and in 1864 he died.

Luther Stearns Cushing was born in Lunenburg, some twenty-five miles northwest of Boston, in 1803 and graduated from Harvard Law School in 1826. He was admitted to the bar shortly thereafter and was called to the bench of the Municipal Court and Court of Common Pleas in 1844. He had served there for four years, when he was named reporter of the Supreme Judicial Court of Massachusetts. He edited a respected legal journal for several years, authored several legal monographs, and served in the Massachusetts House of Representatives.

Jonathan Cogswell Perkins was born in Ipswich about fifteen miles north of Boston in 1809 and graduated from Amherst College in 1832. He studied at the Harvard Law School and was admitted to the bar in 1835. He served as a judge in the Municipal Court and the Court of Common Pleas between 1848 and 1859, when both courts were dissolved. He edited several volumes of Pickerings Reports and contributed to important legal treatises as well as authoring one of his own. He died in 1877.

Ebenezer Rockwood Hoar was born in 1816 in Concord. He prepared at Concord Academy and graduated from Harvard College in 1835. He studied law at Harvard and in the law offices of Emory Washburn. He joined the bar in 1839 and served as a justice of the Municipal Court and the Court of Common Pleas from 1849 to 1853. He was appointed to the Supreme Judicial Court bench in 1859 and served there until 1869, when he was named attorney general of the United States by President Ulysses S. Grant. He served in the Massachusetts Senate, the United States House of Representatives, and in several important posts at the Smithsonian Institution and Harvard College.

George Tyler Bigelow was born in Watertown in 1810. He studied at Boston Latin School and graduated from Harvard College in 1829. He studied law in his father's law offices and was admitted to the bar in 1833. He served several terms in the Massachusetts House and Senate and was appointed to the benches of the Municipal Court and the Court of Common Pleas in 1848. In 1850 he was named to the Supreme Judicial Court bench and in 1860 became chief justice upon the resignation of Lemuel Shaw. He received an honorary LL.D. from Harvard in 1853 and died in 1878.

Pliny Merrick was born in 1794 in Brookfield, thirty-five miles west of Boston. He graduated from Harvard College in 1814, and after studying law was admitted to the bar in 1817. He served as county attorney in Worcester from 1824 to 1843 and was named to the Court of Common Pleas and Municipal Court benches in 1850. In 1853 he was advanced to the Supreme Judicial Court as an associate justice and received an honorary LL.D. degree from Harvard. He died in 1867.

In addition to these renowned jurists several less eminent but equally dedicated men served on the Municipal Court bench. They included Thomas Dawes, Jr. who was born in Boston in 1758 and graduated from Harvard in 1777. He read law in an attorney's office in Boston and was admitted to the bar in 1780. He was appointed to the Probate Court in 1790, and in 1792 he was elevated to the Supreme Judicial Court. He resigned in 1802 and returned to the Probate Court. He served simultaneously on the Municipal Court bench until 1822. He died in 1825.

Peter Oxenbridge Thacher, the sole Municipal Court judge for twenty-one years, served from 1823 to his death in 1843. He was born in Malden in 1776 and graduated from Harvard College in 1796. He was admitted to the Suffolk County Bar in 1801 and practiced law privately until his appointment to the Municipal Court bench. When he died, the legislature authorized justices of the Court of Common Pleas to serve concurrently on the bench of the Municipal Court in the belief that it was detrimental for judges to hear only criminal cases.

John Mason Williams and Willard Phillips were both appointed to the Municipal Court in 1843. Judge Williams served until 1844 and Judge Phillips until 1847. Williams was born in New Bedford in 1780 and graduated from Brown in 1801. He was admitted to the bar in 1803 and became a judge in the Court of Common Pleas in 1821. In 1839 he was named chief justice of that court. He received an honorary LL.D. from Brown in 1843 and died in 1868. Willard Phillips was born in Bridgewater in 1784 and graduated from Harvard College in 1810. After studying law he was admitted to the bar in 1818. He served as representative in the Massachusetts House before being appointed a probate judge in 1839. He continued in that post until 1847, when he was named president of the New England Mutual Life Insurance Company. he received an honorary LL.D. degree in 1873 from Harvard, the year of his death.

Charles Allen was born in Worcester in 1797. He studied at Yale (though he never graduated) and after reading in the law, he was admitted to the bar in 1818. After several years in the Massachusetts House and Senate, he was appointed to the bench of the Court of Common Pleas in 1842. He resigned in 1844 to serve in the Superior Court of Suffolk County, and when it was dissolved in 1859 in favor of the Massachusetts Superior Court, he was named chief justice of the latter court. He died in 1869.

Joshua Holyoke Ward was born in Salem in 1809 and graduated from Harvard College in 1829. He read law with W. Leverett Saltonstall and was admitted to the bar in 1832. He was appointed to the Court of Common Pleas bench in 1844 but died four years later at the age of thirty-nine.

Daniel Wells was born in 1792 in Greenfield in western Massachusetts and graduated from Dartmouth College in 1810. After serving as a county attorney for several years, he was appointed chief justice of the Court of Common Pleas in 1844, succeeding John Mason Williams. He continued in that post until his death in 1854.

Horatio Byington was born in Stockbridge, twenty miles southwest of Boston, and read law there. He was admitted to the bar in 1820 and practiced law until 1846, when he became a justice in the Court of Common Pleas and Municipal Court. He continued as justice until his death in 1856.

Thomas Hopkinson was born in New Sharon, Maine in 1804 and graduated from Harvard College in 1830. He studied law in Lowell and was admitted to the bar in 1833. After serving several terms in the Massachusetts House and Senate, he was appointed to the Court of Common Pleas bench in 1848. He resigned in 1849 to become president of the Boston and Worcester Railroad. He died in 1856.

Edward Mellen was born in Westboro, twenty-five miles from Boston, in

1802 and graduated from Brown in 1823. He joined the bar in 1828 and was raised to the bench of the Court of Common Pleas in 1847. In 1849 he became the Chief Justice of that court, where he remained until 1859 when the Court of Common Pleas was abolished. He died in 1875.

It is interesting that sixteen of these eighteen judges (89 percent) had graduated from college, although during this same period only 48.5 percent of the judges presiding over the federal lower courts had also graduated from college (Hall 1976, 248). Apparently, as a group, Boston's lower court judges were among the better-trained judges in the whole country.

Notes

Chapter 1. The Early Criminal Courts

1. The rigid application of common law doctrine throughout most of the eighteenth century, which is Horwitz's thesis regarding American practice, certainly does not describe English practice during the same period. It is clear, thanks to the work of Beattie (see 420–21, for example) among others, that the criminal law was conceived very directly as an instrument of administration to further government policy.

2. In 1800 fourteen out of nineteen jurisdictions required evidence of an apprenticeship before admission to the bar, but in 1840 only eleven out of thirty did, and by 1860 only nine—mostly in the northeast—of twenty-nine jurisdictions did (Chroust 1965, vol. 2, chap. 3).

3. Among the broader issues disturbing the tranquility were the value of the common law as a foundation for the nation's newly independent courts (Gawalt, 1979, 50–52), and the merit of an independent judiciary with a high degree of professionalism as opposed to a more democratically selected bench (Ellis 1971, chaps. 13–14). In addition, the courts were under severe pressure to simplify their procedures and to reduce the difficulty of achieving justice through them (Handlin 1969, 41–50), but the most immediate issue affecting the Boston criminal courts was the distinctive needs of the town as compared with those of Suffolk County.

4. In a parallel development the Criminal Justice Act (1855) in Great Britain permitted the criminal courts to try summarily (i.e., without a jury) petty theft and simple assault, recognizing apparently their diminishing seriousness in the criminal code.

5. Other researchers have reported the same early rush to the courts. See Steinburg (1986) on Philadelphina, Castan (n.d.) on the south of France, and Konig (1979) on Puritan Salem.

Chapter 2. Responsive Law and Police Power

1. The public corporation was also an early creature of the legislature but its sphere was largely economic and its ties to the state weakened as industrialization advanced (Handlin and Handlin 1969, chap. 7).

2. Things have not changed much in the nearly century and a half since then. Recent research indicates that "half of the convictions were the product of arrests made by a mere 12 percent of officers" (Forst 1983, 169–70).

3. We might ask why the city marshal, Benjamin Pollard, did not step in and regulate the wayward tavern owners? Although he did perform a variety of regulatory tasks, he was not specifically charged with that responsibility, and in the face of the county attorney's interest in these cases, he was obliged to divert his attentions elsewhere.

4. Unfortunately, there are no budgeting data for the prosecutor's office during this period. If such data were available they would probably show similar rises during the 1835–50 period.

5. The Municipal Court held jurisdiction over most state laws because they carried more severe punishments, which only the Municipal Court could administer. The Police Court was restricted to crimes carrying only limited punishments—that is, minor offenses and city ordinances.

6. Commenting on this peculiar arrangement, a contemporary—John C. Park—noted that in Suffolk,

> few if any the complaints under the liquor law are made at the Police Court Room; whereas in the country counties nearly all are made before the Justices of the Peace. In Suffolk, the complaints are made to the Grand Jury. It is true that the law authorizes the Grand Jury to act, by giving to the Municipal Court, concurrent jurisdiction. But such cases are not like felonies. (Park 1852, 4–5)

7. Nardulli (1978, 170–71) found that modern day prosecutors and defense counsels are also much more flexible in negotiating guilty pleas and light sentences for drug cases than with felony cases because aggravated complainants are rare in the former.

8. The attorney general of Massachusetts, James T. Austin, may have been referring to such practices in his Annual Report of 1834:

> To extend the protection of government to a criminal in consideration of services by him to be performed, whereby one *known* offender is in fact pardoned, that another or several who are suspected, may be put on trial, is among the highest and most delicate of official duties. (Austin 1834, 16–17).

But even if Austin did not have plea bargaining in mind, he was certainly describing an atmosphere of cooperation between the underworld and criminal justice officials that was congenial to it when it did develop.

Chapter 3. The Prosecutor Assumes Control

1. Boston's elevation of the prosecutor seems to have preceeded Philadelphia's by at least two decades (Steinberg 1975, 582–86 and 1989, chapt 9).

2. After all these years prosecutors still worry about abdicating their adversarial responsibilities as well as usurping the judges' sentencing powers in plea bargaining (Heumann 1978, 94–102).

3. In the first decade of the nineteenth century the courts in Massachusetts had looked with disfavor on guilty pleas—particularly if they had been negotiated (Wishingrad 1974). By mid-century, however, guilty pleas had become so commonplace that the courts were beginning to change their views. *Greene v. Commonwealth* (1866) for example, upheld a defendant's right to plead guilty, even to a capital offense, if the plea were voluntary.

4. It is interesting that recent court decisions, *Escobedo v. Illinois* (1964) and *Miranda v. Arizona* (1966), essentially were designed to restrict such early discussions between the prosecutors or the police and the accused.

Chapter 4. The Judges

1. More specifically, minor property crimes—larceny, for example—are much less likely to be incarcerated today than in early Boston (see U.S. Department of Justice 1985). Today, in the United States, about 44 percent of convicted larceny offenders are incaracerated as compared with nearly 61 percent in nineteenth-century Boston. At the same time convicted aggravated assault offenders today are incarcerated 50 percent of the time, whereas in early Boston felonies against the person were punished in the same way only 32 percent of the time. Burglary offenders, on the other hand, are incarcerated as compared with nearly 61 percent in nineteenth-century Boston. (50 vs. 55 percent, respectively).

2. Much the same was found in Alameda County, California, though the authors did not comment on this fact (Friedman and Percival 1981, 206–8). See also Beattie (chap. 8) on eighteenth-century Surrey.

3. Actually in the 1830s there were three magistrates in the Police Court: William Simmons who served from 1822 to 1843; John G. Rogers (1831–58); and James C. Merrill (1834–52).

4. Galanter et al. break down the concept of the activist judge into four types: the legalistic, the mission-oriented, the programmatic, and the entrepreneurial judge. The traditional judge that I have described here seems to correspond to their legalistic judge who is forceful in the courtroom but conservative in interpreting the law. My utilitarian judge is probably closest to their programmatic judge who is looking for better ways to do things in the courtroom, though some were also, no doubt, the prototypical trial court judge who serves as an referee in the courtroom with no stake in the outcome. He sees his responsibility as primarily one of applying the rules fairly and impartially. Finally, my professional judge corresponds to their mission-oriented judge who is willing to mold the law like putty to make it fit his legal purposes, although some also seem to resemble their entrepreneurial judge who uses the post as a springboard to higher positions (see also Gibson 1978, and Howard 1977).

5. It is interesting that the northeast (Maine, Rhode Island, and New Jersey) followed a very eccentric path in the late nineteenth and early twentieth centuries with regard to criminal appeals to the state supreme court. Between 1870 and 1925, while the rest of the country was showing a very high but steadily declining success rate for criminal appeals, the northeast was showing a very low but slowly declining level (Meeker 1984, 561). The policy of rejecting nearly all appeals, first established in the Massachusetts Supreme Judicial Court, was followed by two other sister New England states—Maine and Rhode Island, well into the twentieth century.

6. There is some suggestion that similar changes occurred in appeals to the Wisconsin Supreme Court during the late nineteenth century as the state turned its attention to regulation of business practices (Kimball 1965, 102, 114). A high rate of appeals was also found in California during the 1860s when basic changes were underway in that legal system as well (Vernier and Selig 1928, 46–47).

Chapter 5. Crime in Antebellum Boston

1. Philadelphia experienced a very similar transformation (Warner 1968, Parts I and II).

2. Contrast Lane's (1967, chap. 2 and 5) accounts of early Boston and antebellum Boston. See also Dahl (1961, 11–86).

3. Quoted in Schultz (1967, 57).

4. Vinovskis (1981, 63) estimates that nearly 25 percent of women between fifteen

and sixty were employed in industry or domestic service in Massachusetts during the early antebellum period.

5. Much the same happened in Philadelphia around the same time (Warner, 1968, 64–68).

6. The careful reader may object to any attempt in these pages to infer the nature of Boston's crime problem from court records. My answer, however, is that it is possible in these data to distinguish trends in criminal cases that reflect sociocommunal pressures from those that derive primarily from politico-legal pressures. Suffice it to say here that these glimpses of early nineteenth-century crime are of considerable significance to criminologists, particularly as they are coupled with thorough analyses of the legal, judicial, and political changes that accompanied them.

7. There is, of course, a certain hazard in comparing official crime rates between drastically different eras or jurisdictions, and as we shall see, the courts of antebellum Boston differed dramatically from the courts of today. Nevertheless, it is interesting to note that the aggregate crime-rate of both courts in 1824–5,430 per hundred thousand–was not exceeded until the crime waves of the 1880s (Ferdinand 1967), and the aggregate levels of assaultive crime–1,780 per hundred thousand–and property crime–1,400 per hundred thousand–have never been exceeded in Boston.

8. The definition of minor offenses used here includes assault and battery, misdemeanors against the person, misdemeanors against property, offenses against religion, liquor offenses, public disturbances, prostitution, larceny, and violation of lawful authority.

9. The definition of serious offenses used here includes burglary, felonies against property, and felonies against the person.

10. Property crime here includes burglary, felonies against property, forgery, fraud, larceny, and misdemeanors against property. Assaultive crimes include assault and battery, felonies against the person, and misdemeanors against the person; regulatory offenses include city ordinance violations; liquor law violations, and offenses against religion (which were mainly violations of Sunday blue laws). Vice includes prostitution and gambling violations.

Chapter 6. The Offenders

1. Beattie, 1986 (199–202) agrees that court data can reveal as much about crime patterns as about the processing of criminals.

2. In 1850 the juvenile crime rate as measured by charges brought before the Municipal Court (Figure 3.1) was 212.7 per one thousand juveniles in Boston. It was 22 percent higher than the rate of juvenile arraignments in Suffolk County in 1980–182.6 per one thousand (Brown 1982)! The figure for 1850 does not include juvenile arraignments before the Police Court, which must have been even more substantial.

3. There is, of course, no certain way to determine whether the increase in juvenile criminal cases reflected an underlying crime rate or simply a shift toward aggressive policing, but when we consider the close agreement between observers in Boston (the mayor and the prosecutor) and in New York (the Chief of Police, officials of a house of refuge, and a social reformer), as to the causes as well as the actuality of the rise, the conclusion that it was an unusual phenomenon in these two cities inviting wonder and comment seems inescapable. They would not have been so inclined to offer explanations if it had been simply a result of police or court measures.

4. In order to identify the ethnicity of defendants in both courts, their last names were coded as Irish or non-Irish according to Weyl (1967, 219). Although this method is far from precise, it can provide a measure of the changing contribution of Irish

defendants to the overall picture of crime in Boston. Doubtless, many Irish defendants were included among the non-Irish, since not all Irish surnames were easily distinguished from English surnames, and some non-Irish defendants were probably mistakenly classified as Irish since cultural heritage is not perfectly indicated by surname. The category of Irish defendants, however, is probably sufficiently representative of the Irish in Boston to permit reasonable inferences regarding the nature and trends of their criminality.

The fact that Irish crime and delinquency amounted to only between 11 and 15 percent of all crime and delinquency in 1850 (see fig. 6.2 and 6.4) suggests that the identification of Irish defendants by family name was indeed very conservative. We know from other sources that the Irish made up about 25 percent of Boston's population in 1850, and the inference is probably sound that they composed at least that percent of the criminal and delinquent population of the city. I am grateful to Juan Carlos Schiappa-Pietra Cubas for pointing this out.

5. It is interesting that women were consistently identified in the Municipal Court as wives, widows, spinsters, or single women. Men, on the other hand, were always identified by their occupations. Women also held jobs, but that was not their identifying social characteristics. Thanks to Mary Bularzik for pointing this out.

6. The data presented were derived from cases coming before the Municipal Court only. The Police Court did not record the occupation of the defendant and could not be used in this analysis. Since women were not classified in the Municipal Court in terms of occupation (only their marital status), the data reported here regarding occupation apply only to men.

Chapter 7. Modernizing Boston's Lower Courts

1. During this period, for example, the movement to abolish capital punishment gathered considerable momentum (Hindus 1980, 196–99).

2. They resembled Gibson's (1978) activist judges who utilized many extralegal criteria in arriving at their sentencing decisions.

Chapter 8. The Future of America's Responsive Courts

1. Felix Frankfurter and Robert Jackson were among Justices on the other side who favored a more restrained role for the Supreme Court (Simon 1989).

2. Bork's contentious hearing and subsequent rejection by the Senate Judicial Committee is simply a case in point. For both sides now, political alignment competes with legal competence in deciding appointments to the Supreme Court.

3. During the antebellum period the Congress and especially the Senate arranged compromise after compromise (The Missouri Compromise of 1820, the Compromise of 1850, the Kansas-Nebraska Act, 1854), while the president and the Supreme Court (with one disastrous exception, Dred Scott v. Sandford, 1857) left the question of slavery alone.

4. Busing of minorities to nonminority schools, though it is twenty-five years old in Boston, is still a sore spot with many working class whites, and in 1986 Roxbury—a largely black section in Boston—sought unsuccessfully to secede from the city.

Bibliography

Alschuler, Albert W. "The Prosecutor's Role in Plea Bargaining." *University of Chicago Law Review* 36, no. 1 (Fall), 1968: 50–112.

Armeo, Agnes Orsatti. "Devout Legalists–Protestant Reliance on Law in Early Nineteenth Century America." *American Studies* 26, no. 2 (Fall), 1985: 61–73.

Aumann, Francis R. *The Changing American Legal System*. New York: Da Capo Press, 1969.

Austin, James T. *Report of the Attorney General to the Legislature of Massachusetts*. House Document no. 4, 1 January 1834.

_____. "Attorney General Reports." *Massachusetts House Document* no. 20, part I, 1842.

Baker, J. H. "Criminal Courts and Procedure at Common Law 1550–1800." In *Crime in England 1550–1800*, edited by J. S. Cockburn, 15–48. Princeton: Princeton University Press, 1977.

Baker, Jean. "From Belief into Culture: Republicanism in the Antebellum North." *American Quarterly* 37, no. 4 (Fall), 1985: 532–50.

Baltzell, E. Digby. *The Protestant Establishment*. New York: Random House, 1964.

Barney, William L. *The Passage of the Republic*. Lexingon, Mass.: D. C. Heath and Company, 1987.

Beattie, J. M. *Crime and the Courts in England 1660–1800*. Princeton: Princeton University Press, 1986.

Bechtler, Thomas W. *Laws in a Social Context*. Deventer, the Netherlands: B.V. Kluver, 1978.

Bork, Robert H. *The Tempting of America*. New York: The Free Press, 1990.

Brown, Marjorie E., et al. *Population and Crime: A Study of the Juvenile Population and Volume of Juvenile Arraignments in Massachusetts 1940–1980*. Boston Mass.: Department of Probation, 1982.

Castan, Yves. "Social Control and Judicial Recourse in Eighteenth Century Languedoc Villages," unpublished manuscript.

Chroust, Anton-Hermann. *The Rise of the Legal Profession in America* 2, Norman: The University of Oklahoma Press, 1965.

Clark, Charles E., and David M. Trubek. "The Creative Role of the Judge: Restraint and Freedom in the Common Law Tradition." *Yale Law Journal* 71, no. 2, 1961: 255–76.

Clifford, William. *An Introduction to African Criminology*. Nairobi: Oxford University Press, 1974.

Clinard, Marshall, and Daniel J. Abbott. *Crime in Developing Countries: A Comparative Perspective*. New York: John Wiley & Sons, 1973.

Cohen, Lawrence E., James R. Kluegel, and Kenneth C. Land. "Social Inequality and

Predatory Criminal Victimization." *American Sociological Review* 46, no. 5 (October), 1981: 505–24.

Cohen, Stanley. *Visions of Social Control*. Cambridge, England: Polity Press, 1985.

Cott, Nancy F. *The Bonds of Womanhood*. New Haven: Yale University Press, 1977.

Dahl, Robert. *Who Governs? Democracy and Power in an American City*. New Haven, Conn.: Yale University Press, 1961.

Davis, William T. *The Bench and Bar of the Commonwealth of Massachusetts* 1, Boston: The Boston History Co., 1895.

DeFleur, Lois. *Delinquency in Argentina*. Pullman: Washington State University Press, 1970.

Demos, John. *A Little Commonwealth*. New York: Oxford University Press, 1970.

Diner, Hasia R. *Erin's Daughters in America*. Baltimore: The Johns Hopkins University Press, 1983.

Eisenstein, James, and Herbert Jacob. *Felony Justice: An Organizational Analysis of the Criminal Courts*. Boston: Little, Brown & Co., 1977.

Elliott, Delbert, and Harwin L. Voss. *Delinquency and Dropout*. Lexington, Mass. Lexington Books, 1974.

Ellis, Richard E. *The Jeffersonian Crisis: Courts and Politics in the Young Republic*. New York: Oxford University Press, 1971.

Emery, L. A. "The Nolle Prosequi in Criminal Cases." *Maine Law Review* 6, (February), 1913: 199–204.

Engel, Charles Donald. "Criminal Justice in the City: A Study of Sentence Severity and Variation in the Philadelphia Criminal Court System." Ph.D diss., Temple University: Philadelphia, 1971.

Faber, Eli. "Puritan Criminals: The Economic, Social and Intellectual Background to Crime in Seventeenth Century Massachusetts." *Perspectives in American History* XI, Cambridge: Harvard University Press, 1977–78: 261–87.

Feeley, Malcolm M. *The Process Is the Punishment*. New York: Russell Sage Foundation, 1979.

———. "Plea Bargaining and the Structure of the Criminal Process." *Justice System Journal* 7 (Winter), 1982: 338–55.

Fenner, Ball. *Raising the Veil; or Scenes in the Courts*. Boston: James French & Co., 1856.

Ferdinand, Theodore N. "The Criminal Patterns of Boston Since 1849," *American Journal of Sociology* 73, no. 1 (July) 1967: 84–99.

———. "Criminal Justice: From Colonial Intimacy to Bureacratic Formality." In *Handbook of Contemporary Urban Life*, edited by David Street, 261–287. San Francisco: Jossey-Bass, 1978.

———. "Criminality, the Courts, and the Constabulary in Boston," *Journal of Research in Crime and Delinquency* 17, no. 2, 1980: 190–208.

———. "A Brief History of Juvenile Delinquency in Boston and a Comparative Interpretation." *International Annals of Criminology* 24, nos. 1&2, 1986: 59–81.

———. "Juvenile Delinquency or Juvenile Justice: Which Came First?" *Criminology* 27, no. 1 (July), 1989: 79–106.

Figueria-McDonough, Josefina. "Gender Differences in Informal Processing." *Journal of Research in Crime and Delinquency* 22, no. 2 (May), 1985: 101–33.

Forst, Brian. "Prosecution and Sentencing." In *Crime and Public Policy*, edited by James Q. Wilson, 165–82. San Francisco: ICS Press, 1983.

Foucault, Michel. *Discipline and Punish*. New York: Vintage Books, 1979.

Friedman, Lawrence M. *A History of American Law*. New York: Simon and Schuster, 1973.

———. "Courts Over Time: a Survey of Theories and Research." In *Empirical Theories About Courts*, edited by Keith O. Boyum and Lynn Mather, 9–50. New York: Longman, 1983.

Friedman, Lawrence M., and Robert V. Percival. *The Roots of Justice Crime and Punishment in Alameda County, California 1870–1910*. Chapel Hill: The University of North Carolina Press, 1981.

Galanter, Marc, Frank S. Palen, and John M. Thomas. "The Crusading Judge: Judicial Activism in Trial Courts." *Southern California Law Review* 52, 1979: 699–741.

Gatrell, V. A. C. "The Decline of Theft and Violence in Victorian and Edwardian England." In *Crime and the Law*, edited by V. A. C. Gatrell, Brune Lenman, and Geoffrey Parker, 238–337. London: Europa Publications, 1980.

Gawalt, Gerald W. *The Promise of Power The Emergence of the Legal Profession in Massachusetts 1760–1840*. Westport, Conn.: Greenwood Press, 1979.

Gibson, James L. "Judges' Role Orientations, Attitudes, and Decisions: An Interactive Model." *American Political Science Review* 72, 1978: 911–24.

Gilmore, Grant. *The Ages of American Law*. New Haven: Yale University Press 1977.

Glazer, Nathan. *The Limits of Social Policy*. Cambridge: Harvard University Press, 1988.

Goldstein, Abraham S. "History of the Public Prosecutor." In *Encyclopedia of Crime and Justice* 3, edited by Sanford H. Kalish, 1286–1289. New York: The Free Press, 1983.

Greenberg, Douglas. *Crime and Law Enforcement in the Colony of New York, 1691–1776*. Ithaca, N.Y.: Cornell University Press, 1976.

Gusfield, Joseph. *Symbolic Crusade*. Urbana: University of Illinois Press, 1963.

Hall, Kermit L. "Social Backgrounds and Judicial Recruitment: A Nineteenth Perspective on the Lower Federal Judiciary." *Western Political Quarterly* 29, 1976: 243–57.

Handlin, Oscar. *Boston's Immigrants a Study in Acculturation*. Rev. ed. New York: Atheneum, 1968.

Handlin, Oscar, and Mary Flug Handlin. *Commonwealth*. Cambridge: Harvard University Press, 1969.

Haskins, George Lee. *Law and Authority in Early Massachusetts*. New York: Archon Books, 1968.

Hawes, Joseph. *Children in Urban Society*. New York: Oxford University Press, 1971.

Heumann, Milton. *Plea Bargaining*. Chicago: The University of Chicago Press, 1978.

Hindus, Michael. *Prison and Plantation*. Chapel Hill: University of North Carolina Press, 1980.

Hobson, Barbara M. *Uneasy Virtue*. New York: Basic Books, 1987.

Hofstadter, Richard. *The Age of Reform*. New York: Alfred A. Knopf, 1955.

Homans, George. "John Adams and the Constitution of Massachusetts." *Proceedings of the American Philosophical Society* 125 (August) 1981: 286–91.

Horowitz, Donald L. *The Courts and Social Policy*. Washington DC.: Brookings Institution, 1977.

Horwitz, Morton J. *The Transformation of American Law, 1780–1860*. Cambridge: Harvard University Press, 1977.

Howard, J. Woodford, Jr. "Role Perceptions and Behavior in Three U.S. Courts of Appeals." *The Journal of Politics* 39, 1977, 916–38.

Hull, N. E. *Female Felons*. Urbana: University of Illinois Press, 1987.

Hurst, James Willard. *The Growth of American Law*. Boston: Little Brown & Co., 1950.

──────. *Law and the Condition of Freedom in Nineteenth-Century United States*. Madison: The University of Wisconsin Press, 1956.

Huse, Charles P. *The Financial History of Boston*. Cambridge: Harvard University Press, 1916.

Johnson, David R. *Policing the Urban Underworld*. Philadelphia: Temple University Press, 1979.

Kimball, Edward L. "Criminal Cases in a State Appellate Court: Wisconsin 1839–1959" *American Journal of Legal History* 9, 1965: 91–102.

Klonoski, James R., and Robert I. Mendelsohn, eds. *The Politics of Local Justice*. Boston: Little, Brown & Co., 1970.

Knights, Peter R. *The Plain People Boston 1830–1860*. New York: Oxford University Press, 1978.

Konig, David Thomas. *Law and Society in Puritan Massachusetts*. Chapel Hill: The University of North Carolina Press, 1979.

Kornhauser, Ruth Rosner. *Social Sources of Delinguency*. Chicago: University of Chicago Press, 1978.

Lane, Roger. *Policing the City*. Cambridge: Harvard University Press, 1967.

Langbein, John H. "The Criminal Trial Before the Lawyers." *The University of Chicago Law Review* 45 (Winter) 1978: 263–316.

──────. "Understanding the Short History of Plea Bargaining." *Law and Society Review* 13, no. 2, 1979: 261–72.

Levin, Martin A. *Urban Politics and The Criminal Courts*. Chicago: University of Chicago Press, 1977.

Levy, Leonard W. *The Law of the Commonwealth and Chief Justice Shaw*. Cambridge: Harvard University Press, 1957.

Logue, Edward J. "Garrity's Impact and Other Thoughts on Boston." *The Boston Globe* 2 May 1983: 13.

Massachusetts Legislative Documents. *House Document* no. 63, 1843: 1–70.

──────. *House Document*, no. 5, 1845.

Mather, Lynn. "Some Determinants of the Method of Case Disposition: Decision-Making by Public Defenders in Los Angeles." *Law & Society Review* 8, no. 2 (Winter), 1973: 187–216.

──────. *Plea Bargaining or Trial? The Process of Criminal Case Disposition*. Lexington: Lexington Books, 1979.

Matza, David. *Delinguency and Drift*. New York: John Wiley and Sons, 1964.

McCaughey, Robert A. *Josiah Quincy, 1772–1864. The Last Federalist*. Cambridge: Harvard University Press, 1974.

McDonald, William F., ed. *The Prosecutor*. Beverly Hills, Calif.: Sage Publications, 1979.

Meeker, James W. "Criminal Appeals Over the Last 100 Years." *Criminology* 22, no. 4 (November) 1984: 551–571.

Messerli, Jonathan. "The Columbian Complex: The Impulse to National Consolidation." *History of Education Quarterly* 7, no. 4 (Winter) 1967: 417–25.

Nardulli, Peter F. *The Courtroom Elite: An Organizational Perspective on Criminal Justice.* Cambridge: Ballinger Publishing Co, 1978.

Nardulli, Peter F., Roy B. Flemming, and James Eisenstadt. "Criminal Courts and Bureaucratic Justice: Concessions and Consensus in the Guilty Plea Process," *Journal of Criminal Law and Criminology* 76 (no. 4), 1985: 1122–31.

Nelson, William E. *The Americanization of the Common Law.* Cambridge: Harvard University Press, 1975.

Neubauer, David W. *Criminal Justice in Middle America.* Morristown, N.J.: General Learning Press, 1974.

Nonet, Phillippe, and Philip Selznick. *Law and Society in Transition Toward Responsive Law.* New York: Harper & Row Publishers, 1978.

Oberholzer, Emil Jr. *Delinguent Saints.* New York: Columbia University Press, 1956.

Packer, Herbert *The Limits of Criminal Sanction.* Stanford: Stanford University Press, 1968.

Park, John C. "Report to the Mayor and Aldermen of the City of Boston." Pamphlet, 1 January 1852.

Parker, Samuel D. *Report of the Arguments of the Attorney of the Commonwealth, at the Trials of Abner Kneeland, for Blasphamy in the Municipal and Supreme Courts in Boston, January and May, 1834.* Boston: Homer and Company, 1834.

Pickett, Robert S. *House of Refuge.* Syracuse, N.Y.: Syracuse University Press, 1969.

Posten, Richard W. *The Gang and the Establishment.* New York: Harper & Row Publishers, 1971.

Quincy, Josiah. "Remarks on Some of the Provisions of the Laws of Massachusetts Affecting Poverty, Vice and Crime." Cambridge: 1822.

_____. *A Municipal History of the Town and City of Boston During Two Centuries from September 17, 1630 to September 17, 1830.* Boston: Charles C. Little and James Brown, 1852.

Rorabaugh, W. J. *The Alcoholic Republic.* New York: Oxford University Press, 1979.

Rumbarger, John J. *Profits, Power, and Prohibition.* Albany, N.Y.: State University of New York Press, 1989.

Ryan, Mary P. *Womanhood in America.* New York: New viewpoints, 1975.

Sanger, William W. *History of Prostitution.* New York: Harper, 1858.

Sarat, Austin. "Doing the Dirty Business of Coping with Crime: The Contemporary 'Crisis' of American Criminal Courts." In *The Study of Criminal Courts: Political Perspectives*, edited by Peter F. Nardulli, 59–79. Cambridge: Ballinger Publishing Co., 1979.

Savage, Edward Hartwell. *Police Records and Recollections; or Boston by Gaslight for Two Hundred and Forty Years.* Boston: J. P. Dale & Co., 1873.

Scheiber, Harry N. "Property Law, Expropriation, and Resource Allocation by Government, 1789–1910." *Journal of Economic History* 33, no. 1, (March) 1973: 232–51.

Schlesinger, Arthur M., Jr. "The Supreme Court: 1947." *Fortune* 35 (January), 1947: 201–2.

Schnore, Leo, and Peter R. Knights. "Residence and Social Structure: Boston in the

Antebellum Period." in *Nineteenth Century Cities*. Stephen Thernstrom and Richard Sennet, eds. New Haven: Yale University Press, 1969.

Schultz, Stanley K. *The Culture Factory Boston Public Schools, 1789–1860*. New York: Oxford University Press, 1973.

Silberman, Matthew "Judicial Professionalism, Due Process, and Felony Trials." Paper presented at the North Central Sociological Association annual meetings, 1973.

Silver, Allan. "The Demand for Order in Civil Society: A Review of Some Themes in the History of Urban Crime, Police, and Riot." In *The Police*, edited by David Bordua, 1-24. New York: John Wiley & Co., 1967.

Simon, James F. *The Antagonists: Hugo Black, Felix Frankfurter and Civil Liberties in Modern America*. New York: Simon and Schuster, 1989.

Smith, Page. *As a City Upon a Hill*. New York: Alfred A. Knopf, 1966.

Sprague, Henry H. *City Government in Boston*. Boston: n.p., 1890.

Steinberg, Allen. "From Private Prosecution to Plea Bargaining: Criminal Prosecution, the District Attorney, and American Legal History." *Crime and Delinquency* 30, no. 4 (October), 1975: 568–592.

———. "'The Spirit of Litigation': Private Prosecution and Criminal Justice in Nineteenth Century Philadelphia." *Journal of Social History* 20, no. 2 (Winter), 1986: 231–49.

———. *The Transformation of Criminal Justice*. Chapel Hill and London: The University of North Carolina Press, 1989.

Sudnow, David. "Normal Crimes: Sociological Features of the Penal Code," *Social Problems* 12, no. 3 (Winter) 1965: 255–76.

Sutton, John B. *Stubborn Children*. Berleby: The University of California Press, 1988.

Teubner, Gunther. "Substantive and Reflexive Elements in Modern Law." *Law & Society Review* 17, no. 2, 1983: 239–85.

U.S. Department of Justice. Bureau of Justice Statistics. *Felony Sentencing in 18 Local Jurisdictions*. Special Report, 1985. NCJ-97681.

Van Dyke, Jon M. "Jury Trial." In *Encyclopedia of Crime and Justice* 3, Sanford Kalish, 932–41. New York: The Free Press, 1983.

Vernier, C. G., and Philip Selig, Jr. "The Reversal of Criminal Cases in the Supreme Court of California." *Southern California Law Review* 2, 1928: 21–52.

Vinovskis, Maris A. *Fertility in Massachusetts from the Revolution to the Civil War*. New York: Academic Press, 1981.

Warner, Sam Bass Jr. *The Private City Philadelphia in Three Periods of Its Growth*. Philadelphia: University of Pennsylvania Press, 1968.

Warren, Charles. *A History of the American Bar*. New York: Howard Fertig, 1966.

———. *History of the Harvard Law School* 1. New York: Da Capo Press, 1970.

Weyl, Nathaniel. *The Creative Elite in America*. Washington, D.C.: Public Affairs, 1966.

Wilson, William J. *The Truly Disadvantaged: The Inner City, the Underclass, and Public Policy*. Chicago: The University of Chicago Press, 1987.

Wishingrad, Jay. "The Plea Bargain in Historical Perspective." *Buffalo Law Review* 23, 1974: 499–527.

Woodman, Horatio, *Reports of Criminal Cases Tried in the Municipal Court of the City of Boston Before Peter Oxenbridge Thacher, Judge of the Court from 1823 to 1842*. Boston: Charles C. Little and James Brown, 1945.

Zehr, Howard. "The Modernization of Crime in Germany and France, 1830–1913." *Journal of Social History* 8 (Summer), 1975: 117–41.

Index

Abbott, Daniel, 153
Adams, John, 15, 38, 39, 194
Adams, John Quincy, 15, 25
American lawyers: post-Revolutionary training of, 31
Armeo, Agnes, 38
Asylum and Farm School for Indigent Boys, 157
Augustus, John, 182
Austin, James T., 9, 10, 69, 133, 221 n.8

Baker, J. H., 33
Baker, Jean, 39
Baker v. Carr, 369 U.S. 186 (1962), 205
Baltzell, E. Digby, 196, 197, 198
Barney, William, 26, 153, 163, 168
Beattie, J. H., 33, 97, 117, 125, 140, 220 n.1 (chap. 1), 222 n.2 (chap. 4), 223 n.1
Bechtler, Thomas, 203
Bigelow, John, 156
Black, Hugo, 203
Bolling v. Sharpe, 347 U.S. 497 (1954), 205
Bork, Robert, 203, 204, 205, 206
Boylston School for Children of Tender Years, 157
Brace, Charles Loring, 156
Brigham, Peter Bent, 77
Broad Street riot, 159
Brown, Marjorie, 223 n.2
Brown v. Topeka Board of Education, 347 U.S. 483, 202, 204, 209
Bularzik, Mary, 224 n.5
Burger Supreme Court, the, 204, 205

Castan, Yves, 220 n.5
Channing, William Ellery, 15, 38
Chroust, Anton-Hermann, 31, 220 n.2 (chap. 2)
Clark, Charles, 104
Clifford, William, 153

Clinard, Marshall, 153
Cohen, Lawrence, 176
Cohen, Stanley, 196
Commonwealth: the idea of, 40
Commonwealth v. Clark Greene, 13 Allen 251 (1866), 187, 221 n.3
Constables, 44, 45, 95, 96
Cott, Nancy, 163, 164
Court of Common Pleas, 34
Court of General Sessions, 34
Courtroom workgroups, 182–87; adaptabilty of, 189; role in modernization, 192–93
Crime: and occupation, 172–77; types, 142–46
Crime patterns, 137–42; meaning of, 146–48, 149–51, 179–80
Cubas, Juan C., 223–24 n.4
Curley, James Michael, 197

Dahl, Robert, 222 n.2 (chap. 5)
Davis, William, 31
DeFleur, Lois, 153
DeLorean, John, 187, 192
Demos, John, 163
Diner, Hasia, 164, 168
Douglas, William O., 203
Dred Scott v. Sandford, 60 U.S. (19 How.) 393 (1856), 202, 224 n.3
Dukakis, Michael, 208

Eisenstein, James, 183
Eliot, Charles, 197
Elliott, Delbert, 152
Ellis, Richard, 220 n.3 (chap. 1)
Emery, L. A., 71
Engel, Charles, 117
Enlightenment, the, 38
Esobedo v. Illinois, 378 U.S. 478 (1964), 221 n.4 (chap. 3)

Faber, Eli, 22

INDEX

Feeley, Malcolm, 93, 184, 193
Fenner, Ball, 11–12, 104
Ferdinand, Theodore N., 22, 23, 33, 34, 153, 196, 197, 223 n.7
Fifteen gallon law, 26, 43, 178
Figueria-McDonough, Josphina, 117
Flynn, Raymond, 208
Forst, Brian, 220 n.2 (chap. 2)
Foucault, Michel, 23, 195
Frankfurter, Felix, 224 n.1 (chap. 8)
Friedman, Lawrence, 33, 192, 222 n.2 (chap. 4)

Galenter, Marc, 126, 222 n.4 (chap. 4)
Gatrell, V. A. C., 103
Gawalt, Gerald, 31, 220 n.3 (chap. 1)
General Court of Sessions, 34
Gibson, James, 222 n.4 (chap. 4) 224 n.2 (chap. 7)
Gilmore, Grant, 29, 203
Glazer, Nathan, 198
Goldstein, Abraham, 97
Greenberg, Douglas, 67
Griggs v. Duke Power Co., 401 U.S. 424 (1971), 205
Gusfield, Joseph, 41

Hall, Kermit, 219
Handlin, Mary, 42, 220 n.1 (chap. 2)
Handlin, Oscar, 22, 25, 38, 39, 41, 42, 135, 157, 158, 220 n.1 (chap. 2)
Haskins, George, 40
Hawes, Joseph, 152, 153, 156
Heumann, Milton, 221 n.2
Hinckley, John, 192
Hindus, Michael, 142, 224 n.1 (chap. 7)
Hobson, Barbara, 25, 27
Hofstadter, Richard, 198
Homans, George, 39
Horowitz, Donald, 42, 199, 200, 201, 205
Horwitz, Morton, 28, 38, 41, 220 n.1 (chap. 1)
House of Reformation, 156
Howard, J. Woodford, Jr., 222 n.4 (chap. 4)
Hull, N. E., 125
Huntington, Asahel, 69–70
Hurst, James, 31, 42

In re Gault, 387 U.S. 1 (1967), 200
Irish, the, 157–60; and crime, 160–63; and poverty, 158

Jackson, Robert, 224 n.1 (chap. 8)
Jacob, Herbert, 183
Johnson, David, 65
Judges: of Municipal Court, 126–27, 216–19; of Police Court, 222 n.4 (chap. 4); types of, 125–33
Juvenile delinquency, 141–42; in the Municipal Court, 153–57

Kimball, Edward, 222 n.6
Klonoski, James, 35
Knights, David, 22, 169–71
Konig, David, 220 n.5
Kornhauser, Ruth, 152

Lane, Roger, 25, 26, 27, 43, 45, 46, 51, 95, 135, 183, 196, 222 n.2 (chap. 5)
Langbein, John, 33, 48, 186
Lau v. Nichols, 414 U.S. 563 (1974), 200
Law schools: emergence of, 32–33; leadership role, 188
Legal realists, 203
Levin, Martin, 104, 184, 188
Levy, Leonard, 43, 134
Litchfield Law School, 32
Llewellyn, Karl, 29, 203
Locke, John, 15, 25, 39, 40, 198
Logue, Edward, 199
Lower courts: dismissals, 71–72; diversion of minor crimes from, 83–89; jurisdictional shifts, 46–47, 179–80; left-on-file in, 72–74; plea bargaining in, 69–70; widening jurisdictions, 34–36
Lucas v. Forty-Fourth General Assembly, 337 U.S. 713 (1964), 205

McCaughey, Robert, 40
McDonald, William, 65
Mather, Lynn, 48, 71, 182
Matsell, George, 154
Matza, David, 177
Mendelsohn, Robert, 35
Merrill, James C., 110
Messerli, Jonathan, 39
Methods for studying lower criminal courts, 211–15
Minor cases: refusal of, 23, 24
Minor crimes: defined, 223 n.8; severity toward, 107–8
Miranda v. Arizona, 384 U.S. 436 (1966), 221 n.4

INDEX

Modern court system: organization of, 12
Municipal Court: appeals from, 128–30; budget of, 47–48
Municipal Court sentencing, 104–10; and gender, 119–25; of juveniles, 117; and social position, 114–25

Nardulli, Peter, 183, 187, 221 n.7
Nelson, William, 23, 67, 68
Neubauer, David, 35, 184
Neutrality: legal, 206
Nonet, Phillippe, 24

Oberholzer, Emil, 33, 34
Original intent, 205–8

Packer, Herbert, 184
Palen, Frank, 126
Park, John, 221 n.6
Parker, Samuel D., 67, 94, 95, 99, 128, 134, 156, 195
Percival, Robert, 222 n.2 (chap. 4)
Pickett, Robert, 25
Plea bargaining: beginning of, 65–66; explained, 92–97; in Municipal Court, 74–81; in Police Court, 89–92
Police: budgets of, 45–46; the new, 27–28, 43–46
Police Court sentencing, 110–13
Pollard, Benjamin, 27, 43, 220 n.3 (chap. 2)
Posten, Richard, 198
Professional bar: emergence of, 31
Professionalization of the bench, 187–88; offering adaptability, 189; role in modernization, 192–93
Progressive party, the, 198
Property crimes: defined, 223 n.10; severe punishments for, 107
Prosecutor's role: expansion of, 48, 49–61, 68–71
Public schools, 39–40; emergence of, 151–52; meaning of, 152–53

Quincy, Josiah: as judge, 9, 11, 190, 216; as mayor, 13, 25, 40, 41, 137, 140, 151, 179; as moral leader, 15, 194
Quincy, Josiah, Jr., 25

Regulatory crimes: defined, 223 n.10
Responsive law: and autonomous courts, 207–8; and divided society, 197–99; emergence of, 24, 28–30; implications of, 33–34; and politics, 197–202
Reynolds v. Sims, 377 U.S. 533, 205
Riparian rights, 28, 41
Rush, Benjamin, 39

Sanger, William, 167
Sarat, Austin, 34, 181
Savage, Edward, 83
Scheiber, Harry, 42
Schlesinger, Arthur, 203
Schnore, Leo, 135
Schultz, Stanley, 135, 151, 152, 153, 222 n.3
Selig, Philip, Jr., 222 n.6
Selznick, Philip, 24
Serious crimes: defined, 223 n.9; leniency toward, 107–8
Shaw, Lemuel, 15, 42, 127, 128, 189, 190, 194
Silberman, Matthew, 188
Simon, James, 224 n.1 (chap. 8)
Smith, Page, 25
Social Darwinism, 198
Social reform through politics or law, 209–10
Sprague, Henry, 34
State Reform School for Boys, 156
Steinberg, Alan, 220 n.5, 221 n.1
Sudnow, David, 191
Sutton, John, 153

Teubner, Gunther, 29
Thacher, Peter O., 95, 126, 128, 217
Thomas, John, 126
Trubek, David, 104

Ursuline Convent: burning of, 158–59
U.S. Department of Justice, 222 n.1

Van Dyck, Jon, 185
Vernier, C. G., 222 n.6
Vice: campaign against, 13; defined, 223 n.10
Vinovskis, Maris, 135, 152
Violent crimes: defined, 223 n.10; mild punishments for, 107
Voss, Harwin, 152

Warner, Sam Bass, Jr., 222 n.1 (chap. 5), 223 n.5
Warren, Charles, 32, 33

Warren Supreme Court, the, 203, 204, 205
Washburn, Emory, 126, 189, 190, 194, 216
Webster, Daniel, 9, 10
Weyl, Nathaniel, 223–24 n.4

Wilson, William J., 200
Wishingrad, Jay, 221 n.3
Woodman, Horatio, 72

Zehr, Howard, 23